Almost a Revolution

ALMOST A REVOLUTION

Mental Health Law and The Limits of Change

PAUL S. APPELBAUM, M.D.

Arnold Frank Zeleznik
Distinguished Professor of Psychiatry
Director, Law and Psychiatry Program, and
Chair, Department of Psychiatry
University of Massachusetts Medical Center

New York   Oxford
OXFORD UNIVERSITY PRESS
1994

Oxford University Press

Oxford   New York   Toronto
Delhi   Bombay   Calcutta   Madras   Karachi
Kuala Lumpur   Singapore   Hong Kong   Tokyo
Nairobi   Dar es Salaam   Cape Town
Melbourne   Auckland   Madrid

and associated companies in
Berlin   Ibadan

Copyright © 1994 by Oxford University Press, Inc.

Published by Oxford University Press, Inc.,
200 Madison Avenue, New York, New York 10016

Oxford is a registered trademark of Oxford University Press

Library of Congress Cataloging-in-Publication Data
Appelbaum, Paul S.
Almost a revolution : mental health law and the limits of change /
Paul S. Appelbaum.
p.   cm.   Includes bibliographical references and index.
ISBN 0-19-506880-7
1. Mental health laws—United States.
2. Insanity—Jurisprudence—United States.
3. Forensic psychiatry—United States.
I. Title.   KF3828.A97   1994
344.73′044—dc20   [347.30444]   93-37337

2 4 6 8 9 7 5 3 1

Printed in the United States of America
on acid-free paper

For my children—
Binyamin,
Yonaton,
and Avigail.

Preface

The meaning of wisdom, once sought in prayer, in quiet contemplation, or by cleaving to the words of a spiritual teacher, is as likely these days to be pursued by survey research techniques and factor analysis. Indeed, when these approaches were applied to the problem of understanding what people mean when they speak of wisdom, the results were as intriguing as anything that might pass the lips of the most sublime guru.[1]

Wisdom, it turns out, is conceived not as a single quality, but as an amalgam of traits quite distinct one from another. Understanding the factual basis of a situation is part of wisdom, but only the beginning; it fails to distinguish wisdom from mere shrewdness. To move toward wisdom, one must add a practical kind of knowledge that allows one to apply one's understanding to effecting solutions in the living world. And finally, wisdom also encompasses a capacity to place things into persepctive, to bring a body of experience to bear on new events, to discern their meaning and their likely implications.

This last component of wisdom is in some ways the easiest to acquire and in others the most difficult. Perspective comes with experience, with spending years observing (often only intuitively) the ebb and flow of events and seeing which leave their mark and which do not. It is as difficult to avoid gaining perspective as one grows older as it is to acquire it in youth. The peasant who has watched governments come and go, making promises and breaking them while few things change in his life, has acquired such perspective. The young reformer, fresh from university with a radical vision of altering rural life, has not.

Perspective, though, is a double-edged attribute. Rooted in experience, it molds an essentially conservative temperament: that which has happened before is thought likely to happen again; the unprecedented is always dis-

---

1. S. G. Holliday and M. J. Chandler, *Wisdom: Explorations in Adult Competence* (Basel, Switzerland: S. Karger, 1986).

counted. Thus the most experienced observer often fails to see an oncoming cataclysm that may be painfully obvious to the neophyte.

This book embodies the perspective I have gained during nearly two decades of observing and studying the relationship between psychiatry and law. I do not mean to imply that I have attained wisdom during that time. "Who is wise?" asks Ben Zoma in the part of the Mishnah known as the Ethics of the Fathers. "He who learns from every man." Wisdom is a process, not an accomplishment.

Developing an interest in mental health law when I did, at the peak of the most far-reaching period of reform in the field's history, has been both an advantage and a handicap. I am grateful for the opportunity to have witnessed and participated in this unprecedented epoch of change. Yet immersion in the tumult of an era makes it difficult to reflect thoughtfully on the swirl of events. Perspective requires not only the passage of time, but also the leisure to allow one's thoughts to crystallize and to probe their validity. The waning of reform in the second half of the 1980s has permitted those of us who have been students of mental health law to pause long enough to look for the broader patterns and deeper implications of the revolution we observed.

That, in short, is the purpose of this book. My intent is to examine four of the most important reforms in mental health law during the decade and a half when it captured the imagination of the legal world:

- The change in civil commitment laws from statutes allowing confinement on the basis of patients' need for treatment to laws restricting involuntary hospitalization to persons found dangerous to themselves or others, and the accompanying adoption of strict procedural protections based on the criminal model.
- The imposition of liability on mental health professionals for violent acts committed by their patients, when the courts deem that the violence was foreseeable.
- The recognition of the right of psychiatric patients—even those involuntarily hospitalized—to refuse treatment, especially with antipsychotic medications.
- The extensive changes in the insanity defense, including a narrowing of the standard for legal insanity, that followed the trial of John W. Hinckley, Jr., and were intended to limit the number of people found not guilty by reason of insanity.

In each case, after sketching the roots of the law and the motives for reform, I will examine the changes themselves, identify the expectations that accompanied them, assess whether those expectations were met, and (when they were not) inquire into the lessons we can learn about the failure of the reformers to achieve their goals. The final chapter generalizes from the conclusions concerning each area of reform and reflects on the implications of these findings.

The essence of my argument—and the value of perspective—is captured in the title of this book. In the midst of the waves of reform in mental health law in the 1970s and early 1980s, the changes underway seemed of revolutionary proportions. With the perspectives granted by time, it has become clear in many cases that changes in the law had much less impact than anticipated on the functioning of the mental health system. The reasons why it was "almost a revolution" relate to flaws in the ideological and conceptual underpinnings of the reforms, an underestimation of the resistance that would be encountered, and the unanticipated effects of other social forces. Few of us were wise enough to foresee these limits to change. I hope this analysis will increase our collective wisdom in the future.

The impetus for this work was provided by the American Psychiatric Association, which in 1990 was kind enough to confer on me its Isaac Ray Award, "for outstanding contributions to forensic psychiatry and the psychiatric aspects of jurisprudence." Along with the award came the obligation to present one or more public lectures and to prepare them for publication. Chapter 2, on civil commitment, and Chapter 4, on the right to refuse treatment, are expanded versions of my Isaac Ray Lectures given, respectively, at the Massachusetts Mental Health Center in Boston and the Western Psychiatric Institute and Clinic in Pittsburgh. Their presentation here fulfills my duty to the APA.

In the midst of preparing these lectures, I was invited by the School of Law at the University of Virginia to present the P. Browning Hoffman Memorial Lecture, a biennial tribute to a founding father of the academic study of mental health law, who died at a tragically young age. I am grateful to Professor Richard Bonnie and his colleagues for their invitation. Chapter 3, dealing with psychotherapists' duty to protect potential victims of their patients, is a revised version of the lecture I presented at the School of Law in Charlottesville.

Finally, the State Mental Health Forensic Directors Division of the National Association of State Mental Health Program Directors offered me the opportunity to present Chapter 5, on the insanity defense, as the keynote address at their annual meeting. This lecture was designated as the first Saleem Shah Memorial Lecture, in honor of a leading figure in mental health law—and a proponent of the importance of empirical research—who had died in a terrible accident not long before.

Along with my gratitude to the organizations that stimulated this work goes my thanks to friends and colleagues who took the time to read and comment on earlier drafts of one or more of the chapters: Richard Bonnie, J.D.; Thomas Grisso, Ph.D.; Ken Hoge, M.D.; Loren H. Roth, M.D., M.P.H.; and Henry Steadman, Ph.D. My understanding of mental health law issues has been aided immeasurably by my participation in the John D. and Catherine T. MacArthur Foundation's Research Network on Mental Health and the Law, directed by John Monahan, Ph.D.

    I especially appreciate the help afforded by the staff at the American Psychiatric Association Library in Washington, D.C., and by my secretaries, Denise George and Gail Foley, who struggled mightily to keep order among the flurry of drafts and revisions. None of what follows would have been possible without the assistance of my wife, Diana, for all the reasons you can imagine, and also because her unerring instincts as a writer time and again helped me present my thoughts more clearly than I otherwise would have.

Newton, Mass.   P. S. A.
October 1993

Contents

Almost a Revolution

1

Setting the Stage for Reform

An ambitious law school graduate in the early 1960s would have been ill-advised to pursue a career in the law of mental disorder. Although laws dealing with mentally ill people date back to colonial America,[1] little attention had been paid to them since the turn of the century. By and large the principles on which mental health law was based in 1961 were the same ones that prevailed in 1881.[2] The U.S. Supreme Court had never decided a case dealing with the treatment of mental illness, and state courts paid only slightly more attention to the area. Few lawyers specialized in legal aspects of mental disorders; those who did were involved mainly in routine guardianship cases or an occasional insanity defense. Indeed, most observers would have agreed that the field was largely moribund.

The lethargy in mental health law was evident in academia as well. Only a scattering of law professors were writing in the area, on topics ranging from involuntary commitment to competence to enter into a contract.[3] A similarly small group of psychiatrists focused on legal issues in their work, including Manfred Guttmacher, whose textbook, co-authored with attorney Henry Weihofen, dominated the field in the early 1960s.[4] The vast bulk of scholarly attention, however, was fixed on a single issue: the determination of when mentally ill persons should be excused from responsibility for their criminal acts.[5] Apart from the insanity defense—and the related question of what role expert psychiatric witnesses should play in courtroom proceedings—few issues in mental health law generated much fervor in the academic community.

Perhaps a particularly sharp-eyed observer of the legal scene might have had an inkling of what was to come. More likely, though, the signs of change were evident only in retrospect: pinpoints of intellectual ferment

3

scattered across an otherwise barren landscape. In 1949, the newly created National Institute of Mental Health issued a "Draft Act Governing the Hospitalization of the Mentally Ill," setting the stage for a renewed debate on the proper limits of state intervention in the lives of the disordered.[6] Five years later, Judge David Bazelon of the U.S. Court of Appeals for the District of Columbia Circuit attempted a radical revision of the traditional insanity defense in his decision in *Durham v. U.S.*[7]—an approach that contrasted sharply with the more conservative tack taken by the American Law Institute in its new Model Penal Code.[8] In 1960, a physician-lawyer named Morton Birnbaum suggested in the *Journal of the American Bar Association* that the Constitution might be read to afford a right to treatment for mentally ill persons detained against their will.[9] And in 1961, the American Bar Foundation published *The Mentally Disabled and the Law,* a volume it described as the "first American treatise on the law of mental disability," compiling in a single reference the relevant laws of all American jurisdictions.[10]

Though it may have been difficult to anticipate at the time, these were the first stirrings of what would become a thoroughgoing overhaul of law applicable to the mentally ill. Beginning in the late 1960s, for a decade and a half, mental health law underwent a period of intense change, thrusting it to the forefront of legal theory and legal activism alike. What accounted for this transformation?

Legal change has three prerequisites. The first, a perception by significant elements in society that change is required, lies external to the law. But the other two foundational elements reside within the legal system itself: a body of theory that can be applied to extend or alter the law in the desired direction, and a group of legal actors—lawyers, judges, and legislators—sufficiently committed to change to see it through. It took most of the 1960s for these elements to fall into place.

Changes in Attitudes Toward Psychiatry

Labeling Theory and the Reality of Mental Illness

Developments in the law often are exquisitely sensitive to shifts elsewhere in society. And unquestionably attitudes toward the mentally ill and toward the psychiatric system responsible for their care were undergoing a remarkable transition in the middle of the twentieth century. Psychiatry had generally been treated with deference since the late nineteenth century, perhaps as a *quid pro quo* for its willingness to care for a segment of society that most citizens would just as soon ignore. In the late 1950s, however, that deference gave way to a questioning of psychiatry's most basic presumptions. Critics began to ask questions that had not been heard before: Does mental illness really exist? Do psychiatrists and the treatments they render do more harm than good? Are psychiatrists possessed of genuine expertise, such that we should trust them with the powers they have been granted in the hospitals and the influence they have wielded in the courts?

The most fundamental of these questions—concerning the reality of mental illness—arose from the work of a group of sociologists of deviance who propounded what they called "labeling theory" as an explanation for socially nonconforming behavior. Labeling theorists argued that behavior of any sort was not intrinsically deviant, but only became deviant when it was so designated by powerful social forces. Moreover, once a person was labeled as behaving deviantly, the label had a potent effect on subsequent actions of the person and others. Edwin Lemert, the intellectual grandfather of labeling theory, described the process this way:

> As an illustration of this sequence the behavior of an errant schoolboy can be cited. For one reason or another, let us say excessive energy, the schoolboy engages in a classroom prank. He is penalized for it by the teacher. Later, due to clumsiness, he creates another disturbance and again he is reprimanded. Then, as sometimes happens, the boy is blamed for something he did not do. When the teacher uses the tag "bad boy" or "mischief maker" or other invidious terms, hostility and resentment are excited in the boy and he may feel that he is blocked in playing the [positive] role [previously] expected of him. Thereafter, there may be a strong temptation to assume his role in the class as defined by the teacher, particularly when he discovers that there are rewards as well as penalties deriving from such a [deviant] role.[11]

The appeal of this line of reasoning is obvious; it suggests that "there is no such thing as a bad boy," only misguided adults in positions of authority. Within a decade, labeling approaches constituted the dominant school of American criminology. Given the imperialistic tendencies of most theoreticians, which rival those of any colonial power, labeling theory was soon being applied to a wide range of behavior commonly considered deviant, including alcoholism, homosexuality—and mental illness.

Mental illness's susceptibility to being understood in terms of labeling theory lay in the absence of any pathophysiologic process to which most mental disorders could be attributed. Unlike anemia, for example, which can be diagnosed by a microscopic examination of red blood cells, mental illnesses were identified only by the behavior of those afflicted. The sociologists of deviance were always suspicious that the characterization of behavior as abnormal might serve as cover for persons seeking other ends than the well-being of the individual so labeled. Thus, in the late 1950s and early 1960s, they began to question whether there was anything more to mental illness than an arbitrary decision by those with power in society to classify as ill various persons who displayed annoying behaviors, and thus to facilitate their confinement and control.

The essential features of a labeling theory approach to mental illness were described by one critic as:

> first, that virtually everyone at some time commits acts that correspond to the public stereotypes of mental illness; second, that if these acts become public knowledge, the individual may, depending on various contingencies [related to the social status of the person, with the behavior of high-status persons less likely to be called deviant], be referred to the appropriate officials. Third, once the person is reacted to, he or she will routinely be processed as mentally ill and placed in a mental institution. Fourth, . . . this labeling process is the single most important determinant of a career of mental illness.[12] (p. 277)

Scheff, the most influential of the labeling theorists of mental illness, even elaborated an explanation for why mental disorders, if they originated in random deviations from acceptable behavior, so often resulted in patients' having symptoms that were similar to one another's and consistent for each patient. He argued that we all learn as children how "crazy people" are supposed to behave. Once labeled mentally ill, persons feel compelled to act out these images: the mentally ill person's "amorphous and unstructured deviant behavior tends to crystallize in conformity to these expectations, thus becoming similar to the behavior of other deviants classified as mentally ill, and stable over time."[13]

The speculations of the labeling theorists received an enormous boost from the work of a small group of psychiatrists who reached similar conclusions. Thomas Szasz, an upstate New York psychoanalyst, led the charge against traditional conceptions of mental disorder with his first and most famous book, *The Myth of Mental Illness,* which was published in 1961, the same year as *The Mentally Disabled and the Law.*[14] Szasz, using the diagnosis of hysteria as the basis for his conclusions, rejected any analogy between physical illnesses and mental disorders. The seemingly inexplicable symptoms of hysteria—loss of the ability to move a limb or to speak, lapses of memory, an inability to feel pain—were, for Szasz, efforts by the patient to communicate indirectly things that could not be said in words.

Although Szasz believed that persons with symptoms of what were called mental illnesses might legitimately seek treatment to help them recognize the problems at the root of their distress, he completely rejected use of medication, electroconvulsive therapy, and other somatic treatments. Nor did he believe that any justification existed for involuntary hospitalization and treatment. One does not, after all, deprive persons of liberty because they have elected to communicate distress in idiosyncratic ways. Finally, Szasz maintained, in an effort to undercut any possible rebuttal from the profession, psychiatrists' adherence to a disease model was grounded in their efforts to preserve their privileged status, at the expense of persons whose efforts to communicate pain were thus stripped of all meaning.

An echoing voice answered Szasz from across the Atlantic. R. D. Laing, a British psychiatrist, in a series of books aimed at a popular audience, maintained that even symptoms of severe mental disorder should be seen as rational responses to an irrational world. Citing Szasz, Scheff, and other labeling theorists, Laing argued that schizophrenic behavior could only be understood in its social context. Persons called schizophrenics are caught up in "unliveable situations" and are driven to invent strategies of coping that appear irrational but are actually brilliantly adaptive:

> To regard the [bizarre speech patterns of persons called schizophrenic] as due *primarily* to some psychological deficit is rather like supposing that a man doing a handstand on a bicycle on a tightrope 100 feet up with no safety net is suffering from an inability to stand on his own two feet.[15]

Not the patient, but the malevolent social network in which the patient is enmeshed should be the object of treatment. For Laing, labeling a person schizophrenic was a political statement that distracted attention from the disordered system that was at the heart of the problem. Indeed, far from degrading patients by labeling them ill, we should recognize that schizophrenics have access to a higher, transcendent reality to which most of us can only aspire.

The works of the labeling theorists and their psychiatric allies became staples in college curricula, and were trumpeted to the public at large in such works as Ken Kesey's novel, *One Flew Over the Cuckoo's Nest,* published in 1962. They began to be cited in discussions of mental health policy and law,[16] and their implications were profound. Psychiatry was a shell game, a dubious effort at redefining rationally motivated behavior as a particular kind of deviance—illness. Whether consciously or not, psychiatrists acted primarily to preserve the status quo by containing behavior that those in positions of power found problematic.

Now, more than three decades later, Scheff, Szasz, Laing, and their colleagues are no longer fixtures in psychology and sociology courses. Most college and graduate students have never heard of them or their argument that mental illness is a socially derived myth. Academic critics have picked their arguments apart,[17] and though Szasz, for one, is entirely unrepentant, many theorists who denied the existence of mental illness three decades ago are somewhat embarrassed now about their former beliefs. At the time, however, the influence of their arguments was dramatic and raised serious questions about the extent to which greater controls were needed on the psychiatric system.

Doubts About the Benefits of Psychiatric Treatment

A second query, related to the issue of whether mental illness was a legitimate entity, involved the nature and effects of treatment, especially for severe mental disorders. Concern about the state hospital system, where long-term hospitalization of patients with schizophrenia, manic-depressive illness, and other psychotic mental disorders ordinarily took place, began to be expressed in the years following World War II. Two potent exposés of conditions in state hospitals—Albert Deutsch's *The Shame of the States* and Mike Gorman's *Every Other Bed*—called the attention of the nation to the horrible conditions in many state institutions, where half a million severely mentally ill people were hospitalized at any point in time.[18] Congressional hearings followed; and though concrete achievements were few, the hospitalized mentally ill were restored to at least a secondary position on the nation's social agenda.

In a third major book published in 1961, sociologist and labeling theorist Erving Goffman reported on the year he had spent as a participant/observer on the wards of St. Elizabeths Hospital in Washington, D.C.[19] Goffman's *Asylums* drew public attention to what he construed as pernicious and insidious effects of long-term hospitalization. "Total institutions," such as psychiatric hospitals, were places where patients were stripped of their identities and addressed only in their ascribed roles as patients. This process was reinforced throughout the multitude of small humiliations that constituted hospital life, cumulatively amounting to the loss of power to control the most basic aspects of existence: when to sleep, eat, and excrete; whether or not to accept medication; how to express sexuality. To the extent that "inmates" adapted to the requirements of a total institution, they became progressively less fit to survive in the outside world. Their status as patients became permanent, with no hope of reprieve.

Once more, the concerns of the sociologists resonated with those of some psychiatrists, who corroborated their argument about the evils of hospitalization. U.S. Army psychiatrists in World War II had observed that chronic war neurosis (today we might call it post-traumatic stress disorder) could be avoided if soldiers were treated in field hospitals just behind the lines, where they could stay in close touch with their buddies, and from which they could be discharged rapidly to rejoin their units. When the war ended, these Young Turks of psychiatry developed new programs to implement their ideas at home, diverting patients from state hospitals into acute treatment units and mobilizing long-stay patients to return to the outside world.[20] Research seemed to confirm their wartime impressions: prolonged hospital stays might themselves have negative effects on patients, rendering them "institutionalized" and hence incapable of functioning in society.[21]

Many American psychiatrists began to espouse a philosophy of treatment that fell under the rubric of "community psychiatry"—an approach that emphasized early outpatient treatment and short-term hospitalization when necessary to avoid the perils of the state hospitals.[22] These efforts were made possible by the introduction in the mid-1950s of the first effective medication for controlling the symptoms of psychosis: chlorpromazine, more often known by its trade name Thorazine. Leaders of American psychiatry declared the state hospital system morally bankrupt and called for its abandonment.[23] A federal commission agreed in part, arguing for systems of smaller hospitals set up closer to the communities in which patients lived, but avoiding a complete endorsement of the community psychiatrists' agenda.[24]

Ultimately, the confluent concerns of sociological critics of institutional life and of advocates of community psychiatry led to passage of the Community Mental Health Center Act of 1963, a federal commitment to create a nationwide network of community-based psychiatric facilities.[25] Another effect was to call into question the power granted to psychiatrists to hospitalize and treat mentally ill persons with little societal oversight. The profession itself now acknowledged that hospitalization often worked to the detriment of those confined. Even people unwilling to reject the reality of mental illness began to support the idea of imposing limits on the ease with which psychiatrists could deprive people of their right to live freely in society.

Questions About the Limits of Psychiatric Expertise

The prevailing uncertainty about whether mental illness was real and whether its treatment was beneficial inevitably raised a third question: to what extent did psychiatrists' expertise warrant the influence they were granted in society? During the 1960s, psychiatrist-lawyer Jonas Robitscher was beginning to compile his skeptical answer to this query, *The Powers of Psychiatry*.[26] As he later characterized the ethos of the era, it was marked by increasing concern over the extraordinary breadth of psychiatric influence, from providing justifications for abortion (which in the 1960s was tightly controlled in most states) to helping excuse people from punishment for their crimes to defining who was genuinely disabled and thus eligible for indefinite societal support. In many of these cases, Robitscher noted, psychiatrists were not relying on any body of scientific expertise to reach their conclusions; rather, they were expressing their personal biases as if they represented professional opinion.

A stream of critical studies of psychiatrists' behavior contributed to doubts about the nature of their expertise. Researchers comparing diagnostic practices in England and in the United States found that patients who were diagnosed by British psychiatrists as manic-depressive were routinely called schizophrenic in the United States.[27] A psychologist trained eight "pseudopatients" to feign hallucinations; when these persons were admitted without question to twelve psychiatric hospitals, he claimed that psychiatrists could not tell the sane from the insane.[28] Psychiatrists were told that they had little ability to predict which mentally ill offenders were likely to be dangerous in the future.[29] Some courts responded with dismay to variations in psychiatric diagnostic practices, and called for psychiatrists to limit their testimony to bare observations, allowing judges and juries to draw legally relevant conclusions.[30]

These questions about the fundamental capacities of psychiatrists—to distinguish between illness and normality, to treat mental disorders effectively and avoid harm to patients, and to provide meaningful expertise to the decisionmaking organs of society—were in the air at the beginning of the 1960s and grew through the course of the decade. With these motive forces, mental health law was destined to become one of the era's most active legal areas. But first, two more pieces of the machine that would drive this effort had to be put into place.

Developments in the Legal System

For social pressure to stimulate legal reform, a legal theory is required in which efforts at change can be grounded, and a cadre of activists must be created to guide the process. Most significant in regard to doctrinal developments in mental health law were the aftereffects of the civil rights revolution of the 1950s. I examine the development of specific legal doctrines in subsequent chapters; the general themes are my concern here. Civil rights litigation in the South in the 1950s brought the U.S. Supreme Court out of a period of lethargy into which it had slid in response to the excesses of an activist conservative court in the first third of the century. Suddenly the equal protection and due process clauses of the Constitution were imbued with new meaning, providing potent tools for dismantling state-sponsored segregation. Longstanding civil rights statutes, which had been largely ignored for decades, were invoked with unprecedented success. Courts, especially the U.S. Supreme Court, were seen as the focal point of efforts to guarantee equal rights to the dispossessed.

What began with civil rights litigation on behalf of Southern blacks soon spread to other groups that lacked the political clout to protect their own interests. Defendants' rights became a prominent concern of the courts in the 1960s, with prisoners' rights not far behind.[31] Juveniles, especially those who had fallen into the hands of the criminal justice system, were another focus of attention.[32] Addressing the status of these groups, the courts formulated general principles that appeared to be relevant to other persons who were deprived of liberty, including the mentally ill. Due process required a hearing before confinement, with notice of charges, the right to representation, and the right to appeal.[33] The state bore the burden of proof in these efforts; if it failed, the detainee was to be set free. By the end of the decade, the U.S. Supreme Court had begun applying these principles to a hybrid group of mentally ill persons who had been confined in the criminal justice system.[34] Their broader application to the civil mental health system seemed imminent.

Accelerating these changes was the emergence of a new cadre of law school professors whose primary concern was mental health law. Among the earliest of these were psychiatrists who taught at the nation's most prestigious schools: Andrew Watson at Michigan, Alan Stone at Harvard, and Jay Katz at Yale. In contrast to their less distinguished predecessors, they had full-time law school appointments. Often, they collaborated with lawyers who were similarly occupied with mental health law issues. Neither group was content to describe the system as it was. Impelled by the critiques of psychiatry and of the mental health system that were abroad in the land, they brought the critical writings of sociological and psychiatric dissenters into the classroom and took the classroom to the state hospital to convey to their students the problems besetting the system. Their students developed an appreciation for the problems of the mentally ill, the limits of psychiatric expertise, and the potential for a transformation of mental health law.

Literature addressing mental health law proliferated. Among the new works were theoretical appraisals of existing law, often with pointed suggestions for change.[35] In addition, empirical studies demonstrating how the system actually worked began to appear on the scene. The earliest studies came from the pens of the sociological critics of psychiatry, but they were followed by studies conducted by law professors and their students, and by psychiatrists and psychologists as well.[36] Policy makers now had at their disposal detailed descriptions of what was wrong with the current system and detailed prescriptions for using the law to effect needed change.

As the new generation of law students graduated, eager to extend the rights revolution to the mentally ill, they gravitated to legal aid organizations that fought for the rights of the underprivileged in general. In places, specialty legal services programs developed, focused specifically on the problems of mental illness. The most influential of these was the Mental Health Law Project (MHLP), based in Washington, D.C., which opened its doors in 1968. Many of the major pieces of litigation pursued over the next two decades would be initiated or markedly influenced by MHLP lawyers.

Mental health professionals responded to the growing interest in legal issues in their field in reciprocal fashion. Psychiatrists organized the American Academy of Psychiatry and the Law, and psychologists formed the American Psychology-Law Society, both in 1969.[37] Each founded a journal and ran regular meetings to educate their members about the evolving law and the role of clinicians in its applications.[38] Moreover, each group stimulated academic attention to theoretical and empirical issues in mental health law, and the resulting studies were often used to shape the process of reform further. Other journals were created to publish this work[39] and to help legal and mental health practitioners keep up with the flood of new information available.[40] Fellowship training programs were developed to produce clinicians who could work knowledgeably within the new legal system. And a cohort of experts became available to work with litigators to continue the process of reform.

The Stage Is Set

By the end of the 1960s, the elements necessary to make mental health law a priority on the nation's legal agenda were at hand, and reform was already underway. The changes that ensued were of astonishing scope and intensity, continuing into the early 1980s, before their force was spent. Now, more than a decade has passed since the most important reforms were initiated; and in some cases, over two decades of experience are available. The surge of academic interest and research funding for studies of the changes in mental health law have created a body of data that permits us to assess the results of this process.

The chapters that follow focus on four of the major reforms of this remarkable era: the reorientation of commitment laws from a focus on patients' need for treatment to an examination of their dangerousness; the creation of a new form of liability for mental health professionals as a consequence of their patients' violent acts; the adoption of a right on the part of involuntarily committed psychiatric patients to refuse treatment; and the manifold reforms in the law governing the defense in criminal cases of not guilty by reason of insanity.

These are not the only reforms of the period that could be examined, but they are among the most important; and of particular significance for this work, each of them is characterized by a body of research that allows us to examine in considerable detail the changes that followed in its wake. The questions to be asked are: What drove the reforms? How were they crafted? What outcomes were anticipated? Were the desired changes realized? And if they were not, what factors prevented achievement of the goals of reform?

I write at a particularly fortuitous time for a work of this sort. The pace of reform has slowed considerably; some commentators might even argue that the clock has been turned back in selected areas, as the initiatives of the 1970s have been reversed.[41] Whatever interpretation one puts on recent developments, it seems clear that we are in a period of consolidation, rather than one of rapid change. Each of the areas under examination, though, is likely to be the focus of further attention in the future. We surely will be better prepared for that future if we strengthen our understanding of the complex interaction of forces involved when the law is applied to the mentally ill.

References

1. A. Deutsch, *The Mentally Ill in America,* 2d ed. (New York: Columbia University Press, 1949).
2. F. T. Lindman and D. M. McIntyre, eds., *The Mentally Disabled and the Law* (Chicago: American Bar Foundation, 1961).
3. See, e.g., W. Curran, "Hospitalization of the Mentally Ill," *North Carolina Law Review* 31: 274–298 (1952–53); and M. D. Green, "Judicial Tests of Mental Incompetency," *Missouri Law Review* 6: 141–165 (1941). Other examples of scholarly legal work during this era include F. Flashner, "Analysis of Legal and Medical Considerations in Commitment of the Mentally Ill," *Yale Law Journal* 56: 1178–1209 (1947); H. A. Ross, "Commitment of the Mentally Ill: Problems of Law and Policy," *Michigan Law Review* 57: 945–1018 (1959); and C. W. Whitmore, "Comments on a Draft Act for the Hospitalization of the Mentally Ill," *George Washington Law Review* 19: 512–30 (1951). See also *infra* note 5.
4. M. S. Guttmacher and H. Weihofen, *Psychiatry and the Law* (New York: W. W. Norton, 1952).
5. Note the comment of Sheldon Glueck in 1962: "Too great effort has been expended upon the very small proportion of criminal cases which involve the defense of insanity and not nearly enough on the much larger area of constructive possibilities of professional cooperation in the general run of cases." The comment appears in Glueck's Isaac Ray Award Lectures, which ironically are devoted almost entirely to the insanity defense. S. Glueck, *Law and Psychiatry: Cold War or Entente Cordiale?* (Baltimore: Johns Hopkins University Press, 1962). For a selection of works of the era on the insanity defense, see J. Biggs, *The Guilty Mind* (New York: Harcourt, Brace & Co., 1955); J. Hall, "Psychiatry and Criminal Responsibility," *Yale Law Journal* 65: 761–85 (1955–56); H. Kalven, "Insanity and the Criminal Law: A Critique of *Durham v. United States,*" *University of Chicago Law Review* 22: 317–30 (1954–55); P. Roche, *The Criminal Mind* (New York: Farrar, Straus & Cudahy, 1958); H. Wechsler, "The Criteria of Criminal Responsibility," *University of Chicago Law Review* 22: 367–76 (1954–55); and H. Weihofen, *Mental Disorder as a Criminal Defense* (Buffalo, N.Y.: Dennis & Co., 1954).
6. A Draft Act Governing Hospitalization of the Mentally Ill (revised). Public Health Service Publication No. 51 (Washington, D.C.: U.S. Government Printing Office, 1952).
7. *Durham v. U.S.,* 214 F.2d 862 (D.C. Cir. 1954).
8. American Law Institute, *Model Penal Code,* Tentative Draft No. 4 (Philadelphia: American Law Institute Publishers, 1955).
9. M. Birnbaum, "The Right to Treatment," *American Bar Association Journal* 46: 499–505 (1960).
10. Lindman and McIntyre, *supra* note 2.
11. E. M. Lemert, *Social Pathology* (New York: McGraw-Hill, 1951), p. 77.
12. W. R. Gove, "The Current Status of the Labelling Theory of Mental Illness," in W. R. Gove, ed., *Deviance and Mental Illness* (Beverly Hills, Calif.: Sage Publi-

cations, 1982), pp. 273–300. Gove is characterizing the work of Thomas Scheff, the most widely known of the sociologists who applied labeling theory to mental disorders. See T. J. Scheff, *Being Mentally Ill: A Sociological Theory.* (Chicago: Aldine, 1966).

13. T. J. Scheff, "Cultural Stereotypes and Mental Illness," *Sociometry* 26: 438–52 (1963), p. 446.

14. T. S. Szasz, *The Myth of Mental Illness: Foundations of a Theory of Personal Conduct* (New York: Dell, 1961).

15. R. D. Laing, *The Politics of Experience* (New York: Ballantine Books, 1967), p. 102.

16. P. E. Dietz, "Social Discrediting of Psychiatry: The Protasis of Legal Disenfranchisement," *American Journal of Psychiatry* 134: 1356–60 (1977).

17. M. S. Moore, "Some Myths About 'Mental Illness,' " *Archives of General Psychiatry* 32: 1483–97 (1975); and R. Pies, "On Myths and Countermyths: More on Szaszian Fallacies," *Archives of General Psychiatry* 36: 139–44 (1979); Gove, *supra* note 12.

18. A. Deutsch, *The Shame of the States* (New York: Harcourt, Brace, 1948); and M. Gorman, *Every Other Bed* (Cleveland: World Publishing, 1956).

19. E. Goffman, *Asylums: Essays on the Social Situation of Mental Patients and Other Inmates* (New York: Doubleday, 1961).

20. See especially the work of Gerald Grob, including "World War II and American Psychiatry," *Psychohistory Review* 19: 41–69 (1990); "Mental Health Policy in America: Myths and Realities," *Health Affairs* 11: 7–22 (1992); and *From Asylum to Community: Mental Health Policy in Modern America* (Princeton, N.J.: Princeton University Press, 1991).

21. Much of the research was performed in England. See, e.g., R. Barton, *Institutional Neurosis* (Bristol, U.K.: John Wright, 1959); D. Martin, "Institutionalisation," *Lancet* II: 1188–90 (1955); and J. Wing, "Institutionalism in Mental Hospitals," *British Journal of Social and Clinical Psychology* 1: 38–51 (1962).

22. J. R. Ewalt and P. L. Ewalt, "History of the Community Psychiatry Movement," *American Journal of Psychiatry* 126: 41–52 (1969); B. Rubin, "Community Psychiatry: An Evolutionary Change in Medical Psychology in the United States," *Archives of General Psychiatry* 20: 497–507 (1969); and Grob, *supra* note 20.

23. H. C. Solomon, "The American Psychiatric Association in Relation to American Psychiatry," *American Journal of Psychiatry* 115: 1–9 (1958).

24. Joint Commission on Mental Illness and Health, *Action for Mental Health* (New York: Basic Books, 1961).

25. M. Levine, *The History and Politics of Community Mental Health* (New York: Oxford University Press, 1981).

26. J. Robitscher, *The Powers of Psychiatry* (Boston: Houghton Mifflin, 1980).

27. J. E. Cooper, R. E. Kendell, B. J. Gurland, L. Sharpe, J. R. M. Copeland, and R. Simon, "Psychiatric Diagnosis in New York and London: A Comparative Study of Mental Hospital Admissions," Maudsley Monograph No. 20 (London: Oxford University Press, 1972).

28. D. L. Rosenhan, "On Being Sane in Insane Places," *Science* 179: 250–58. (1973).

29. See the critiques of J. Goldstein and J. Katz, "Dangerousness and Mental Illness: Some Observations on the Decision to Release Persons Acquitted by Reason of Insanity," *Yale Law Journal* 70: 225–39 (1960); J. Livermore, C. Malmquist, and P. Meehl, "On the Justifications for Civil Commitment," *University of Pennsylvania Law Review* 117: 75–96, 1968; and B. Diamond, "The Psychiatric Prediction

of Dangerousness," *University of Pennsylvania Law Review* 123: 439–52 (1974). These critiques began to be affirmed in the 1970s by empirical studies, including H. Kozol, R. Boucher, and R. Garofalo, "The Diagnosis and Treatment of Dangerousness," *Crime and Delinquency* 18: 371–92 (1973); H. Steadman and J. Cocozza, *Careers of the Criminally Insane* (Lexington, Mass.: Lexington Books, 1974); and T. Thornberry and J. Jacoby, *The Criminally Insane: A Community Follow-up of Mentally Ill Offenders* (Chicago: University of Chicago Press, 1979).

30. *Blocker v. U.S.*, 274 F.2d 572 (D.C. Cir. 1959); *McDonald v. U.S.*, 312 F.2d 847 (D.C. Cir. 1962); *Washington v. U.S.*, 390 F.2d 444 (D.C. Cir. 1967). For a retrospective account of the argument in these opinions, all authored by Judge David Bazelon, see D. L. Bazelon, "Veils, Values and Social Responsibility," *American Psychologist* 37: 115–21 (1982).

31. On defendants' rights, see *Mapp v. Ohio*, 367 U.S. 643 (1961); *Gideon v. Wainwright*, 372 U.S. 335 (1963); *Miranda v. Arizona*, 384 U.S. 436 (1966); and *U.S. v. Wade*, 388 U.S. 218 (1967). With regard to prisoners' rights, see *Morrissey v. Brewer*, 408 U.S. 471 (1972); and *Wolff v. McDonnell*, 418 U.S. 539 (1974).

32. *Kent v. U.S.*, 383 U.S. 341 (1966); *In re Gault*, 387 U.S. 1 (1967); and *In re Winship*, 397 U.S. 358 (1970).

33. See cases cited *supra* note 32.

34. *Baxstrom v. Herold*, 383 U.S. 107 (1966); and *Specht v. Patterson*, 386 U.S. 605 (1967).

35. See, e.g., F. Cohen, "The Function of the Attorney and the Commitment of the Mentally Ill," *Texas Law Review* 44: 424–69 (1966); A. Goldstein, *The Insanity Defense* (New Haven, Conn.: Yale University Press, 1967); J. Katz, "The Right to Treatment: An Enchanting Legal Fiction?" *University of Chicago Law Review* 36: 755–83 (1969); A. Leifer, "The Competence of the Psychiatrist to Assist in the Determination of Incompetency: A Skeptical Inquiry into the Courtroom Functions of Psychiatrists," *Syracuse Law Review* 14: 564–75 (1963); Livermore et al., *supra* note 29; and "Note: Civil Commitment of the Mentally Ill: Theories and Procedures," *Harvard Law Review* 79: 1288–1350 (1966).

36. See, e.g., Contemporary Studies Project, "Facts and Fallacies About Iowa Civil Commitment," *Iowa Law Review* 55: 895–980 (1970); L. Kutner, "The Illusion of Due Process in Commitment Proceedings," *Northwestern University Law Review* 57: 383–99 (1962); D. Miller and M. Schwartz, "County Lunacy Commission Hearings: Some Observations of Commitments to a State Mental Hospital," *Social Problems* 14: 25–36 (1966); R. S. Rock, M. A. Jacobson, and R. M. Janopaul, *Hospitalization and Discharge of the Mentally Ill* (Chicago: University of Chicago Press, 1968); and D. L. Wenger and C. R. Fletcher, "The Effect of Legal Counsel on Admissions to a State Mental Hospital: A Confrontation of Professions," *Journal of Health and Social Behavior* 10: 66–72 (1969).

37. T. Grisso, "A Developmental History of the American Psychology-Law Society," *Law and Human Behavior* 15: 213–31 (1991); and T. Grisso, "The Differences Between Forensic Psychiatry and Forensic Psychology," *Bulletin of the American Academy of Psychiatry and the Law* 21: 133–45 (1993).

38. The *Bulletin of the American Academy of Psychiatry and the Law* began publication in 1973; *Law and Human Behavior,* sponsored by the American Psychology-Law Society, first appeared in 1977.

39. The *Journal of Psychiatry and Law* first appeared in 1973, and *International Journal of Law and Psychiatry* began publication in 1978.

40. In 1976, the Commission on the Mentally Disabled began publishing the *Mental*

Disability Law Reporter (now the *Mental and Physical Disability Law Reporter*), which, in contrast to the other periodicals, consists primarily of summaries of recently decided court cases.

41. J. Q. Lafond and M. L. Durham, *Back to the Asylum: The Future of Mental Health Law and Policy in the United States* (New York: Oxford University Press, 1993).

2

Involuntary Commitment of the Mentally Ill:
Civil Liberties and Common Sense

On October 29, 1971, Alberta Lessard was picked up by two police officers in front of her house in West Allis, Wisconsin, and taken to her local mental health center. Once there, the officers completed a form requesting her "emergency detention for mental observation," and she was admitted against her will. What led the officers to believe that she required hospitalization? Was she sitting calmly on her stoop, enjoying the evening breeze? Or was she pacing the street, cursing under her breath at the children who passed? To our regret, we do not know.

In fact, the record tells us little about this woman who was to have such a profound impact on the law of civil commitment in the United States. We know that she harbored some unusual ideas, such as her conviction that the National Education Association was infiltrated by communists. At one point, she may have been arrested for making harassing telephone calls to nearby Marquette University. There is a hint that she might have attempted to kill herself several weeks before her detention, but there is no evidence that she was actually suicidal at the time she was taken into custody.

What happened next to Alberta Lessard, however, is clearly etched in legal history. Three days after her involuntary hospitalization, the two police officers who had picked her up appeared before County Court Judge Christ T. Seraphim, without Ms. Lessard present, to repeat the allegations that formed the basis of their decision to apply for her detention. Judge Seraphim authorized an additional ten days of hospitalization.

A few days after the initial hearing, a psychiatrist from the mental health center indicated to the court his belief that the patient was suffering from schizophrenia, and he recommended "permanent commitment." On

17

the basis of this evidence, Judge Seraphim extended Ms. Lessard's detention, and he did the same at a subsequent hearing, each time without her
being told of the proceeding or being given a chance to respond to the
claims made concerning her illness. Although the court by now had appointed a guardian *ad litem* to represent her interests, he apparently played
no role in these hearings.

Alberta Lessard, however, as is often true of people with a somewhat
conspiratorial view of the world, appears to have been endowed with an
unusual measure of spunk. She obtained representation on her own initiative from Milwaukee Legal Services. Even so, on November 24, 1971,
when a formal commitment hearing was finally held in Judge Seraphim's
court, Ms. Lessard was ordered committed for an additional thirty days on
the grounds—further unexplicated—that she was "mentally ill."

Belying her need for the permanent commitment her psychiatrist had
recommended, Alberta Lessard was released from the hospital just three
days later on "outpatient parole." Neither she nor her attorney, however,
was content to let matters rest there. Just a few days after Lessard contacted
Milwaukee Legal Services, a suit was brought in federal court on her behalf
and on behalf of all other persons subject to involuntary commitment in
Wisconsin. When an opinion was issued in the case nearly one year later,
the result was a complete repudiation of the bases for and procedures associated with Ms. Lessard's commitment.[1]

I consider in due course the details of the court's opinion and the
changes it stimulated in courts and legislatures around the country. To understand the magnitude of the alteration the decision in *Lessard v. Schmidt*
required in the law of civil commitment, however, one must have some
grasp of the history of traditional commitment law and of the legal engines
used to topple it. It is to that task that I now turn.

Evolution of the Law of Civil Commitment

The laws that governed the commitment of Alberta Lessard had their antecedents in the earliest American statutes regulating the involuntary hospitalization process, first adopted in the second quarter of the nineteenth century. Development of public asylums for the treatment of mental disorders,
the forerunners of today's state hospitals, stimulated passage of these acts.[2]

Prior to the 1830s, only a few hospitals of any sort existed in the
United States, and these generally made no distinction between the admission of patients for treatment of physical disorders and the admission of
patients for treatment of mental disorders. The same doctors cared for both.
Private institutions established their own rules for admission, which often
required only that a family member or friend guarantee payment of the

patient's bill, and that one of the hospital's attending physicians certify the patient for admission.[3] Family members usually requested admission for patients who were too confused or debilitated to speak for themselves, blurring the distinction between voluntary and involuntary hospitalization. The right of family members and friends to act in patients' interests was supported by a number of early court decisions.[4]

Only a small fraction of mentally ill persons, of course, could be accommodated in the young nation's few hospitals. Many more were confined in county jails when they became disorderly or merely vagrant, and still others were detained on orders of the overseers of the poor in county almshouses—ubiquitous institutions in nineteenth-century America. The detailed memoranda of Dorothea Dix, who combed much of the nation in the 1840s and 1850s to document the need for hospitals to treat the insane, reveal that nearly every county had its share of deranged jail inmates, confined in abominable conditions. Their counterparts lodged in the almshouses might have been marginally better off, but still they often were housed in dirty and disorderly conditions, tossed together with the indigent physically ill and disabled, alcoholics, the retarded, the senile, and the slothful.[5]

Dix, like other lay and medical reformers, was inspired by English models for moral treatment of the mentally disordered, which offered the first basis for optimism in an era previously marked by therapeutic despair.[6] They fought for a more humane alternative to jails and almshouses—for institutions dedicated exclusively to treatment of the mentally ill—guided by the premise that mentally ill people were more like than unlike their "normal" counterparts. Such institutions would offer shelter from the stresses of the outside world (hence the name "asylums") and opportunities for patients to resume responsible functioning as members of a more intimate society.[7] In response to their efforts, the states began to assume responsibility for the care of indigent mentally ill persons and to build facilities where active treatment could take place. A great surge of construction of state-run asylums moved across the country, beginning with Worcester State Hospital in Massachusetts in 1833.[8]

Although the law had, to this point, little to do with hospitalization of the mentally ill, state involvement brought a need for enabling legislation and for some modicum of outside control. In many states, under the new statutes that were passed, commitment could still be effected by concerned family members who were willing to pay the costs of care; but if the state assumed the costs, judicial certification of the need for treatment, along with medical approval, generally was required. In the early days of the formal commitment system, judicial involvement sometimes functioned more as a form of cost control and allocation than as a mechanism for the protection of individual rights.[9] In some states, for example, paupers already supported in almshouses could be committed to state mental hospitals by overseers of the poor, and the costs charged back to the county, with no further legal intervention. On what basis would the superintendents of the new asylums decide to admit mentally ill persons (contemporary statutes ordinarily spoke of "lunatics" or the "insane") whose families sought their care? The sole requirement was that they be in need of or likely to benefit from treatment. The intent was to exclude the most chronic cases, but few others. It was assumed that all patients would be admitted involuntarily, since mental illness was thought to compromise the faculties of reason to such an extent that patients would not be capable of requesting care on their own behalf.[10]

Thus, the theoretical underpinnings for the Wisconsin law under which Alberta Lessard was detained—and for its counterparts in most states— were in place by the start of the Civil War. Commitment was predicated simply on a mentally ill person's requiring care. Asylums, run by the state, were assumed to be the best place to care for almost all such people. Entry was designed to be as simple as possible, and it was essentially left in the hands of family members and physicians whenever practicable. And given the presumed effects of mental disorder on cognition, coercion was viewed as essential if needed treatment was to be obtained.

To the extent that commitment law evolved over the next century, the changes focused almost entirely on the procedures associated with the commitment process. Following the Civil War, allegations began to be heard that persons had been railroaded into mental institutions by greedy relatives and conniving physicians.[11] The most prominent of the former patients who crusaded for statutory changes to halt these abuses was Mrs. E. P. W. Packard, a prolific author and speaker.[12] She fought in particular for jury trials for persons faced with involuntary hospitalization, at which allegations concerning their disorder and need for treatment could be adjudicated.

The claims of Mrs. Packard and others had a cumulative effect that led to two categories of change in commitment laws: legal regulation was extended to private facilities; and procedural safeguards, generally borrowed from the criminal justice system, were introduced. States began to require that hospitalization be preceded by a hearing at which the allegedly mentally ill person could object to the proposed confinement. Respondents in many states were required to have a jury make the ultimate commitment decision, and in other states they could elect to have a jury do so. Physicians were required to examine patients before signing affidavits testifying to their need for commitment and to state that they were not related to the patients and had no financial interest in their hospitalization.

Succeeding decades saw further tinkering with the procedural aspects of commitment, with something of a cyclic quality. When public attention was directed primarily toward the obstacles placed in the path of rapid hospitalization and treatment, a push was made to loosen or do away with criminal-style procedures. In contrast, when the abuse of civil liberties held the public's eye, such moves were resisted and greater oversight supplied.

During the Progressive Era, for example, in the years prior to World War I, concern was expressed regarding the difficulty of obtaining prompt hospitalization under many statutes, especially in cases of recent onset. With the development in many major cities of psychopathic hospitals dedicated to caring for acute cases, the impetus grew for special procedures that would bypass complex and time-consuming judicial hearings. As a result, many states adopted emergency commitment provisions, allowing physicians to hospitalize patients for brief periods of time without court review.[13] The police, too, were sometimes given the right to initiate emergency admissions.

By the 1930s, 1940s, and 1950s, concern again was growing over the potentially adverse consequences of rigorous, criminal-style procedures. States without physician-controlled, emergency commitment procedures were still utilizing sheriffs and other law enforcement personnel to pick up and detain mentally ill persons in jails pending their hearings in court. In the late 1930s, it was estimated that 64 percent of patients were transported to state hospitals by law enforcement personnel, and that 29 percent spent at least some time in jail on the way.[14] Proposals were offered for the abolition of mandatory judicial hearings, with the power to commit left in the hands of one or two physicians, and with patients given the right to request a hearing after the fact, if they desired.[15] For states that retained required hearings, it was urged that the decision about whether to inform the patient of the proceeding should be left in the judge's hands.[16] A number of states, including Wisconsin, adopted such measures, especially after the issuance of the highly influential "Draft Act Governing Hospitalization of the Mentally Ill" by the National Institute of Mental Health in 1949.[17]

Each period of reform and reaction left its mark on the statute under which the West Allis police officers detained Alberta Lessard. The standard that she was found to meet to qualify for commitment—"mentally ill or infirm or deficient and . . . a proper subject for custody and treatment"— echoes the earliest commitment laws of the nineteenth century. Progressive Era reforms had their impact in allowing the police to initiate her detention and to set in motion a process that could have resulted in her being hospitalized for up to 140 days before a hearing took place. And mid-twentieth-century concern for the adverse impact on a mentally ill person of having to appear in court is reflected in the judge's failure to afford her notice of any of the preliminary hearings in her case.

Yet the procedural reforms of the postbellum era had an effect as well. Judicial oversight of police and medical decisions regarding commitment was provided, and a formal hearing was held. Though the outcome of the hearing may demonstrate how difficult it is for a judge to controvert the opinion of the treating psychiatrist, Ms. Lessard was afforded representation and an opportunity to be heard. And her suit in federal court, which had so great an impact on the future of commitment law, was filed under a federal civil rights statute (designed to protect citizens against the power of the state) that dated back to the post–Civil War era, too.

What must now be explained is how, given this legal pedigree and the intricate balance of interests it represented, the federal judges of the Eastern District of Wisconsin were able to fashion what was, in many respects, a dramatically different approach to the law governing involuntary hospitalization. To do that, we require an excursus into the turbulent world of constitutional law and related legal developments in the years just after the midpoint of this century.

Legal Basis for Challenges to Traditional Commitment Laws

In retrospect, like a geologist reading the history of time in the sediments of a series of rock formations, one can discern the layers of legal thought that provided the foundation for the *Lessard* court's decision. While those sediments were being deposited, however, it must have been difficult to make sense of what was happening in the nation's courts.

Judicial activism in the early part of this century meant using the courts and the federal Constitution to block legislative reform, particularly when it had economic implications. In what came to be known as the "*Lochner* era," after one of the leading cases of this mold, the U.S. Supreme Court repeatedly rejected efforts by Congress and the states to regulate working conditions, employer–employee relations, and other aspect of the business of doing business.[18] These decisions were based on a sweeping interpretation of the fourteenth amendment's prohibition of deprivation of "life, liberty, or property" without due process of law. The Court emphasized the perhaps oxymoronic notion of "substantive" due process, rather than focusing on the procedural aspects of legal intervention that the common-sense usage of the term would imply. By substantive due process, the Court meant to designate certain categories of state intervention in a person's (or corporation's) affairs that were impermissible, regardless of the procedures employed.

In contrast to the alignment of forces to which we have grown accustomed today, in the first half of this century the progressive and liberal block argued for judicial restraint, while the conservatives trumpeted the ultimate dispositive authority of the Constitution and its interpreters, the courts. This conflict came to a head in the late 1930s, as an aging, conservative Court repeatedly struck down key pieces of New Deal legislation on substantive due process grounds. Although President Roosevelt's effort to "pack" the Court by appointing additional justices failed, his appointment power ultimately produced a set of justices willing to restrain their own powers and thus to permit vastly more scope to the people's legislative representatives.

By the mid-1950s, however, under the leadership of Chief Justice Earl Warren, the Supreme Court was eager to flex its muscles again. This time the Court's primary target was legislation or state practices that infringed on individual liberty, rather than on property. Since the doctrine of substantive due process was now in disfavor (although, as we shall see, it could be called into action if needed), the Court required new tools as well. These it found in the equal protection clause of the fourteenth amendment and in a "procedural" analysis of that same amendment's due process clause.

The signal case for what was to come was the Court's famed decision in *Brown v. Board of Education,* striking down state-sponsored school segregation on equal protection grounds.[19] As the Court's consideration of individual rights accelerated, the Court began to move into areas that would have an even greater and more direct impact on commitment law. Two series of opinions are most relevant to our analysis here.

In a string of cases from the mid-1960s to the early 1970s, the Supreme Court considered a variety of statutes addressing classes of persons whose status straddled the criminal justice and mental health systems. These included persons who were adjudicated as sexually dangerous offenders in hearings lacking full-scale criminal trial procedures and then were indefinitely committed to treatment programs[20]; sex offenders who were facing recommitment without a formal hearing[21]; prisoners who had been transferred to mental hospitals without formal hearings prior to the expiration of their sentences and had been held indefinitely thereafter[22]; and defendants who were found incompetent to stand trial and were subsequently held indefinitely, even when it was clear they would not regain competence.[23]

The opinions of the Supreme Court in these cases conveyed a dual message. Explicitly, the Court ruled that civil proceedings resulting in detention with allegedly therapeutic intent cannot be used as a cover for indefinite confinement of persons who are believed to be likely to commit criminal acts. Sex offenders must be found guilty of having performed the acts of which they stand charged in criminal hearings with full procedural protections before they can be committed to a treatment facility.[24] Recommitment requires procedures similar to those used in the civil system.[25] If the state wishes to hold a prisoner in a mental hospital after the expiration of his or her sentence, the usual procedures for authorizing civil commitment must be employed.[26] And the state's power to confine anyone must be supported by a legitimate state interest; thus, indefinite "treatment" of an incurably incompetent defendant makes no constitutional sense.[27]

Underlying the actual holdings of the Court in these cases was another message. Confinement in a hospital for "treatment" is confinement none-theless. In a phrase that was much cited in subsequent lower court decisions, the Court characterized commitment as a "massive curtailment of liberty."[28] Therapeutic labels cannot be used in these circumstances to justify the denial of due process to which the person would otherwise be entitled. Further, harkening back to the doctrine of substantive due process, the Court implied that there might be circumstances in which the state has no legitimate interest in confining a person—and therefore no power to do so—regardless of the procedures utilized.

A second series of U.S. Supreme Court opinions, beginning with *Kent v. U.S.* in 1966, addressed the procedural aspects of another system with combined punitive and therapeutic elements, and reinforced and extended these conclusions.[29] Juvenile delinquents, since roughly the turn of the century, had been adjudicated in hearings that lacked many of the characteristics of criminal trials. Once again, the justification was that the proceedings were intended to benefit wayward children by finding the most appropriate disposition to help them alter their course. The Court, though, had some doubts whether this was the way the system worked in practice:

> While there can be no doubt of the original laudable purpose of juvenile courts, studies and critiques in recent years raise serious questions as to whether actual performance measures well enough against theoretical purpose to make tolerable the immunity of the process from the reach of constitutional guaranties applicable to adults . . . [T]here may be grounds for concern that the child receives the worst of both worlds: that he gets neither the protections accorded to adults nor the solicitous care and regenerative treatment postulated for children.[30]

Again the Court relied on the due process clause to find that the Constitution required similar procedures for juvenile delinquency hearings as for adult criminal trials. These procedures included adequate notice of the hearing and representation by counsel; application of the rules of evidence, including exclusion of hearsay; the right to remain silent to avoid self-incrimination; and a burden on the state to prove the relevant facts alleged beyond a reasonable doubt.[31] Trial by jury, interestingly, was not found to be guaranteed by the Constitution in juvenile proceedings.[32]

Taken together, the quasi-criminal commitment cases and the juvenile delinquency cases suggested that the state was not entirely free to decide whom it might confine and what procedures it would employ to reach its decisions. Although the Court had not addressed civil commitment *per se,* the analogies between the systems it had considered and the civil commitment system seemed apparent. The categories of persons subject to civil commitment were often ill-defined, and the state's interest in their involuntary hospitalization might be questioned. Procedures in commitment cases gave authorities markedly more discretion than their counterparts in the criminal justice system enjoyed. And as the Supreme Court feared was true for juvenile delinquents, the promise of therapeutic assistance was probably unfulfilled for many of the mentally ill as well.[33]

Indeed, for observers who were slow to see the potential applicability of these cases to civil commitment of the mentally disordered, the Court itself underscored the point. Justice Blackmun, writing the majority opinion in *Jackson v. Indiana,* the case that limited confinement of incurably incompetent defendants, noted: "Considering the number of persons affected, it is perhaps remarkable that the substantive constitutional limitations [on a state's commitment] power have not been more frequently litigated."[34]

Other lines of cases may have been significant building blocks of the later commitment decisions,[35] but one line in particular was critically important in easing the path for plaintiffs into federal court. In the early 1960s, the U.S. Supreme Court revived a statute that dated to the post–Civil War era, but had largely lain dormant since.[36] Title 42, Section 1983 of the United States Code permits citizens to bring suit in federal court when they have been deprived of their federal statutory or constitutional rights by someone acting under color of state law. By allowing such suits to be brought as a matter of right, even if other remedies were available under state law, the Court created a tool of enormous utility to litigators. Under Section 1983, lawyers could seek relief for named plaintiffs or for an entire class of persons. Compensatory damages and punitive damages were both available. And injunctive relief offered the opportunity to prohibit state officials from enforcing unconstitutional statutes. Later Congress would authorize the courts to award attorneys' fees to victorious plaintiffs, thus compelling states to fund successful litigation against themselves. Perhaps most important of all, in an era in which federal courts were often thought to support individual rights more strongly than state courts did, Section 1983 allowed plaintiffs to avoid the conservative state courts in favor of a more sympathetic venue.[37]

Despite these incentives, when Alberta Lessard was detained for observation, the courts had not yet extended the U.S. Supreme Court's precedents to the civil commitment of the mentally ill. But as is often the case, commentators in the law reviews were already anticipating the directions the courts would later take. State justifications for involuntary commitment were under fire,[38] as were the actual practices in the commitment process. One of the more influential papers was a massive report of an empirical study by law students at the University of Arizona of that state's system for civil commitment.[39] As they documented problems at each stage of the commitment process—for example, the cursory nature of most commitment hearings, at which psychiatrists' conclusions regarding a patient's committability were accepted at face value, without even a superficial exploration of the supporting evidence—the students pointedly contrasted the situation with the constitutional guarantees that appeared to be promised by the new cases. The call for judicial enforcement of individual rights could not have been more direct.

By focusing on the courts as the initiators of change in this area, I have so far neglected the pioneering role of two jurisdictions where legislative models of commitment law reform arose. In 1964, under the leadership of Senator Sam Ervin (after whom the law came to be known), Congress passed a statute altering commitment standards and procedures in the District of Columbia.[40] The law limited commitment to persons who were mentally ill and dangerous to themselves or others, and it provided additional procedural protections.

In a similar vein, California's Lanterman–Petris–Short (LPS) Act, passed in 1967 and implemented two years later, rested the state's power to commit on a mentally ill person's dangerousness, although it included an additional provision for those who were so gravely disabled as to be unable to meet their physical needs.[41] Far more radical than the Ervin Act, California's law limited commitment for danger to self to a duration of only 31 days; commitments for danger to others were renewable after the first 17 days, but a full rehearing was required every 90 days. Persons deemed to be still dangerous to self after 31 days could be held against their will only if they were also gravely disabled and thus qualified for a conservatorship of their person.[42] The state's power was restricted to emergency intervention, except with regard to persons clearly unable to meet their own needs. Significant procedural protections were included.

The Ervin Act and the California statute reflected a view of the proper reach of state power that was to grow in popularity in the following two decades. It was based on the libertarian belief that the state is justified in infringing individual liberty only when one person's actions endanger others, and perhaps in a limited set of circumstances when people act irrationally to endanger themselves. Many commentators argued that precisely this vision of liberty inspired our founding fathers, and that state actions that transcend these limits lack constitutional legitimacy.[43] It is also likely that legislators' concerns about the cost of institutional care—and its poor quality despite the sums expended on it—contributed to their endorsement of stricter commitment standards.[44] The poor care in many state institutions appeared to substantiate arguments that the state's benevolent intentions inevitably degenerated into cruel and abusive realities.[45] And this desire to limit the legal basis for involuntary commitment was supported by the claims of community psychiatrists that chronically ill patients could be treated better as outpatients than as residents in state hospitals.[46] Thus, a potent set of arguments, ranging from the philosophical to the fiscal to the clinical, supported restricting the scope of commitment laws. The California experience, in particular, was watched carefully around the nation.

The courts not only had relevant constitutional precedents and commentators offering advice on how to apply them; they had statutory models of commitment laws to adduce and examples of systems that had functioned successfully under the approach they would embrace. The federal district court sitting in Milwaukee was now ready to make use of each of these elements in responding to the complaint of Alberta Lessard.

Lessard and the Reformulation of Commitment Law

On October 18, 1972, just short of a year after Ms. Lessard was detained on the streets of West Allis, the court issued its opinion. The plaintiff's attorneys had alleged that the standard under which she was committed—"mentally ill . . . and a proper subject for custody and treatment"—was vague and overbroad and did not embody the principle of "less drastic means." [47] The court appeared to accept all these arguments; but rather than striking down the statute as unconstitutional, it took the somewhat unusual path of "interpreting" the statute in such a way as to avoid that course.

Having argued in a prologue to its actual holding that the state's legitimate powers are limited to preventing harm to others under its police powers (citing the libertarian philosopher John Stuart Mill for the point) and to preventing imminent harm to oneself under a very narrow reading of its powers as *parens patriae*, [48] the court now "saved" the statute by reading it as comporting with these views. It quoted the opinion of the U.S. Supreme Court in *Humphrey v. Cady*, one of the sex offender cases referred to earlier, which suggested in *dicta* [49] that Wisconsin's commitment statute implicitly requires that a person's "potential for doing harm, to himself or to others, is great enough to justify such a massive curtailment of liberty."

In making that requirement explicit, the court held that "the state must bear the burden of proving that there is an extreme likelihood that if the person is not confined he will do immediate harm to himself or others" (p. 1093). This finding of dangerousness must be based on a recent overt act, attempt, or threat to inflict substantial harm. As if to emphasize the restrictive nature of this standard, the judges commented in a footnote, "Even an overt attempt to substantially harm oneself cannot be the basis for commitment unless the person is found to be 1) mentally ill and 2) in immediate danger at the time of the hearing of doing further harm to oneself" (p. 1093).

The court also addressed the question of the procedures that must attend the commitment process. It ruled that a preliminary hearing must be held within 48 hours of detention to determine whether probable cause existed to believe that the person was committable, with rights to notice, to attendance, and to representation by counsel. A full hearing was required within 10 to 14 days. Here the delinquency cases, particularly *In re Gault,* were cited to support the requirements for appointment of counsel, a right against self-incrimination, exclusion of hearsay evidence, and proof by the state of the respondent's committability beyond a reasonable doubt. Commitment could be ordered only if no less restrictive alternatives were available.

Lessard dispensed with the historic standard for civil commitment and, in a stroke, substituted a vastly constricted dangerousness requirement. Simultaneously, it imported a rigorous set of procedures from the criminal law that went far beyond those imposed during any previous period of reform. How influential was *Lessard* in subsequent developments? The decision came at a time when some states had already changed their commitment laws in the directions suggested by the opinion and others were considering doing so. If *Lessard* had not been decided when it was, some other federal or state court would probably have reasoned from the same precedents to a similar conclusion. *Lessard* reflected the ethos of its era.

Yet we must not underestimate its influence either. Other courts frequently cited *Lessard* for support in striking down their states' commitment laws.[50] *Lessard's* visibility—due in part to the tortuous procedural history that kept the case alive for three more years following the district court's decision[51]—undoubtedly helped persuade other states to change their statutes before they were challenged in court. And perhaps most important of all, *Lessard* came to symbolize a desire to subordinate the therapeutic impulses that once drove civil commitment law to the civil libertarian concerns that were then in ascendence.

Whether *Lessard* merely reflected its era or actually molded it—and it probably did both—the degree to which commitment law in the subsequent decade came to resemble its vision is striking. In 1959, only five states restricted involuntary hospitalization to persons who were "dangerous"; and in 1971, the number was nine.[52] Moreover, even in these states, danger to self or others was likely interpreted so broadly as to place few limits on the commitment of putatively mentally ill persons.[53] By the end of the 1970s, however, every state either had changed its statute to restrict hospitalization to persons who were dangerous to themselves or others (including dangerousness by virtue of "grave disability," defined as an inability to meet one's basic needs) or had interpreted its preexisting statute in this way so as to "save" it from being found unconstitutional.[54] The triumph was complete for those who believed that the state's power to confine the mentally ill, although legitimate, represented a massive invasion of liberty that could only be permitted in the most limited circumstances.

Reactions to the Transformation of Commitment Law

Mental health professionals, reacting in the early and mid-1970s to this dramatic alteration in civil commitment law, were by no means entirely negative about the changes.[55] In fact, with community models of psychiatry at the peak of their influence and with psychiatrists sharing the society's general concern over abuses of state power and support for individual rights, many psychiatrists had reasonably favorable reactions to the changes.

Some authorities expressed relief at the reduced discretion afforded psychiatrists under the new laws. "[P]sychiatrists have not been entirely unwilling to see their practices attacked," noted forensic psychiatrist and educator Seymour Halleck. "Many of us have long anguished over the power we hold over patients and have welcomed greater community control of that power." Pointing to the relatively weak initial response from the profession to commitment law changes, he continued, "The efforts of reformers in this area receive quick reinforcement because psychiatrists themselves have offered little resistance to change."[56]

Indeed, psychiatrists were positively enthusiastic about some aspects of the reforms. The Committee on Psychiatry and Law of the American Psychiatric Association (APA) formulated a "Position Statement on the Involuntary Hospitalization of the Mentally Ill," which was approved by the APA's Board of Trustees in March 1972, while *Lessard* was still being considered by the Wisconsin federal district court.[57] The statement began by endorsing a move away from involuntary hospitalization, insofar as that could be accomplished: "The American Psychiatric Association is convinced that most persons who need hospitalization for mental illness can be and should be informally and voluntarily admitted to hospitals in the same manner that hospitalization is afforded for any other illness. . . ."

The statement noted, however, that involuntary hospitalization would still be required for "a small percentage of patients" who, because of illness, were unable to make informed decisions and for those who might constitute a danger to themselves or others. To be justified in such cases, however, involuntary hospitalization should only proceed with careful attention to due process, including availability of legal counsel for the patient, examination by an independent psychiatrist if the patient desired it, a prompt judicial hearing on the need for hospitalization, frequent and periodic reports to the courts on the patient's condition, and rehearings every six months (at a minimum) on the need for continued hospitalization, with the burden resting on the treating agency to prove that continued hospitalization was needed.

The APA position statement clearly indicates that the organization, although shying away from accepting the restriction of involuntary hospitalization solely to persons who were dangerous to themselves or others, approved of substantial limitations on the use of commitment and, in particular, endorsed a panoply of criminal-style procedures. That the organization's position comported with the views of the majority of its members is suggested by the results of a series of surveys of psychiatrists, conducted from 1969 until 1978.[58] The polls reveal a high degree of consensus on the desirability of providing procedural rights in the commitment process, albeit considerably less agreement as to whether civil commitment should be limited only to persons found dangerous to themselves or others.

As the changes in commitment law gained momentum, however, the critics of the new approach became more vocal and more visible, probably reflecting the concerns of their colleagues at large.[59] Their negative reactions appear to have been based on experiences they encountered while working under the new statutes, which they came to blame for a variety of bad outcomes for their patients and a series of adverse effects on the mental health system as a whole.

The best known of the early critics of a *Lessard*-type approach to civil commitment was Darryl Treffert, a Wisconsin psychiatrist. Reporting his experiences after the court decision in *Lessard,* he coined a phrase that would become a battle cry for opponents of commitment law reforms. Patients, said Treffert, were "dying with their rights on," an idea he elaborated in two publications with that title.[60] Treffert described one case in which a judge refused to commit a woman with anorexia nervosa, saying that her danger to self was not imminent. The woman died of starvation three weeks later at home. A second case involved a college student who was released from a medical hospital following a suicide attempt, after lawyers advised the patient's family that she probably would not qualify for hospitalization under the *Lessard* standard. She hanged herself at home the following day. Finally, Treffert detailed a case from a neighboring state with a strict dangerousness standard in which two girls picked up by police from a street corner, where they had been staring at each other mutely for hours, were released after city attorneys opined that the girls would not meet the standard for commitment. Two days later the girls were found ablaze, having set each other alight in a suicide pact.[61]

Treffert did not offer a discrete plan at that time for remedying the problems he saw, but he argued that the pendulum had swung too far in excluding from involuntary hospitalization all patients who were not imminently dangerous to themselves or others. Severely ill people had rights to freedom, he argued, but also rights to be rescued from the consequences of their illnesses. The situation could be corrected by moving commitment standards back to "some reasonable middle ground" between unlimited hospitalization of all persons diagnosed as mentally ill and the current restrictive approach.

Clearly, Treffert's articles and call to action struck a chord among practicing psychiatrists. A number of authors followed in Treffert's footsteps, offering other examples of patients harmed by restrictive commitment laws.[62] Forensic psychiatrist Jonas Rappeport called psychiatry "belegaled," a word that seemed to capture the profession's mood.[63]

In many ways the most influential critic of the new approach to civil commitment was Alan Stone, a psychiatrist who was professor of law and psychiatry at Harvard Law School and who served as president of the American Psychiatric Association in the late 1970s. In the introduction to his 1975 book *Mental Health and Law: A System in Transition,* Stone noted his perception that "[f]ive years into the decade of the 1970s . . . the United States is engaged in an all out legal war over the fate of the mentally ill."[64] Stone generally supported the due-process-oriented procedural changes, even noting that the absence of due process might be countertherapeutic.

On the other hand, Stone had a bone to pick with particular procedural requirements, such as the *Lessard* mandate for a *Miranda*-type warning from psychiatrists to patients that their statements made during an examination might be used against them in a commitment hearing, and the use of proof beyond a reasonable doubt as the standard at commitment hearings. The latter he characterized as "impossible of fulfillment," (p. 57) and taking the *Lessard* opinion as a whole, Stone maintained that "if followed exactly, [it would] put a virtual end to involuntary confinement" (p. 52).

As for the substantive criteria for hospitalization, Stone opposed reliance on a dangerousness standard. He offered in its place what he called his "Thank You Theory" of civil commitment. Under this approach, a set of criteria would be developed, emphasizing patients' need for treatment, incapacity to make their own decisions, and reasonable expectations that they might benefit from care, with the goal of identifying a group of patients who could reasonably be expected to be grateful, at the conclusion of their hospitalization, that commitment had occurred.

In his later book, *Law, Psychiatry, and Morality,* Stone elaborated on the impediments that the new laws, including those governing commitment, had created to the delivery of psychiatric care:[65]

> There is a pervasive conviction in public mental hospitals that the law has made it impossible to treat people who don't want treatment, so why bother . . . A typical reaction is for psychiatrists to assume that patients cannot be involuntarily confined . . . [T]he [psychiatrist's] bottom line is this: I am helpless to do anything because of the law and I am not responsible.

Stone pointed to legal regulation as a prime factor motivating the flight of psychiatrists from the public sector.

By the early 1980s, the opposition to a dangerousness-based standard and to some of the procedural changes coalesced around several similar designs for proposed changes in the laws. Stone was the primary architect of the American Psychiatric Association's model law, which relied heavily on his "Thank You Theory" of commitment.[66] The model law would allow commitment (besides in the usual dangerousness-based situations) if the patient "will if not treated suffer or continue to suffer severe and abnormal mental, emotional, or physical distress, and this distress is associated with significant impairment of judgment, reason, or behavior causing a substantial deterioration of his previous ability to function on his own." In addition, committed patients must lack "capacity to make an informed decision concerning treatment"; treatment must be available at the facility to which the patient will be sent; and commitment must be "consistent with the least restrictive alternative principle."[67]

Treffert offered a proposal based on similar ideas.[68] He suggested allowing commitment when the patient "is unable to make an informed decision regarding treatment and evidences a substantial probability of serious mental or emotional deterioration unless treatment is provided and is incapable of expressing an understanding of the advantages and disadvantages of accepting treatment and the alternatives to the particular treatment offered after the advantages, disadvantages, and alternatives have been explained."

Although opponents of the *Lessard* reforms generally focused on the harms suffered by patients who might have been seriously ill but failed to meet narrow dangerousness criteria, this was not the only basis on which attacks were launched. It was also argued that the restrictive nature of the new laws would divert patients who needed treatment into the criminal justice system.[69] They would be arrested for behaviors (usually misdemeanors) that previously would have resulted in their being brought to the state hospital. Then, found incompetent to stand trial as a result of their mental illness, they would be committed to the state hospital for treatment until competence was restored. At that point, the charges against them would be dismissed, having served their intended purpose. Even worse, they might simply be convicted and sent to jails, where they would languish untreated.

Other concerns were expressed, as well. Some critics worried that the new standards would force psychiatrists to make determinations regarding dangerousness for which they had no training and which, in any event, might not be possible to make reliably. The effect on the facilities themselves was also a matter of concern; Stone, among others, argued that selecting patients on the basis of their dangerousness, rather than on the basis of their amenability to treatment, might create a system in which hospitals became quasi-penal institutions.[70]

Overall, psychiatrists' initial neutral or even positive reactions to the revolution in commitment law that took place in the early 1970s substantially evaporated by the end of the decade. Although most psychiatrists still endorsed the procedural changes designed to make a commitment hearing more like a criminal trial, strong opposition had developed to the substantive criteria for commitment, which were based on predicting patients' dangerousness to themselves or others.

The critique of the commitment system offered by psychiatrists was based heavily on anecdotal evidence, with few empirical data to support the cause. Indeed, some of the most prominent authors repeated their anecdotal case reports in article after article and occasionally recounted cases previously published by other opponents of the reforms. Yet the critics made specific predictions about the effects of commitment law reform that were empirically testable. Either patients in need of treatment were being turned away in large numbers or they were not. Either the criminal justice system was absorbing some of the resulting burden or it wasn't. Whatever the reality, carefully designed studies could be expected to reveal it.

Studies of the Effects of Commitment Law Reforms

Need for Empirical Data

What kind of data would validate the predictions of the opponents of commitment law reform? If we begin with the everyday experience of most contemporary Americans, who see around them the sorry condition of the homeless mentally ill, can we doubt that restrictive statutes make it too difficult for psychiatrists to hospitalize people in need of care? Cast adrift in our society, mentally ill people who might once have been housed in state hospitals now live by the thousands on the streets of our major cities. We step over and around them on our way to work, to shop, and to play. They seem to offer mute testimony to the failure of two decades of commitment law reform.

The hard numbers of the researchers seem to support these impressions. Surveys of the homeless, who appear to number from 400,000 to more than 2 million,[71] have found that 25 to 50 percent have major mental disorders, with many of the remainder suffering from alcohol and drug abuse or severe personality disorders.[72] Less apparent are the even larger numbers of mentally ill persons living in board-and-care homes, with minimal psychiatric services.[73] There is no question that they reflect the inadequacy of our systems for dealing with mental disorder.

Another kind of evidence from day-to-day experience comes from the pages of our newspapers and magazines, filled with accounts of patients turned away from mental health facilities, often because they are said not to be involuntarily committable under present law, only to perpetrate horrendous violence on others or to endure shameful degradation themselves.[74] The psychotic man who slashes his way across the deck of the Staten Island ferry; the depressed worker who slaughters his colleagues and then turns his gun on himself; and the deranged woman who opens fire in a shopping mall on helpless passers-by have become prototypical casualties of an imperfect society. Indeed, the stories of such episodes that appear periodically on the front pages of newspapers are so similar in many respects that they gradually merge with one another in our memories.

And if the question is whether other institutions of society have picked up the burdens shed by the mental health system, the reports coming out of our jails and prisons appear to provide the answer. Studies of the prevalence of mental disorders in correctional facilities show substantial rates of severe mental disorders in prisons where convicted felons are held, with 10 percent a commonly accepted figure.[75] But even this figure doesn't tell the whole story. In local jails, which are used to detain defendants prior to trial and to incarcerate misdemeanants and others with short sentences, astronomical rates of severe mental illness are found.[76] Indeed, the Los Angeles County Jail has been described as the largest mental hospital in the United States.[77]

In the face of a hard-edged reality such as this, it seems difficult to question the impact of the changes in commitment law inspired by the Ervin Act, California's LPS statute, *Lessard,* and their ideological offspring. Many citizens and lawmakers, in fact, look no further. When changes in commitment law are sought these days, usually in the direction of loosening commitment criteria and easing procedural rules, the myriad homeless mentally ill and the random acts of violence committed by those who are refused involuntary hospitalization are most often cited in support.[78]

But do these commonsensical data provide a truly adequate basis for assigning responsibility for the situation? The mental health system is a complex agglomeration of organizations, the functioning of which is affected by (among other factors) changes in political goals, funding sources, availability of treatment facilities, new methods of treatment, cooperation of related systems (such as the criminal justice system), and the availability and competence of clinical staff, in addition to legal rules.[79] Although everyday observations and the data on the incidence of mental illness among the homeless and in correctional facilities make a good case that something has gone wrong with our mental health services, they do not demonstrate by themselves that the blame rests with the new generation of commitment laws. It might be, for example, that the system began to fail before the laws were revised and that the new statutes had relatively little impact on the course of events.

To establish a causal link, therefore, we need to obtain a clearer idea of exactly what impact the revised commitment laws themselves had on decisions to hospitalize mentally ill people. That question can be addressed on two levels. Studies of aggregate data, such as admission statistics from mental health systems in transition, can tell us something about the magnitude of changes associated with the new statutes. If no gross changes occurred, the likelihood that the statutes had any important effect on individual hospitalization decisions is small. But while aggregate data can tell us about the size of an effect, they cannot tell us precisely what its nature is. For example, a sharp decrease in the number of commitments following the implementation of a new law could indicate that more restrictive criteria are being taken seriously and are having the desired effect of limiting hospitalization to dangerous persons. Equally plausible, however, is the possibility that the restrictions are having a random effect, with fewer commitments occurring as the process becomes more difficult to manage, but with no change in the overall mix of patients. To separate out these possibilities, we need to inspect data that tell us something about individual cases. Fortunately, both sorts of data exist.

Studies of Aggregate Data

Studies of the aggregate effects of new commitment statutes, of which about two dozen have now been performed, usually examine the rates of commitment for a given jurisdiction (often a whole state) from some time prior to the implementation of the new law to some point afterward. The first study of this type was carried out in Massachusetts by A. Louis McGarry, a psychiatrist, and his colleagues in the early 1970s.[80] Massachusetts had been one of the earliest states to follow California's lead in revising its commitment statute, with McGarry himself spearheading the effort to rewrite the law in 1971. The new statute replaced need-for-treatment criteria with typical dangerousness-based criteria and incorporated a panoply of procedural protections drawn from the criminal model.

Striking results appeared in data on admissions gathered from all public in-patient facilities in the state. McGarry found sharp decreases in total admissions, first admissions, and judicial commitments, with a concomitant increase in the rate of voluntary admissions. The latter was apparently stimulated by a new requirement that all patients be offered the opportunity to sign themselves into the facility before emergency commitment occurred. To this day, the Massachusetts study remains one of the most impressive demonstrations of the impact a more restrictive commitment law can have.

A more recent study with similar conclusions comes from Florida and examines the effects of a 1982 change in that state's commitment statute, known as the Baker Act.[81] This statutory change, part of a second wave of reform, further tightened provisions of Florida's dangerousness-based statute, requiring the state to demonstrate that overt behavior indicating a patient's dangerousness has occurred within 20 days of the commitment hearing, and using more precise language to define grave disability. Emergency commitments were reduced in duration from five to three days, and judges were instructed to review all "less restrictive treatment alternatives" before committing patients.

Roger Peters and his co-workers applied sophisticated time-series analyses to the records of the in-patient censuses at Florida's state hospitals.[82] They showed a significantly greater decline for the year following the new statute than had occurred, on average, for the three preceding years.[83] Hospital admissions fell more than would have been expected given contemporary trends, and the drop was limited to involuntary patients. The authors of the study concluded that the new law had a significant effect on hospitalization practices.

Not all studies examining the effects of the new commitment laws, however, produced comparable results. When an interrupted time-series design was used to examine commitment patterns for 20 months before and after implementation of Nebraska's new dangerousness-based statute, researchers found a temporary fall-off in the number of commitments, followed by a rapid return to levels that occurred under the previous statute.[84] A ten-year study of all commitments in a single county in Washington state revealed a continuous increase in the number of both emergency and judicial commitments, despite the introduction of a strict dangerousness-based law in 1973.[85] In fact, reports showing little or no effect of commitment law changes on aggregate commitment rates are somewhat more common than those suggesting an impact.

How can these divergent findings be reconciled? A fascinating reanalysis of the published data by two Canadian psychologists, R. Michael Bagby and Leslie Atkinson, offers a way out of the dilemma.[86] They noted a peculiar pattern in research on commitment law effects. When researchers limited their post-reform observations to a short period of time, often just one year, a significant fall-off in commitments was commonly noted. Researchers who extended their studies beyond the first year, however, almost always found a rise in commitment rates, and in some cases a return to or an increase above the original levels. In their words, "15 of the 17 independent data sets showed that increases in civil commitment rates followed initial post-reform decreases. All three studies which included extended post-reform observations revealed that admission rates eventually approached pre-reform levels."

This analysis, as intriguing as it is, was based solely on data offered by the authors of the original studies. Thus, if the original authors failed to extend their observations sufficiently to test the theory that rates of commitment would rebound toward their previous baseline, Bagby and Atkinson did not obtain data independently to test the hypothesis. Beyond that, to say that rates of commitment increased after an initial decline is not to say that the original reform failed to have a lasting effect. Commitment rates may never have reached previous levels in some states, attaining equilibrium somewhere between the *status quo ante* and the maximal decrement noted in the first year. Nonetheless, the difficulty researchers have had in demonstrating a clear effect of the new statutes in restricting admissions is impressive.[87]

Studies of Individual Cases

Studies that have examined data at the level of individual cases have had a similarly difficult time identifying consistent restrictive effects of the new laws. One might anticipate that statutes with more rigorous definitions of dangerousness and grave disability would lead to commitment of a sicker, perhaps more chronic population. Certainly, one would expect the post-reform group to be more likely to meet the new dangerousness criteria than a pre-reform sample. But these effects too have been difficult to demonstrate.

In California, for example, an evaluation of the impact of the landmark Lanterman-Petris-Short Act was undertaken by the ENKI Research Institute just as the law was taking effect.[88] Comparing data on 236 patients sampled before the change in the law with information on 335 patients obtained after implementation of the new statute, the research team found no difference between the groups on numerous demographic and diagnostic variables. Of particular interest was the researchers' finding that between 21 and 53 percent of patients committed (depending on the jurisdiction within the state) apparently failed to meet dangerousness criteria both before and after the new statute was implemented.

A study from Pittsburgh, conducted by psychiatrist Mark Munetz and colleagues following a tightening of Pennsylvania's dangerousness-oriented law, gave roughly similar results.[89] Examining the records of three groups of fifty patients each, taken from the pre-reform, immediately post-reform, and two-year post-reform periods, the Pittsburgh psychiatrists found no significant differences in the demographic or diagnostic composition of their subject groups. Fewer patients were committed on the basis of suicidality after the change in the law, and more on the grounds of inability to care for their basic needs. In addition, the authors were under the impression that the latter category constituted a catch-all for patients who did not meet specific criteria but for whom hospitalization appeared to be warranted on clinical grounds.

A final study conducted at the individual case level that is worth examining was performed as part of the Florida study described earlier.[90] Peters and his colleagues argued that their aggregate data supported a significant effect for the revised commitment statute. As part of their research, however, they also observed and recorded eighty commitment hearings in a single court, split evenly between cases heard before and after the statutory change. The researchers found no differences in the number of commitment petitions filed or the number of hearings held in the two periods, suggesting that the new law had not greatly altered the flow of potential involuntary committees before the court. This was confirmed by the finding that, although patient-respondents after the statutory change were rated as somewhat more dangerous according to objective criteria when dangerousness was the basis for the commitment petition, they still averaged only 2.6 on a 10-point scale and rarely had actually harmed anyone. Further, when grave disability served as the grounds for commitment, respondents were *not* rated as less able to care for themselves after the new law took effect. Before the change in the law, thirty-eight of forty patients were committed, with six being given dispositions other than admission to the state hospital. Under the new law, forty of forty patients were committed, and only one patient was sent to an alternative placement. Despite the stricter criteria and some evidence of procedural changes, this study, too, failed to demonstrate any clear-cut effect of the new law on the type of patients who were committed.[91]

These three case-level studies are typical of those found in the literature. Indeed, I have been unable to identify a single study that demonstrates marked changes in the characteristics of committed patients from before to after a statutory change. If the restrictive commitment statutes have had an overall effect in decreasing the number of patients committed, therefore, we have yet to see evidence that the effect is consistent with the goals of the statutory reforms.

Studies of Persons Not Committed

It is worth considering a final set of studies that address the purported effects of restrictive commitment statutes most directly. While case-level studies of committed patients tell us something about persons who are committed, they cannot reveal the characteristics of those who are turned away. Given that the debate over restrictive statutes has focused heavily on the allegation that large numbers of patients in need of care are denied access to mental health facilities, surprisingly few attempts have been made to determine the extent of this problem directly.

One of the few research reports that tried to answer this question derived from a larger project conducted in the emergency room of the Western Psychiatric Institute and Clinic by psychologist Edward Mulvey and sociologist Charles Lidz.[92] The investigators asked the evaluating clinicians to rate 390 patients whose examinations were observed by the research team on a number of dimensions, including need for immediate treatment and committability under Pennsylvania's dangerousness-oriented statute. Using two different analytic strategies, they attempted to identify patients who were rated high on need for treatment but low on committability. This is precisely the group that critics of restrictive commitment laws charged would be the primary victims of the new statutes. Their best efforts, however, resulted in the identification of only one patient who appeared to need hospital treatment, resisted voluntary hospitalization, and appeared not to qualify under existing commitment criteria.[93]

This exception is worth considering in detail. She was a very psychotic woman, who, though clearly in need of treatment to control her delusions, was not threatening to herself or others and appeared to be able to meet her basic needs. The dilemma she presented was the subject of a good deal of agonizing by the clinical team. They believed she would benefit enormously from hospitalization and treatment, but they found it difficult to fit her into one of the categories in the state's commitment statute. In the end, however, they decided to commit her under the statute's grave disability provisions, although they believed that she did not truly meet those strict criteria. Thus, in a substantial sample from an urban emergency room, researchers could identify only one patient who fell into the problematic category, and she was dealt with by bending the commitment statute to justify commitment.

A different way of approaching this issue was taken by Steven Segal and his colleagues at the University of California at Berkeley.[94] They observed emergency room evaluations of 251 cases. The research team independently rated patients' dangerousness under the California standard, as well as the severity of symptoms the patients experienced. Segal found a strong correlation between severity of symptoms and the presence of indicators of dangerousness. In addition, symptomatology and dangerousness indices together were highly accurate predictors of ultimate disposition. Although, unlike researchers in the Pittsburgh study, Segal did not break his data down to the case level to look specifically for severely impaired patients who might have ranked low on indicators of dangerousness, he drew two relevant conclusions from his aggregate data: it is unlikely that many severely ill patients who are unwilling to volunteer for hospitalization are going uncommitted, since they also tend to be the most dangerous; and dangerous persons who are not in need of treatment do not appear to be entering the hospital system in substantial numbers.

Of course, both the Pittsburgh and California studies are limited by a crucial aspect of their methodology. They dealt only with patients who were seen in psychiatric emergency rooms, not with the population of all mentally ill persons. If referral sources have learned not to send patients who may need treatment but do not meet commitment criteria—because their experience is that such people simply will be turned away—we would not expect to see any such persons turn up in the samples. The possibility of bias of this sort cannot be ruled out. But the emergency rooms in each study cared for a broad population of mentally disordered persons in varying degrees of distress, many of whom appeared on their own initiative, while others were brought by family members or the police. If substantial numbers of seriously distressed people could not be committed because of statutory limitations, we would expect to see some evidence of them in these studies.

Summarizing the Data

It has been remarkably difficult for researchers to demonstrate any of the presumed consequences of the new statutes. To the extent that consistent findings are available, they tend to show that the statutes have had less impact than expected (and in some cases minimal effect) on overall rates of commitment and on the nature of committed populations. Nor has it been possible to identify individual patients who are "dying with their rights on" in the very small number of carefully performed studies.

Does this mean that such cases do not exist, and that massive changes in commitment law have had no effect at all? Undoubtedly not. I believe that some patients are turned away from emergency rooms who desperately need care. The anecdotal evidence to this effect in the writings of Treffert and others is too strong to ignore. Although the data suggest that the number of such people is not very large, it seems likely that regional variations make the problem prominent in some places and nonexistent in others. Further, the preceding data show, at least for an initial period, strong effects of new laws on lowered commitment rates. But these findings, too, vary greatly across jurisdictions and are a far cry from the predictions made by opponents of restrictive statutes that civil commitment would be nearly impossible to effect and that widespread suffering would result. Whatever the impact of the new laws, it has been sufficiently subtle to defy easy characterization.

How can we explain the discrepancy between the predictions and the outcome? If only imminently dangerous persons could be committed, it was reasonable to conclude that many nondangerous persons who needed care would be excluded from hospitalization, that the nature of committed populations would change, and that commitment rates would fall. If mental illness and dangerousness had to be proved in court beyond a reasonable doubt, and if patients were provided with aggressive attorneys who demanded that the state satisfy its burden of proof, how could psychiatry, beset by the inherent uncertainties of human nature, ever meet that standard? Did reason not lead inexorably to the conclusion that the entire commitment system would shrink, perhaps even wither, as a result of the reforms?

Perhaps it did. But this is one case where reason seems to have misled us. The result poses a challenge to our understanding of mental health law: what happened to prevent the civil commitment system from grinding to a halt?

Commitment Law in Practice: Explaining the Data

Attorneys and Judges: The "Commonsense" Model

One of the most important insights of the legal realism movement, which flourished in the second quarter of this century, was that laws are enforced by people; they do not enforce themselves. Unless a law is generally accepted as being worthy of respect, it will be widely ignored. Our unsuccessful experiment with Prohibition is the classic example of a law undermined from the start by a lack of popular support and a reluctance on the part of the criminal justice system, especially the police, to enforce it. In our own time, efforts to compel drivers to use seat belts have met with a comparable degree of resistance. Law, like psychotherapy, cannot change behavior unless people are willing to change.

Therein lies the answer to the question of why, despite two decades of extensive reform in the standards and procedures for civil commitment, it is so hard to find measurable effects of the new laws. For a century-and-a-half, the major participants in the civil commitment system—family members, mental health professionals, attorneys, and the courts—had collaborated in hospitalizing mentally ill people whom they believed were in need of care. In the early 1970s, they were asked to change. No longer would mental illness and an evident need for care be sufficient as a predicate to involuntary commitment. Patients' rights to liberty, *Lessard* declared, required that nonconsensual hospitalization be limited to situations in which imminent physical harm was likely. Moreover, demonstration of that harm required adherence to procedures that might often result in exclusion of relevant evidence, on the grounds that its admission would violate legal norms of fairness.

Powerful justifications were offered for the new approaches. They were grounded in principles, such as respect for individual autonomy and due process of law, that are widely regarded as fundamental to our political system. At a time when concern for the powerless was high on our political agenda, extension of additional rights to the mentally ill—a group that always had been at the bottom of the social ladder—was enormously appealing. Advocates for the new laws asked only that the state treat mentally ill people as it would any other people before depriving them of freedom.

But these appeals were not enough. Even when they were embraced in principle, they often were abandoned in practice. Confronted with psychotic persons who might well benefit from treatment, and who would certainly suffer without it, mental health professionals and judges alike were reluctant to comply with the law and release them. They simply could not give credence to a calculus that placed rights above suffering. Attorneys trained to fight for the exculpation of felons whom they knew or suspected to be guilty could not bring themselves to do the same for mentally ill people, whose freedom seemed of dubious value compared with treatment and a place to sleep. The new laws did not alter the behavior of these key actors in the system, because they did not want to change.

These phenomena are evident in the work of sociologist Carol Warren, who spent years observing hearings in a California mental health court.[95] Warren found that the major participants in the hearings she observed— psychiatrists, assistant district attorneys, public defenders, and the judge— all shared a "commonsense model" of the people whose hospitalization was in question in the court. They were evidently "sick" or "crazy," and generally not able to decide what was best for themselves. There might be reasons in particular cases to void their commitment (the judge apparently believed that families, not the state, should be responsible for the care of mentally ill relatives), but the underlying consensus was that these were people in need of care.

The dominance of the commonsense model was best illustrated in a process Warren calls "plea bargaining," a term evocative of procedure in criminal courts. Warren studied petitioners who were appealing emergency commitments, and was struck by an oddity she noticed in the distribution of grounds on which commitment was based.[96] At the time of initial hospitalization, on emergency 72-hour holds, the majority of patients had been characterized by the committing psychiatrists as meeting more than one of the criteria for commitment—danger to self, danger to others, and grave disability. In fact, 44 percent of the patients were said to meet all three criteria. Yet when the papers were filed to extend hospitalization for an additional 14 days, more than half of the patients were labeled gravely disabled alone.

Warren believed that this shift, in many cases, was the result of a bargaining process among the parties involved. If the psychiatrist would agree to drop alternative grounds for commitment and to rely solely on grave disability, the public defender would not contest the commitment aggressively, and the judge would go along, too. All parties to this arrangement achieved some objective associated with their respective roles by agreeing to call the patient "gravely disabled." In Warren's words:

The public defenders' office reduces the likelihood of their clients being labeled as dangerous. The district attorney's office does not have to show imminent and predictable danger to others. The judge is not required to release
most of the petitioners (which he might if the dangerousness label were retained), and the psychiatrist is enabled to return patients to "needed treatment." (p. 193)

This description does not reflect an adversarial process aimed at forcing the state to rigorous proof of narrow grounds for commitment. Rather,
what we see through Warren's eyes is a mechanism by which participants
with ostensibly different—and even conflicting—roles cooperatively reach
an outcome that they all agree is desirable: hospitalization of a person whom
they believe is clearly in need of care. What makes this degree of consensus
possible? Warren sums up her account of the plea bargaining process with
these thoughts:

Like the defense attorneys, the judge of Metropolitan Court acquiesced to the
topos [commonsense understanding] of madness in his judgment that the persons processed through his court are indeed crazy and need help. He was
therefore willing to facilitate their continued hospitalization when this appeared commonsensically necessary.[97] (pp. 193–94)

It is important to underscore that Warren's findings on plea bargaining
do not mean that California's commitment law was largely disregarded by
the participants in the mental health court. To the contrary, the vast majority of patients whose commitments were upheld met the state's dangerousness criteria, and public defenders frequently fought for patients' release.
But at the margins, when it came to the type of cases that most concerned
the opponents of the restrictive statutes, the impact of the new laws was
mitigated by a general willingness to achieve what appeared to be the most
sensible result.

Data from other jurisdictions indicate that this tendency to round off
the edges of dangerousness-based commitment laws is widespread. As far
as judges' behavior is concerned, for example, sociologists Virginia Hiday
and Lynn Smith found evidence of similar effects in North Carolina.[98] They
reviewed affidavits submitted to the courts by petitioners and examining
psychiatrists in 1,226 cases in which judicial commitment was sought under
a dangerousness-based statute. The affidavits were submitted on prescribed
forms, with areas designated for information indicating the respondents'
dangerousness. Looking only at affidavits from hearings that resulted in a
judge's decision to commit, Hiday and Smith found that in 16.1 percent of
these cases no evidence was offered of the respondents' potential dangerousness (including danger to self, danger to others, and grave disability).
Turning the data around, they found that in 47.5 percent of the cases in
which the affidavits lacked any information concerning the statutory dan-

gerousness criteria, patients were committed anyway. Like Warren, Hiday and Smith concluded that, despite the requirements of the new laws, commitment is not being limited to persons who meet the narrow terms of the statutes.[99]

The failure of patients' attorneys to assume an adversarial posture has been widely reported as well.[100] Psychiatrist Robert Miller and colleagues, in another North Carolina study, produced some of the most striking findings.[101] As part of a larger study, they closely examined eighty-nine commitment hearings in which the special counsel appointed to represent patients recommended a particular disposition to the courts. In nearly 43 percent of the cases, patients' attorneys advocated a more restrictive disposition than the patients desired—either in-patient or out-patient commitment—rather than outright release. When interviewed, they endorsed a role in which they sought patients' best interests, as they understood them, rather than advocating patients' expressed wishes. The pervasiveness of such views among attorneys has been confirmed in other studies.[102]

In the face of studies with similar results from both the pre- and post-reform eras, psychologist Norman Poythress undertook an instructive attempt to alter attorneys' behavior.[103] Identifying a group of attorneys in one Texas county who often represented patients in commitment hearings, he developed a training program designed to encourage them to be more aggressive and adversarial in their defense of patients at commitment hearings. The training consisted of a seminar covering techniques that could be used to cross-examine psychiatric experts in areas in which their opinions might be vulnerable (such as in the prediction of future dangerous behavior) and included a handbook with specific questions that could be asked.

Poythress then observed attorneys' behavior at commitment hearings, comparing trained and untrained groups. He stated his results succinctly:

> The statistical analysis of data collected in this study suggest the following epigram as an appropriate subtitle for this paper: "You can lead a horse to water but you can't make him drink." Essentially no significant changes in attorney behavior were effected by the training intervention.

Of particular note is the fact that not a single attorney attempted to challenge a psychiatric witness by utilizing the research data Poythress had compiled. Discussions with the attorneys after the training revealed the expected finding: they simply did not see their role as being to oppose commitment of people who were "really sick" and who, in their judgment, clearly needed to be in a hospital.[104]

Mental Health Professionals and Families: The Survival of Beneficence

When judges and attorneys fail to endorse the rationale underlying strict limits on civil commitment, their consequent behavior can greatly influence the outcome of the commitment process. Judges, after all, are the ultimate decision makers at hearings, and studies confirm that the absence of a vigorous defense by respondents' attorneys markedly increases the likelihood of commitment.[105] A more subtle finding involves the residual discretion that psychiatrists and other mental health professionals retain and the influence this allows them to exert at several stages of the process.

Although the architects of current commitment statutes adopted models of due process that borrowed heavily from those in place in the criminal justice system, one part of the commitment process in most jurisdictions remains entirely under mental health professionals' control. In an emergency, when harm to a mentally ill person or to others is thought likely to occur unless immediate steps are taken to detain the person, psychiatrists and certain other classes of mental health professionals have the power to initiate short-term civil commitment.[106]

These provisions were designed as exceptions to the usual rule that commitment should occur only after a hearing before a judge, but they have become a surprisingly common path of entry into the commitment system.[107] Just as rivers follow the easiest route to the sea, persons seeking commitment of mentally ill people find the least complicated means of accomplishing that end.

In making emergency commitment decisions, mental health professionals are supposed to conform to the criteria laid down in the statutes—usually the same criteria by which decisions are made at formal commitment hearings. But several factors confer a good deal of discretion on these clinical decision makers. To begin with, the belief of advocates of commitment law reform in the 1970s that statutes based on dangerousness would be inherently more precise in their requirements than the old "need for treatment" laws turns out to have been mistaken. The wording of the statutes themselves is frequently vague, permitting considerable individual judgment in determining who meets the dangerousness criteria.[108] Definitions of dangerousness are often circular, as in this example drawn from Connecticut's statute: "Dangerous to himself or others means there is a substantial risk that physical harm will be inflicted by an individual upon his or her own person or upon another person. . . ."[109] Given this vagueness, and in the absence of data clearly indicating how to identify persons likely to inflict harm on themselves or others,[110] mental health professionals have great leeway in making these determinations.

Enhancing the discretion of mental health professionals to admit patients who may be in need of treatment are the provisions governing commitment of the "gravely disabled," a category often neglected in discussions of dangerousness-based commitment laws. Beginning with California in the late 1960s, the vast majority of states that enacted new laws included in their definitions of circumstances under which commitment might take place a category covering persons who might come to harm by reason of an inability to meet their basic human needs. California's wording is typical: grave disability is "a condition in which a person, as a result of mental disorder, is unable to provide for his basic personal needs for food, clothing, or shelter."[111]

Not only does such a provision, by its express terms, cover many of those persons about whom the greatest concern was expressed by critics of the new laws, but again the imprecision involved in determining when someone cannot meet their "basic personal needs" allows hospitalization to occur in ambiguous cases. Indeed, in the Pittsburgh study discussed earlier in which 390 emergency room evaluations were examined to determine whether patients who needed treatment were being excluded by stringent commitment criteria, researchers found that almost all patients who ranked high on need for treatment but low on danger to others or self, and who resisted voluntary hospitalization, were committed on grave disability grounds.[112] It appears that grave disability provisions provide the flexibility for clinicians in emergency settings to hospitalize many patients whom they believe truly require care. This helps explain why studies repeatedly find that grave disability is cited as the criterion for commitment in one-third to one-half or more of cases.[113]

Interestingly, while the literature is replete with studies of judges and attorneys bending rigid commitment laws in what they perceive as the patients' best interests, documentation of clinicians' behaving similarly has been harder to obtain. Inferential data come from efforts to examine commitment petitions completed by clinicians, which almost always show that evidence documenting compliance with statutory criteria is missing.[114] It is difficult to know, however, to what extent these findings represent sloppy paperwork, as opposed to circumvention of legal requirements. Two studies that asked psychiatrists to rate patients about whom actual commitment decisions were being made, on dimensions of committability and other characteristics (including need for treatment), found the legal criteria to be most closely associated with the commitment decision.[115] But this may have constituted self-justification by clinicians who were making their decisions on other grounds. Studies looking at hypothetical decisions based on standardized vignettes—a methodology that mitigates the emotional impact of having to release a psychotic person in need of treatment—have reached conflicting conclusions, even in the hands of the same research group.[116]

But despite the difficulty of finding clear documentation of clinicians using their discretion to expand the scope of commitment statutes by admitting patients who might not qualify under strict criteria but are thought to be in need of care, clinical experience suggests that it occurs regularly. Clinicians talk casually among themselves about acting in this way. The absence of change in the characteristics of emergency committed patients after implementation of more restrictive statutes, including their failure to meet dangerousness criteria, strongly indicates that this is the case.[117] Moreover, the vagueness of the relevant statutes permits the process to occur unconsciously, as clinicians reinterpret intrinsically malleable criteria to fit the perceived needs of the patients sitting before them.

The impact of another group of participants in the commitment process—family members—is often neglected, but these individuals also help modify the effects of restrictive commitment laws. An ingenious, though somewhat complicated, study by Marx and Levinson of a metropolitan county in a southeastern state addresses these effects.[118] They looked at an alternative to clinician-controlled emergency commitment that exists in some states, the use of an "order to apprehend" (sometimes called a warrant of apprehension). These orders, in the jurisdiction the researchers examined, could be issued by a judge on the request of two petitioners, usually relatives of the allegedly committable person, if the judge had probable cause to believe that the commitment criteria would be met. Issuance of an order allowed a sheriff to apprehend the person and transport him or her to a psychiatric facility for examination.[119]

Marx and Levinson examined petitions granted for orders to apprehend spanning a four-year period, roughly in the middle of which a statutory change occurred. In the county studied, this change had the effect of adding a grave disability provision to a standard that previously had limited involuntary commitment to cases involving individuals dangerous to others or self.[120]

There were no significant differences in the numbers of petitions signed before and after the effective broadening of the commitment criteria, through the addition of the new grave disability language. This finding is consistent with much of the research on the effect of commitment law changes I have already discussed. Review of the petitions themselves, however, showed that the subjects were characterized quite differently before and after the change. More potential patients were described as dangerous to themselves or others before the law was broadened, when those were the only statutory criteria applied. After the change in the law to permit gravely disabled persons to be committed, fewer subjects were described as dangerous and more as unable to care for themselves. In fact, the differences were accounted for almost entirely by individuals in subgroups that were statistically least likely to manifest assaultive behavior (older, female, and white subjects).[121] Prior to the availability of a grave disability criterion, they were much more likely to be portrayed as dangerous than they were after grave disability became available as an alternative.

Marx and Levinson suggest that their data are compatible with overall stability in the characteristics of subjects for whom petitions were approved (recalling that the total number of orders signed was constant), but with substantial differences in the way in which the subjects were portrayed. These portrayals were apparently molded by the commitment criteria in force in that county. In other words, petitioners, presumably acting on the advice of the clinicians they consulted,[122] said whatever they needed to say to get patients committed. As Marx and Levinson concluded, "[R]ather than being passive objects of statutory changes, participants in the mental health system may actively adapt to the changes and look for ways to cope within the framework to obtain desired outcomes."[123]

That conclusion serves as an apt summary of the major reasons why restrictive civil commitment statutes failed to have the massive effects that both their proponents and antagonists predicted. It seems clear that the relevant actors in the system—judges, lawyers, clinicians, and family members—developed means of implementing what Warren referred to as the "commonsense model," the idea that people in need of care and unprepared to obtain it for themselves should be hospitalized against their will. To the extent that the new statutes ignored the feelings of those most directly involved in carrying them out, they were doomed never even to approach fulfillment of their goals.

Legal Reactions to Commitment Law Reform: The Pendulum Changes Direction

As important as informal factors were in modifying the implementation of commitment law in practice, we should not neglect another group of developments that set a more formal limit on the effects of the new statutes. As is often the case in social reform movements, the earliest changes in commitment law were the most radical. California's Lanterman-Petris-Short Act, for example, limited commitment of suicidal patients to 31 days.[124] It was presumed that, if treatment were not successful within that period of time, patients would be released. This provision was responsible for a good deal of the early criticism of the new law, with many people horrified at the thought that treatment of suicidal mentally ill persons effectively might be abandoned.[125]

Lessard v. Schmidt, the first of the major civil commitment cases to be decided, established by far the most sweeping changes. The criteria imposed by the *Lessard* court required not just findings of dangerousness, but a demonstration that these were associated with a recent overt act and that there was a likelihood that immediate harm would occur without intervention. A strict set of criminal-style procedures, including a burden of proof beyond a reasonable doubt on petitioners and the right for respondents to remain silent under examination by a psychiatrist, were also decreed. These provisions, too, attracted considerable concern.[126]

Many predictions of the deleterious effects of the new laws were based on the assumption that the laws would follow the most radical examples available. In fact, that did not occur. No state adopted restrictions similar to California's on the prolonged hospitalization of suicidal patients.[127] *Lessard*'s more stringent procedural rules, in particular, were rejected by many courts and omitted by most legislatures.[128] Whether the critics' predictions of doom led to adoption of more moderate options, or whether this would have occurred anyway as less extreme voices among the advocates of change became dominant, is impossible to say. But the attractiveness of the most drastic approaches to restricting civil commitment was clearly overestimated by critics of the new laws.

Furthermore, even when highly restrictive mechanisms were adopted by state legislatures, these have tended since the late 1970s to be relaxed. Substantive standards for commitment have been broadened in a number of states to include justifications other than an immediate likelihood of harm to others or self. Washington State led the way in 1979 by redefining grave disability to include likely severe deterioration in the person's condition.[129] North Carolina broadened the definition of danger to self to include an inability to exercise self-control, judgment, and discretion in daily responsibilities or social relations; grossly irrational or inappropriate behavior, or other signs of severely impaired insight and judgment create a presumption that patients are unable to care for themselves.[130] Alaska, Arizona, Colorado, Hawaii, Kansas, Rhode Island, and Texas have all made it easier to hospitalize certain classes of mentally ill persons by expanding their commitment criteria.[131] Procedures, in general, have been less subject to revision, but a number of jurisdictions have created procedures for commitment of out-patients, in some cases allowing compulsory community treatment of patients who would not qualify for involuntary hospitalization.[132]

The motives for these changes were varied. In many cases, they were based on a growing consensus that restrictive laws were excluding patients in need of treatment.[133] Others were motivated by a fear that dangerous mentally ill people who should have been hospitalized were escaping from a net that was being too tightly drawn.[134] Overall, however, their effect has been to complement the informal mechanisms discussed previously and to limit further the effects of commitment law reforms.

An Alternative Explanation for Limitations on Admissions to Mental Hospitals

Accepting the conclusion that the wholesale rewriting of civil commitment statutes in the 1970s had far less than the expected impact on the hospitalization of mentally ill people in need of care, we are left with something of a conundrum. Our eyes do not deceive us. A visit to any major urban area (or to any of a number of smaller cities and towns) reveals persons who are undoubtedly mentally ill living in the streets, bus stations, and parks. They mutter unintelligible responses to the voices they alone hear, shriek at and assault unseen demons, or cower autistically in doorways, as if to avoid even the glances of other people. In the winter they huddle on steam grates or walk the bitterly cold streets in clothing torn to rags. People who believe that mental illness is a myth may be able to shut their eyes to the desperate need for treatment of many of these unfortunates, but to most observers it is all too clear. If changes in commitment law have not prevented us from hospitalizing these people, why do they still suffer? If as much flexibility exists in the statutes as this analysis suggests, why can't the homeless mentally ill be confined for their own good?

The answer probably lies in the fact that the changes in commitment law over the last two decades occurred simultaneously with another enormous upheaval in the mental health system: the deliberate effort to achieve attrition in the in-patient populations of our public psychiatric hospitals—the controversial policy of deinstitutionalization. The history of deinstitutionalization is just now being written, but its outlines are clear.[135] The first attempts to whittle away at the population of hundreds of thousands of mentally ill patients held in state hospitals (the total peaked at 550,000 in 1955[136]) began after World War II.[137] Along with the introduction of antipsychotic medications in the United States in 1954, the policies of what turned out to be the first stage of deinstitutionalization led to a slow but steady decline in state hospital populations, continuing into the early 1960s. At that point, however, the possibilities suggested by the initial successes precipitated a whole new approach. If some patients could be discharged from the state hospitals, why couldn't they all?

As a result of the confluence of the forces described in Chapter 1— including the opinions of community psychiatrists who disliked institutionalization and the underfunding of state facilities by penurious legislators— deinstitutionalization took a new turn in the mid-1960s, with states committing themselves to rapid reductions in in-patient populations. Beds were eliminated and buildings closed to prevent the numbers of in-patients from ever growing again.[138] So great was the enthusiasm for turning mental patients out of state hospitals that, in 1973, Ronald Reagan's administration in California confidently announced a plan to phase out the state's public in-patient facilities entirely by 1982.[139] The effect of the new policy was staggering. The number of state and county-operated in-patient beds in the United States fell from 558,922 in 1955 to 475,202 in 1965, to 137,810 in 1980, and ultimately to about 110,000 today.[140]

Unfortunately, once discharged by the state hospitals, former in-patients in many jurisdictions were essentially abandoned.[141] It turned out that schizophrenia and other major mental disorders—not the effects of institutional life—were the real stumbling blocks that prevented mentally ill people from functioning on their own.[142] From the start, a large proportion of those discharged had little chance of coping with life outside a total institution. For many of the others, who might have been able to make it on their own, the community-based services they needed, which had been proposed as a less costly alternative to hospitalization, gave way to a still cheaper option—no services at all. In the absence of such supports, rather than being restored to a functional life in the community, hundreds of thousands of former state hospital patients were moved to nursing homes (many with locked wards designated specifically to house them) or to board-and-care homes with minimal psychiatric services.[143] The policy of deinstitutionalization, observers concluded, might better be termed a policy of "trans-institutionalization."

Of the formerly institutionalized patients who rejected the option of congregate living, many ended up on the streets. Some were simply too disorganized to care for themselves. Without question, though, the incidence of homelessness also increased as gentrification struck our major cities, inner-city real-estate prices rose, and inexpensive housing—such as the single-room occupancy hotels and boarding houses that offered a traditional refuge for economically marginal members of society—became scarcer and scarcer.[144] For many, a steam grate or a bench in a bus terminal became the only affordable domicile.

The saga of deinstitutionalization, therefore, provides a competing hypothesis to explain the phenomena often attributed to the overhaul of commitment law in the fifty states. When mentally ill people, particularly the chronically ill and indigent among them, fail to gain admission to psychiatric facilities, this may not be due to restrictive standards or overly complex procedures. Rather, there may simply be no place to put them, as public-sector psychiatric beds have disappeared and community-based services to replace them have never been created.

In the absence of alternative services, the decrease in available beds exerts influence in several ways. If beds existed, some proportion of the homeless mentally ill, perhaps a sizable segment, might be willing to admit themselves voluntarily, mooting the effect of rigorous commitment standards. More subtly, the unavailability of places in public psychiatric hospitals can influence decisions about patients who are unwilling to enter voluntarily. Since commitment laws are permissive and not mandatory (that is, they allow but do not require a clinician to hospitalize an eligible patient), clinicians faced with a situation in which there are more patients who could be committed than there are beds to put them in might well engage in a sort of triage. The patients who are thought to be most in need of hospitalization are committed, while patients who constitute somewhat less urgent cases, although still meeting commitment standards, are turned away. This low-visibility decision process depends not on judges' enforcing the state's commitment law, but on emergency room and admitting office clinicians' attempting to protect their institutions from being overwhelmed.[145]

The process of excluding patients who meet commitment criteria might also occur after they are admitted to the in-patient unit. As newly admitted patients arrive, the need to find a bed for them forces the premature discharge of other patients, who technically may still be committable and may be only marginally better able to cope than the new arrivals. Discharged patients end up on the street and in shelters not because the law prevented their being admitted, but because the pressure to empty beds disallowed their being retained. In either case, the standards for commitment, in effect, are made progressively more stringent as the imbalance grows between the demand for hospitalization and the supply of beds. Law *per se* plays no role in this process.

Therefore, at least one plausible explanation, apart from strict commitment laws, can account for the breakdown we see around us in care for the severely mentally ill. Indiscriminate deinstitutionalization, without concomitant creation of community services to support patients who might be able to survive successfully outside of a hospital, offers an extralegal mechanism to explain highly restrictive admission policies, the rapid discharge of unstable patients, and the consequences of these approaches.[146]

The Future of Commitment Law

Is the debate over the standards that govern involuntary hospitalization of the mentally ill irrelevant? Given the large investments of effort and emotion in the issue for more than two decades, this would be an ironic conclusion indeed. Nonetheless, some commentators have suggested that it is time to stop arguing over which standards are applied. In the absence of data indicating that restrictive criteria deprive large numbers of patients of needed treatment, they see little reason to change current standards. To the extent that reforms are desired to make the commitment process more efficient, they suggest that efforts be directed at altering the behavior of the major participants in the system, not the statutory standards or procedures, since the decision makers at the "street level" (to borrow a phrase used by Marx and Levinson) determine how the system really works.[147]

The preceding data and analysis clearly can be used to support these arguments. If strict commitment standards have had much less impact than anticipated on commitment practices, devoting extensive attention to finding the most satisfying combination of words to describe those eligible for commitment would seem inefficient and fruitless. Attention might better be concentrated, for instance, on expanding the funding for and provision of mental health services, since these may well be the limiting factors in many jurisdictions.

There is some sense to this approach. Changing commitment laws as a means of addressing the problems of the homeless mentally ill—a frequently offered justification—makes little sense, at least as a first step. Rather, services should be provided in the community for those who can benefit from them, and in-patient capacity should be adjusted, if necessary, to allow those who seek care voluntarily or can be committed involuntarily under existing law to receive treatment. If, at that point, it becomes clear that restrictive statutes are still excluding a substantial group of mentally ill persons from needed care, statutory modifications might be considered.

Nor is it logical to look to statutory change as a means of protecting society from random, albeit shocking, violent acts perpetrated by mentally ill persons. The extreme and probably inherent difficulties that attend predicting violent behavior mean that some unanticipated violence will inevitably occur. When persons are suspected of having a strong propensity for violence, they are very likely to meet criteria under existing statutes. Even when they do not meet the explicit requirements of the law, such as when they have not committed an overt act indicating future dangerousness in states with that provision, clinicians or judges are very unlikely to release them, if violence seems a probable outcome.[148] Improving current performance in hospitalizing violent mentally ill persons depends on making advances in research that will allow their more accurate identification—not on statutory changes.[149]

Clearly, there are many wrong reasons to support reform of standards for commitment. What may be less obvious is that there may remain several good reasons not to abandon completely the goal of modifying restrictive statutes.

As a preliminary matter, it is important not to overstate the lack of impact of the new laws. Although the effects of these laws have been much less than anticipated, even the review by Bagby and Atkinson indicates that restrictive statutes have some effect on overall commitment rates, although the tendency over time is for rates to return to baseline.[150] Furthermore, their analysis of data from a small number of states suggests that liberalization of commitment criteria and procedures may lead to steady increases in commitment rates, in contrast to the less stable effects that are observed when statutes are tightened.[151]

Thus, commitment statutes are not irrelevant to the commitment process. The challenge for sensible reformers is to identify negative effects that might be susceptible to amelioration by statutory changes. Whether such changes are then enacted into law depends on the extent to which the harms they might remedy exceed the possible negative aspects of the changes.

For example, broadening criteria always means limiting some persons' liberty for the sake of their mental health. Moreover, some percentage of persons not requiring commitment will be swept up along with those at whom the change is aimed. Rational efforts at reform must balance the harms that flow from infringing on individual liberty and from inaccurately implementing the statute against the benefits that are likely to accrue. Such a weighing process is not easy to accomplish, but it leads to far different conclusions than a blanket assumption that statutory reform is not worth attempting in the first place.

Under what circumstances does it make sense to consider altering commitment statutes, particularly their substantive criteria defining classes of committable persons? The studies that suggest a limited impact of statutory reforms focus on undifferentiated samples of mentally ill persons. It is entirely possible that subgroups of people who are being harmed by existing laws are lost in the aggregate data. A recent statutory change in Colorado offers an example.[152]

Relatives of mentally ill persons complained that the wording of Colorado's grave disability standard, which required that provision for patients' basic needs be unavailable in the community before they could be committed, created an impossible dilemma for families. As their mentally ill relatives deteriorated, family members were precluded from obtaining an order for early involuntary hospitalization on the grounds of grave disability by the fact that they could and did help their mentally ill relatives meet their needs for food, clothing, shelter, medical care, and the like. The only alternative to waiting until patients became dangerous to themselves or others was to throw them out on the street, at which point they would be considered gravely disabled and hospitalization could occur. Merely threatening to evict a mentally ill relative, however, was not sufficient. The psychotic person actually had to be experiencing the rigors of the street before the statute allowed involuntary commitment to occur.

This provision of the statute was cruel, illogical, and decidedly counterproductive. It discouraged families from taking care of their mentally ill relatives, and it refused treatment to a class of persons the state already had agreed needed commitment and care. Thus, it was entirely sensible for family members to fight for a change in the law. As modified, the statute now permits commitment to take place if patients who are being cared for by family members would otherwise be considered gravely disabled, if they are deteriorating in a manner that previously led to hospitalization, and if (retaining something of a legal fiction) the relatives announce their intention to terminate the patients' care.

Another subgroup of mentally ill persons that may require particular statutory modification consists of patients who cycle rapidly into and out of mental hospitals.[153] When hospitalized and treated with medications, they recompensate quickly and are soon discharged. Once outside, however, they stop taking their medications and begin an inevitable slide toward rehospitalization. Some patients have gone through this cycle dozens of times, with each hospitalization merely stabilizing them for a short period.

Several jurisdictions have tried, in different ways, to short-circuit this process. Washington State modified its commitment statute to permit involuntary hospitalization of patients who are in the midst of deterioration that will predictably result in their meeting commitment criteria.[154] Other states, such as Georgia, Hawaii, North Carolina, and Tennessee, have created systems of mandatory out-patient treatment for persons with histories of recurring deterioration and rehospitalization.[155] This approach, although not entirely free of problems,[156] is aimed at avoiding in-patient stays by maintaining this group of patients in the community.

To the extent that subgroups of patients who would benefit from commitment law reform can be identified, it seems unjust to reject that option on the grounds that "changing commitment standards has no effect." The data cannot be generalized so broadly. Of course, it is desirable to demonstrate the exact nature and magnitude of the problem in need of correction before embarking on statutory reform and to have some sense of the costs of the change. But judicious approaches to rewriting flawed parts of the commitment laws should be welcomed.

Regional problems may constitute another legitimate basis for altering commitment standards. Studies showing minimal effects of restrictive statutes come from a minority of United States jurisdictions. On the other hand, strong anecdotal data suggest that strict commitment standards and procedures are taken seriously in some areas. Philadelphia has been singled out by experts and the media as a locale where rigid standards are applied and where mentally ill persons whom most observers would agree are in need of hospitalization end up on the streets.[157] It is meaningless to cite studies showing that the same Pennsylvania statute has little limiting effect in Pittsburgh,[158] when Philadelphians can see the impact of the state's narrow criteria with their own eyes. If denial of care to persons who consequently undergo considerable suffering is documented in a given jurisdiction, a rationale exists for considering statutory change, regardless of national trends.

Thus far, the justifications identified for considering further commitment law reform suggest that focal changes may be required, but not a massive overhaul comparable to the changes of the 1970s. This conclusion is consonant with an evaluation of commitment law that focuses narrowly on the question of its effectiveness in hospitalizing persons who—recalling Warren's "commonsense model"—most people would agree require in-patient care. Since demonstrating that large numbers of such people are denied care has been difficult, one might conclude that the commitment system is functioning adequately, or at most that some minor changes are required.

A broader perspective, however, suggests that other costs of the current process need to be taken into account before we rest content with what *Lessard* has wrought. To the extent that few people who fit a commonsense model of commitment are denied care, the price is massive transgression of the clear terms of many commitment statutes. The studies are nearly unanimous in indicating that, when the law goes against the grain of popular opinion concerning the legitimate scope of commitment, the law gives way. Persons in need of treatment are called "dangerous" by clinicians in the absence of good evidence that they are. Judges accept the characterization of patients as "gravely disabled" when what they really believe is that these persons are suffering and would be better off receiving care. Lawyers who claim to be advocates for mentally ill respondents at commitment hearings provide them with inadequate assistance or actually work against their expressed wishes. The question for us to consider is whether these are desirable states of affairs.

Law represents an embodiment of the moral sentiments of the community. When those sentiments can be honored only by violating the terms of the law, a tension is created between law and morality. Whichever side wins in an individual case, in the long run the legitimacy of the law suffers. It is unclear, in the case of commitment law, how generalizable the damage to the law is. Perhaps everyone involved recognizes mental health law as an aberrant area that requires extraordinary behavior. But perhaps not. It may be that all those who come into contact with the commitment system— clinicians, judges, lawyers, family members, and patients—have their view of the legitimacy of law eroded by their experiences. These effects would seem to be well worth investigating.[159]

Even if the effect on the general perception of the law is small, one may wonder why this divergence between "commonsense" opinion and law on the books should be sustained. Advocates of restrictive commitment statutes spoke on behalf of fundamental values of freedom. Their arguments were based on the belief that freedom should be valued more highly than treatment for disabling mental disorders, except in extraordinary circumstances. That was a legitimate and appealing position to advance. The events of the last two decades, however, suggest that the balance they wished society to strike has been rejected by the majority of Americans. Perhaps it is time to seek redress.

Many proposals have been offered for restoring an overtly therapeutic element to commitment law, permitting involuntary hospitalization not merely when people endanger their own lives or the lives of others, but when they are suffering mightily and help is at hand.[160] We are probably already achieving much of the effect these proposals seek to produce, but only by means of substantial contortions in our implementation of commitment laws. The experiment that began with the Ervin Act in the District of Columbia in 1964, continued in California with the adoption of the Lanterman-Petris-Short Act in 1969, and reached its high-water mark when Alberta Lessard was picked up on the streets of West Allis in 1971 needs to be reconsidered. We have not yet developed a set of commitment statutes that are simultaneously fair, reasonable, and compassionate. We still have work to do.

References

1. *Lessard v. Schmidt,* 349 F. Supp. 1078 (E.D. Wis. 1972).
2. G. N. Grob, *Mental Institutions in America: Social Policy to 1875* (New York: Free Press, 1973), pp. 193ff.
3. T. G. Morton, *History of the Pennsylvania Hospital, 1751–1895.* (Philadelphia: Times Printing House, 1895).
4. *Matter of Josiah Oakes,* 8 Law Reporter 122 (Mass. 1845); *Hinchman v. Richie,* Brightly 143 (C.P. Phila. 1849).
5. See, e.g., D. L. Dix, "Memorial Soliciting a State Hospital for the Insane," submitted to the Legislature of Pennsylvania, February 3, 1845 (Harrisburg, Penn.: J. M. G. Lescure, 1845). The influence of Dix's memorials is catalogued in Grob, *supra* note 2, Appendix 1.
6. N. Dain, *Concepts of Insanity in the United States, 1789–1865* (New Brunswick, N.J.: Rutgers University Press, 1964).
7. E. T. Carlson and N. Dain, "The Psychotherapy That Was Moral Treatment," *American Journal of Psychiatry* 117: 519–24 (1960).
8. The history of this movement is most comprehensively chronicled in Grob, *supra* note 2. An older version, found in Albert Deutsch's *The Mentally Ill in America: A History of Their Care and Treatment from Colonial Times,* 2d ed. (New York: Columbia University Press, 1949), was highly influential during the period of commitment law reform in the 1970s, often being cited by commentators and courts. David J. Rothman presents a more polemical view of these developments (he believes that the asylums developed primarily as instruments of social control and not to afford treatment to their patients) in *The Discovery of the Asylum: Social Order and Disorder in the New Republic* (Boston: Little, Brown, 1971).
9. P. S. Appelbaum and K. N. Kemp, "The Evolution of Commitment Law in the Nineteenth Century," *Law and Human Behavior* 6: 343–54 (1982); E. Dwyer, "Civil Commitment Laws in Nineteenth-century New York," *Behavioral Sciences and the Law* 6: 79–98 (1988).
10. The first statute authorizing voluntary hospitalization of the mentally ill was not enacted until 1881 in Massachusetts, and even then applied only to patients with the means to pay for their care. See S. J. Brakel, "Voluntary Admission," in S. J. Brakel, J. Parry, B. Weiner, *The Mentally Disabled and the Law,* 3d ed. (Chicago: American Bar Foundation, 1985), pp. 177–201.
11. Just how accurate those allegations were remains a matter of dispute to this day. G. Grob, "Abuse in American Mental Hospitals in Historical Perspective: Myth and Reality," *International Journal of Law and Psychiatry* 3: 295–310 (1980).

12. E. P. W. Packard, *Modern Persecution, or Insane Asylums Unveiled, as Demonstrated by the Report of the Investigating Committee of the Legislature of Illinois* (New York: DeCapo Press, 1973 [reprint of 1875 edition]).

13. By 1939, eighteen states had such provisions in their laws. G. A. Kempf, "Laws Pertaining to the Admission of Patients to Mental Hospitals Throughout the United States," Public Health Reports, Supplement No. 157 (Washington, D.C.: USGPO, 1939).

14. Ibid., p. 28.

15. Ibid.; Group for the Advancement of Psychiatry, "Commitment Procedures," Report No. 4 (Topeka, Kans.: GAP, April 1948); U.S. Public Health Service, "A Draft Act Governing Hospitalization of the Mentally Ill (Revised)" (Washington, D.C.: USGPO, 1952).

16. See Kempf, *supra* note 13, and "Draft Act," *supra* note 15.

17. "Draft Act," *supra* note 15.

18. *Lochner v. New York*, 198 U.S. 45 (1905); *Adair v. U.S.*, 208 U.S. 161 (1908); *Coppage v. Kansas*, 236 U.S. 1 (1915); *Adkins v. Children's Hospital*, 261 U.S. 525 (1923).

19. *Brown v. Board of Education*, 347 U.S. 483 (1954).

20. *Specht v. Patterson*, 386 U.S. 605 (1967).

21. *Humphrey v. Cady*, 405 U.S. 504 (1972).

22. *Baxstrom v. Herold*, 383 U.S. 107 (1966).

23. *Jackson v. Indiana*, 406 U.S. 715 (1972).

24. *Specht v. Patterson*, *supra* note 20.

25. *Humphrey v. Cady*, *supra* note 21.

26. *Baxstrom v. Herold*, *supra* note 22.

27. *Jackson v. Indiana*, *supra* note 23. The argument that the state lacks a legitimate interest in confining or otherwise restricting a person is a variant on substantive due process analysis. When this approach is applied to statutory interpretation, it is often framed as an "overbreadth" contention; that is, the statute is characterized as overbroad in its scope in that it encompasses persons whose liberty the state has no legitimate basis for limiting (e.g., in the case of *Jackson*, incurable incompetents), as well as those it does (e.g., defendants whose competence can be restored).

28. *Humphrey v. Cady*, *supra* note 21, p. 509.

29. *Kent v. U.S.*, 383 U.S. 541 (1966); *In re Gault*, 387 U.S. 1 (1967); *In re Winship*, 397 U.S. 358 (1970).

30. *In re Kent*, *supra* note 29, p. 555.

31. *In re Kent*, *supra* note 29; *In re Gault*, *supra* note 29; *Winship v. U.S.*, *supra* note 29.

32. *McKeiver v. Pennsylvania*, 403 U.S. 528 (1971).

33. Exposés of conditions in many state hospitals made clear that conditions were often abysmal, staff minimal, and therapeutic activities or interventions all but nonexistent. See A. Deutsch, *The Shame of the States* (New York: Harcourt, Brace, 1948); M. Gorman, *Every Other Bed* (Cleveland: World Publishing, 1956). For an example of the role that concern over conditions in state hospitals played in motivating judicial restrictions on civil commitment, see *State ex rel Hawks v. Lazaro*, 202 S.E.2d 109 (W.Va. 1974).

34. *Jackson v. Indiana*, *supra* note 23, pp. 1857–58.

35. One line of cases that should not go unmentioned involves the "void for vagueness" doctrine. According to the Supreme Court's vagueness cases, a person has a right under the due process clause to know with reasonable precision what behavior will result in the imposition of criminal sanctions. Statutes that are so vague in detailing proscribed behavior that they fail to afford adequate notice are unconsti-

tutional. Vagueness also complicates the function of judicial review by impairing appellate courts' ability to overrule arbitrary action by the executive branch or by lower courts. The Supreme Court, during the period under consideration, struck down public vagrancy statutes, among others, as unacceptably vague (*Papachristou v. City of Jacksonville,* 405 U.S. 156 [1972]; *Giaccio v. Pennsylvania,* 382 U.S. 399 [1966]). Although the rationale for applying the vagueness rule to civil commitment statutes has been questioned ("Developments in the Law: Civil Commitment of the Mentally Ill," *Harvard Law Review* 87: 1190–1406 (1974), at 1253), it played an important role in a number of cases. See P. S. Appelbaum, "Is the Need for Treatment Constitutionally Acceptable as a Basis for Civil Commitment?" *Law, Medicine & Health Care* 12: 144–49 (1984).

36. *Monroe v. Pape,* 365 U.S. 167 (1961).
37. P. S. Appelbaum, "Civil Rights Litigation and Mental Health: Section 1983," *Hospital and Community Psychiatry* 32: 305–6 (1981).
38. J. M. Livermore, C. Malmquist, and P. E. Meehl, "On the Justifications for Civil Commitment," *University of Pennsylvania Law Review* 117: 75–96 (1968).
39. D. B. Wexler, S. E. Scoville, et al., "The Administration of Psychiatric Justice: Theory and Practice in Arizona," *Arizona Law Review* 13: 1–258 (1971).
40. D.C. Code Secs. 21-501 to 21-591 (Supp. V. 1966), reprinted in R. C. Allen, E. Z. Fertser, and J. G. Rubin, *Readings in Law and Psychiatry* (Baltimore: Johns Hopkins University Press, 1975), pp. 277–84.
41. California Welfare and Institutions Code, Sec. 5150ff.
42. Good descriptions of LPS can be found in C. A. B. Warren, *The Court of Last Resort: Mental Illness and the Law* (Chicago, University of Chicago Press, 1982); see also ENKI Research Institute, *A Study of California's New Mental Health Law (1969–1971)* (Los Angeles: ENKI Corporation, 1972).
43. A. M. Dershowitz, "Two Models of Commitment: The Medical and the Legal," *The Humanist* (July–August, 1971); N. N. Kittrie, *The Right to Be Different: Deviance and Enforced Therapy* (Baltimore: Penguin, 1973); T. S. Szasz, *Law, Liberty, and Psychiatry* (New York: Collier, 1968).
44. E. F. Torrey, *Nowhere to Go: The Tragic Odyssey of the Homeless Mentally Ill* (New York: Harper & Row, 1988).
45. W. Gaylin, I. Glasser, S. Marcus, and D. Rothman, *Doing Good: The Limits of Benevolence* (New York: Pantheon, 1978). This view is epitomized by Lionel Trilling's comment that: "Some paradox in our nature leads us, once we have made our fellow men the objects of our enlightened interest, to go on to make them the objects of our pity, then of our wisdom, ultimately of our coercion." Cited by Rothman in ibid.
46. R. J. Isaac and V. C. Arnot, *Madness in the Streets: How Psychiatry and the Law Abandoned the Mentally Ill* (New York: Free Press, 1990); B. Rubin, "Community Psychiatry: An Evolutionary Change in Medical Psychology in the United States," *Archives of General Psychiatry* 20: 497–507 (1969).
47. "Less drastic means," later more commonly referred to as "the least restrictive alternative," is another doctrine of constitutional law given broader scope by the Warren Court. Applied to state-imposed restrictions on individual liberty, it requires the state to choose the alternative that is least restrictive of the person's freedom in pursuing its legitimate interests. The classic expression of this doctrine is found in *Shelton v. Tucker,* 364 U.S. 479 (1960).
48. *Parens patriae* powers are derived from the state's inherent power to care for those who are incapable of caring for themselves. They date to the medieval English kings, who exercised their *parens patriae* powers to protect the estates and persons of incompetent nobles. See "Developments in the Law," *supra* note 35; and R.

Neugebauer, "Medieval and Early Modern Theories of Mental Illness," *Archives of General Psychiatry* 36: 477–83 (1979).

49. *Dicta* are elements of a court's opinion that do not directly refer to the issue in dispute in a case. The parts of the opinion that comment directly on issues in the litigation are referred to as the "holding" of the court. A holding of an appellate court creates binding precedent in its jurisdiction. *Dicta* do not. Nonetheless, *dicta* may be useful in laying out the court's view of the legal and factual setting in which the case it is hearing is decided, and sometimes they suggest how the court might rule on other issues that may come before it in the future. Walker DM: *The Oxford Companion to Law*. Oxford, Clarendon Press, 1980.

50. A good overview of the influence of *Lessard* is provided in M. Perlin, *Mental Disability Law: Civil and Criminal*, vol. 1 (Charlottesville, Va.: Michie, 1989).

   My colleague, Steven K. Hoge, M.D., a psychiatrist who teaches at the University of Virginia School of Law, offers a somewhat different perspective on the role of *Lessard*. Had *Lessard* not come along when it did, he argues that a very different series of decisions might have resulted. A delay of only a few years before a major court test of the constitutionality of commitment laws, during which deinstitutionalization accelerated, and public concern grew about its progress, might have led the courts to be more circumspect about sacrificing professional (i.e., treatment-oriented) values. Hoge points to the decision in *Project Release v. Prevost*, 722 F.2d 960 (2nd Cir. 1983), which rejected many of the procedural requirements of *Lessard,* as proof of what might have been. In the meantime, rising pressure to improve the terrible conditions in many facilities and to reorient systems to community care might have led political leaders to institute substantial systemic reform.

51. *Lessard v. Schmidt,* 349 F. Supp. 1078 (E.D. Wis. 1972); *vacated and remanded,* 414 U.S. 473 (1974); *on remand,* 379 F. Supp. 1376 (E.D. Wis. 1974); *vacated and remanded,* 421 U.S. 957 (1975); *reinstated,* 413 F. Supp. 1318 (E.D. Wis. 1976).

52. S. J. Brakel and R. Rock, *The Mentally Disabled and the Law,* 2d ed. (Chicago: American Bar Foundation, 1971), p. 36.

53. This was one of the findings of the Arizona study, *supra* note 39.

54. New York is an example of the latter; see *Scopes v. Shah,* 398 N.Y.S.2d 911 (App. Div., 1977). See generally S. J. Brakel, "Involuntary Institutionalization," in Brakel, Parry, and Weiner, *supra* note 10, pp. 21–176.

55. The debate that followed the court decisions and the enactment of the new statutes was dominated by psychiatrists, due no doubt to the law's assignment to physicians of nearly exclusive rights to initiate emergency commitments, seek prolonged judicial commitment, and testify at commitment hearings. That situation has changed in recent years, as psychologists in many states have gained equivalent powers in the commitment process; and other mental health professions, such as social work and nursing, are beginning to make similar inroads.

56. S. L. Halleck, "A Troubled View of Current Trends in Forensic Psychiatry," *Journal of Psychiatry and Law* 2: 135–55 (1974), p. 147.

57. "Official Actions: Position Statement on the Involuntary Hospitalization of the Mentally Ill," *American Journal of Psychiatry* 128: 1480 (1972).

58. L. R. Kahle, B. D. Sales, and S. Nagel. "On Unicorns Blocking Commitment Law Reform," *Journal of Psychiatry and Law* 6: 89–105 (1978).

59. In 1977, the American Psychiatric Association, reflecting a growing antagonism toward the new laws, rescinded its 1972 position statement. See "APA Rescinds Hospitalization Statement," *Psychiatric News* 12(16): 1ff (1977).

60. D. A. Treffert, "Dying with Their Rights On" [letter], *American Journal of Psychiatry* 130: 1041 (1973); D. A. Treffert, "Dying with Their Rights On," *Prism* 47–52 (1974).

61. Interestingly—and illustrative of the differences within the psychiatric profession on this issue—P. Browning Hoffman, a psychiatrist who taught at the University of Virginia Law School, examined Treffert's anecdotal cases critically and reached somewhat different conclusions about their meaning. He noted that the woman with anorexia nervosa had died three weeks after discharge and asked why family members or physicians did not initiate involuntary commitment again as her situation worsened and the threat of harm became more imminent. With regard to the case of the student who had previously attempted suicide, in which lawyers' advice was accepted despite psychiatrists' beliefs that the patient would come to harm if not hospitalized, Hoffman argued that proceeding to a judicial hearing and allowing a judge to make the decision about committability would have been the proper course. Finally, he inquired why the police turned to lawyers and not psychiatrists in evaluating the committability of the two girls found staring at each other on a street corner. In sum, Hoffman suggested that too great a readiness on the part of people involved in the system to believe that the new law would result in unfortunate and irrational consequences might have been the real culprit in these cases. Further, it was not clear that the bad outcomes in these cases were predictable or that, in the long run, commitment would have prevented them. He argued that, "Patients should not die with their rights on. But they should not live with their rights off, either" (p. 68). P. B. Hoffman, "Living with Your Rights Off," *Bulletin of the American Academy of Psychiatry and the Law* 5: 68–74 (1977).

62. See, e.g., R. Peele, P. Chodoff, and N. Taub, "Involuntary Hospitalization and Treatability: Observations from the District of Columbia Experience," *Catholic University Law Review* 23: 744–53 (1974); and P. Chodoff, "The Case for Involuntary Hospitalization of the Mentally Ill, *American Journal of Psychiatry* 133: 496–501 (1976).

63. J. R. Rappeport, "Belegaled" [editorial], *Bulletin of the American Academy of Psychiatry and the Law* 5: iv–vii (1977). *Psychiatric News,* the newspaper of the American Psychiatric Association, is often a good source from which to gauge the sentiments of the profession; see, e.g., "Braceland Chides Law School Dean on Commitment Issue," 8(9): 19 (1973); W. Singer, "A Troubled Life" [letter] 8(8): 2 (1973); M. L. Sharp, "Commitment" [letter], 8(10): 2, 1973; L. S. Kubie, "Commitment," 8(6): 2 (1973); "Goals for Mentally Ill Not Met, Psychiatrist Says," 11(10): 1ff (1976); and D. D. Burford, "Another View of 'Rights' " [letter], 12(3): 2 (1977).

64. A. A. Stone, *Mental Health and Law: A System in Transition* (Rockville, Md.: NIMH, 1975), p. 2.

65. A. A. Stone, *Law, Psychiatry, and Morality* (Washington, D.C.: American Psychiatric Press, 1984), p. 142.

66. The model law is presented with commentary in C. D. Stromberg and A. A. Stone, "A Model State Law on Civil Commitment of the Mentally Ill," *Harvard Journal of Legislation* 20: 275–396 (1983). For the quoted language, see p. 330.

67. Psychiatrist Loren Roth weighed in with a widely cited proposal very similar to Stone's. See L. H. Roth, "A Commitment Law for Patients, Doctors and Lawyers," *American Journal of Psychiatry* 136: 1121–27 (1979).

68. D. A. Treffert, "The Obviously Ill Patient: A Fourth Standard for Civil Commitment," *Hospital and Community Psychiatry* 36: 259–64 (1985), p. 263.

69. M. F. Abramson, "The Criminalization of Mentally Disordered Behavior: Possible

Side-effect of a New Mental Health Law," *Hospital and Community Psychiatry* 23: 101–5 (1972).

70. A. A. Stone, "Recent Mental Health Litigation: A Critical Perspective," *American Journal of Psychiatry* 134: 272–79 (1977); M. A. Peszke, "Is Dangerousness an Issue for Physicians in Emergency Commitment?" *American Journal of Psychiatry* 132: 825–28 (1975).

71. E. L. Bassuk, "The Homelessness Problem," *Scientific American* 251: 40–45 (1984).

72. P. J. Fischer, "Estimating the Prevalence of Alcohol, Drug, and Mental Health Problems in the Contemporary Homeless Population: A Review of the Literature," *Contemporary Drug Problems* 16: 333–89 (1989). Some studies have shown even higher percentages of the homeless to be mentally ill; see, e.g., E. L. Bassuk, L. Rubin, and A. Lauriat, "Is Homelessness a Mental Health Problem?" *American Journal of Psychiatry* 141: 1546–50 (1984).

73. See, e.g., the work of psychiatrist Richard Lamb and colleagues on the situation in board and care homes in Los Angeles: H. R. Lamb, "The New Asylums in the Community," *Archives of General Psychiatry* 36: 129–34 (1979).

74. J. Barbanel, "Brooklyn Double Murder: Mental Patient and a Flawed System," *New York Times,* March 2, 1988, p. B-1; M. T. Kaufman, "A Killer in St. Patrick's: Hospital to Jail to Death," *New York Times,* September 23, 1988, p. A-1; R. Smothers, "Mental Patient and Shootings Puzzle Georgians," *New York Times,* April 26, 1990, p. A-25; R. Sullivan, "State Panel Criticizes Emergency Psychiatric Care," *New York Times,* August 3, 1986, p. 27.

75. N&C/AY/SCC Consortium, "Current Description, Evaluation, and Recommendations for Treatment of Mentally Disordered Criminal Offenders," vol. 1, "Introduction and Prevalence" (San Rafael, Calif.: California Department of Corrections, June 1989); L. H. Roth "Correctional Psychiatry," in W. J. Curran, A. L. McGarry, and C. S. Petty, eds., *Modern Legal Medicine, Psychiatry, and Forensic Science* (Philadelphia: F. A. Davis, 1980), pp. 677–719.

76. L. A. Teplin, "The Prevalence of Severe Mental Disorder Among Male Urban Jail Detainees: Comparison with the Epidemiologic Catchment Area Program," *American Journal of Public Health* 80: 663–69 (1990). H. R. Lamb and G. W. Grant, "The Mentally Ill in an Urban County Jail," *Archives of General Psychiatry* 39: 17–22 (1982); H. R. Lamb and P. W. Grant, "Mentally Ill Women in a County Jail," *Archives of General Psychiatry* 40: 363–68 (1983).

77. P. A. Hilts, "U.S. Returns to 1820's in Care of Mentally Ill, Study Asserts," *New York Times,* September 12, 1990, p. 28.

78. T. Morganthau, "Abandoned," *Newsweek,* January 6, 1986, pp. 14–18; R. Peele, B. Gross, B. Arons, and M. Jafri. "The Legal System and the Homeless," in H. R. Lamb, ed., *The Homeless Mentally Ill: A Task Force Report of the American Psychiatric Association* (Washington, D.C.: APA, 1984), pp. 261–78; G. L. Pierce, M. L. Durham, and W. H. Fisher, "The Impact of Public Policy and Publicity on Admissions to State Mental Health Hospitals," *Journal of Health Politics, Policy and Law* 11: 41–66 (1986).

79. L. R. Faulkner, J. D. Bloom, B. H. McFarland, and T. O. Stern, "The Effect of Mental Health System Changes on Civil Commitment," *Bulletin of the American Academy of Psychiatry and the Law* 13: 345–57 (1985); L. R. Faulkner, B. H. McFarland, and J. D. Bloom, "An Empirical Study of Emergency Commitment," *American Journal of Psychiatry* 146: 182–86 (1989).

80. A. L. McGarry, R. K. Schwitzgebel, P. D. Lipsitt, and D. Lelos, *Civil Commitment and Social Policy: An Evaluation of the Massachusetts Mental Health Reform Act of 1970* (Rockville, Md.: NIMH, 1981).

81. R. Peters, K. S. Miller, W. Schmidt, and D. Meeter, "The Effects of Statutory Change on the Civil Commitment of the Mentally Ill," *Law and Human Behavior* 11: 73–100 (1987).
82. A time-series analysis is useful when existing trends are likely to interfere with the evaluation of the hypothesized effect. When state hospital populations are examined to detect the impact of new laws, researchers must take into account underlying patterns of change in hospitalization practices. Since 1955, the average census of state hospitals around the country has dropped steadily. Consequently, a demonstration of decline in census after implementation of a new law says nothing about a causal influence. The pressures that accounted for previous declines in in-patient populations—usually deliberate policies of deinstitutionalization—might simply have continued to exert their effect. Use of a time-series analysis allows researchers to determine whether the effect seen after a particular event is greater than expected, given the underlying trend.
83. Interestingly, this effect disappeared when the first post-reform year was compared only with the last pre-reform year. Researchers always have a great deal of discretion in choosing which data analyses to present and to emphasize in their discussions. This is one major way in which preconceptions can shape the outcome of an "objective" research project. Most readers, especially those with policy rather than empirical backgrounds, read the research literature for its conclusions and pay relatively little attention to methods. Thus, a paper comes to be known as supporting the conclusions the authors have selected for their discussion, while potentially conflicting data—even if presented openly in the text of the paper—tend to be ignored. Such has been the fate of the Peters et al. paper, which is often cited as a major study demonstrating a clear impact of commitment reforms.
84. J. W. Luckey and J. J. Berman, "Effects of a New Commitment Law on Involuntary Admissions and Service Utilization Patterns," *Law and Human Behavior* 3: 149–61 (1979).
85. T. Hasebe, J. McRae, "A Ten-year Study of Civil Commitments in Washington State," *Hospital and Community Psychiatry* 38: 983–87 (1987).
86. R. M. Bagby and L. Atkinson, "The Effects of Legislative Reform on Civil Commitment Rates: A Critical Analysis," *Behavioral Sciences and the Law* 6: 45–62 (1988).
87. In contrast, Bagby and Atkinson note that, when legislatures attempted to increase clinicians' prerogatives by loosening commitment procedures and criteria, a uniform effect was found in the expected direction: steady and sustained increases in the rates of commitment occurred in all jurisdictions studied. A more recent analysis by psychiatrist Robert Miller, however, calls even this conclusion into question. Miller found that commitment rates were more likely to decrease than increase following relaxation of commitment laws in eight states in the 1980s. See R. D. Miller, "Need-for-Treatment Criteria for Involuntary Civil Commitment: Impact in Practice," *American Journal of Psychiatry* 149: 1380–84 (1992).

Bagby and Atkinson also consider in their analysis the possibility that post-reform commitment rates might be inflated by an increase in readmissions. If this were the case, it would indicate that commitment law changes had succeeded in restricting the class of committed persons, although members of the class were being committed more frequently than prior to reform. The authors conclude that existing data do not support this possibility. Even when readmission rates increase, the gain is not substantial enough to account for the overall increases over time in commitment numbers.
88. ENKI Research Institute, *supra* note 42.

89. M. R. Munetz, K. R. Kaufman, and C. L. Rich, "Modernization of a Mental Health Act: I. Commitment Patterns," *Bulletin of the American Academy of Psychiatry and the Law* 8: 83–93 (1980).
90. Peters et al., *supra* note 81.
91. Even the finding of a drop-off in the rate of commitments statewide, discussed earlier, can be questioned. The aggregate data offered in support of the contention that commitment rates fell came exclusively from state hospitals. If the same number of patients were being committed after the statutory change, but a larger percentage was being sent to other facilities (private psychiatric, VA, or general hospital units), the authors would not have been able to detect this. In fact, Peters et al. report some data that suggest this interpretation may be correct. They note that the rate of voluntary admissions to state facilities decreased in proportion to the decrease in involuntary admissions, pointing to a general pressure to reduce censuses at the state hospitals by diverting patients elsewhere. Indeed, the authors report a steady trend predating the statutory reform toward reduced in-patient populations in state facilities. Unfortunately, the published data are inadequate to prove the point one way or the other.
92. S. Cleveland, E. P. Mulvey, P. S. Appelbaum, and C. W. Lidz, "Do Dangerousness-oriented Commitment Laws Restrict Hospitalization of Patients Who Need Treatment? A Test," *Hospital and Community Psychiatry* 40: 266–71 (1989).
93. First, the researchers identified the subjects in the sample who ranked high on need for treatment but low on all of the three standards for committability (danger to self, danger to others, or grave disability). Of the eleven patients in this category, two were committed, five consented to voluntary hospitalization, and four agreed to referrals for out-patient treatment—an arrangement with which the emergency room clinicians were comfortable. The hypothesized group of patients unable to obtain needed care simply was not found.

   In an effort to account for this finding, the researchers wondered whether the patients they were seeking might have been rated high on the scale measuring inability to care for self and, having been committed on that basis, thus failed to appear in their first sample. To test this possibility, seventeen additional patients were identified from the group ranked high on need for treatment but low on dangerousness to self or others, with no restrictions on ratings of grave disability. Of these, eleven were admitted voluntarily, and four were committed on the basis of grave disability; only two were not admitted. One of these was considered a marginal case, and the final patient escaped before she could be transferred to another hospital. Even in this larger group, everyone who truly needed treatment (and remained in custody) received it. This strategy led to identification of the single problematic patient, who is described in the text.
94. S. P. Segal, M. A. Watson, S. M. Goldfinger et al., "Civil Commitment in the Psychiatric Emergency Room: I. The Assessment of Dangerousness by Emergency Room Clinicians; II. Mental Disorder Indicators and Three Dangerousness Criteria; III. Disposition as a Function of Mental Disorder and Dangerousness Indicators," *Archives of General Psychiatry* 45: 748–52, 753–58, 759–63 (1988).
95. C. A. B. Warren, "Involuntary Commitment for Mental Disorder: The Application of California's Lanterman-Petris-Short Act," *Law and Society Review* 11: 629–49 (1977); Warren, *supra* note 42.
96. Warren's subjects had been involuntarily committed on the certification of one psychiatrist for a period of up to 72 hours. Most of the patients had been recommitted by the hospital for an additional 14 days. If the facility had wanted to detain them further, these patients would have been entitled to a court hearing at the end of

the 14-day period; the statute also granted them the right at any point before then to bring a writ of *habeas corpus* requesting immediate release. Filing the writ triggered a prompt hearing before a judge. It was these hearings, in a specially designated mental health court, that Warren studied.

97. The utility of plea bargaining to all parties was evident in a recent Pennsylvania court case. Public defenders joined with state officials in contesting an attempt to strike down an overt plea-bargaining process that allowed patients to be hospitalized for less than the maximum period allowed under the law, but without a finding of dangerousness. The appellate courts, however, which do not make commitment decisions themselves, struck down the practice as a blatant violation of the statute. See *In the Matter of J.F.*, No. 2168-CD-1990 (Pa. Commonwealth Ct., Sept. 25, 1991).

98. V. A. Hiday and L. N. Smith, "Effects of the Dangerousness Standard in Civil Commitment," *Journal of Psychiatry and Law* 15: 433–54 (1987).

99. Note should be taken of a methodological problem with this and similar studies (see, e.g., S. D. Stier and K. J. Stoebe, "Involuntary Hospitalization of the Mentally Ill in Iowa: The Failure of the 1975 Legislation," *Iowa Law Review* 64: 1284–1458 [1979]) that rely on review of records or documents submitted to the courts. Judges at commitment hearings obviously have access to much more evidence than is contained on commitment forms. Even when the form provides no evidence of a patient's dangerousness, such evidence may have been presented by witnesses at the hearing itself. Thus, the conclusion is unwarranted that judges were going beyond the criteria contained in the statute in *all* cases in which allegations of dangerousness were missing from the documents.

100. See, e.g., E. Andalman and D. L. Chambers, "Effective Counsel for Persons Facing Civil Commitment: A Survey, a Polemic and a Proposal," *Mississippi Law Journal* 45: 43–91 (1974); F. Cohen, "The Function of the Attorney and the Commitment of the Mentally Ill," *Texas Law Review* 44: 424–69 (1966); and Stier and Stoebe, *supra* note 99.

101. R. D. Miller, R. M. Ionescu-Pioggia, and P. B. Fiddleman, "The Effect of Witnesses, Attorneys, and Judges on Civil Commitment in North Carolina: A Prospective Study," *Journal of Forensic Sciences* 28: 829–38 (1983).

102. V. A. Hiday, "The Attorney's Role in Involuntary Civil Commitment," *North Carolina Law Review* 60: 1027–49 (1982): Stier and Stoebe, *supra* note 99.

103. N. G. Poythress, "Psychiatric Expertise in Civil Commitment: Training Attorneys to Cope with Expert Testimony," *Law and Human Behavior* 2: 1–23 (1978).

104. Several studies have turned up an additional factor that may dissuade attorneys from aggressively pursuing their clients' release. Judges may discourage such behavior, either because they believe most "really crazy" respondents should be committed or because they are loath to expend the additional time that fully adversarial hearings would require. Warren's book, *supra* note 42 (pp. 195–96), offers an anecdotal example of what happens to public defenders who offend judges' wishes in this regard. Poythress's subjects, who depended on judicial appointment to represent respondents for a meaningful segment of their income, also expressed reluctance to annoy judges with an overly aggressive stance.

105. M. L. Durham and J. Q. LaFond, "The Empirical Consequences and Policy Implications of Broadening the Statutory Criteria for Civil Commitment," *Yale Law and Policy Review* 3: 395–446 (1985); D. L. Wenger and C. R. Fletcher, "The Effect of Legal Counsel on Admissions to a State Mental Hospital: A Confrontation of Professions," *Journal of Health and Social Behavior* 10: 66–72 (1969);

T. K. Zander, "Civil Commitment in Wisconsin: The Impact of *Lessard v. Schmidt,*" *Wisconsin Law Review* 1976: 503–62.

106. These procedures vary substantially from state to state. Some jurisdictions limit authority for emergency detention to physicians only, even if they are not psychiatrists. Others allow doctoral-level psychologists, as well as physicians, to initiate commitment; still others authorize psychiatric nurses or social workers to perform this function. A few jurisdictions require that all emergency commitments—or at least all those that will be paid for by public funds—be screened and approved by designated personnel who may (or may not) have training in one of the mental health disciplines. There are also large differences in the periods of time for which emergency commitments are effective without formal review—ranging from three days to several weeks. See generally Brakel, *supra* note 54.

107. See, e.g., G. E. Dix, "Acute Psychiatric Hospitalization of the Mentally Ill in the Metropolis: An Empirical Study," *Washington University Law Quarterly* 1968: 485–591; L. R. Faulkner, J. D. Bloom, and K. Kundahl-Stanley, "Effects of a New Involuntary Commitment Law: Expectations and Reality," *Bulletin of the American Academy of Psychiatry and the Law* 10: 249–59 (1982); L. R. Faulkner, J. D. Bloom, M. R. Resnick et al., "Local Variations in the Civil Commitment Process," *Bulletin of the American Academy of Psychiatry and the Law* 11: 5–15 (1983); L. R. Faulkner, B. H. McFarland, and J. D. Bloom, "An Empirical Study of Emergency Commitment," *American Journal of Psychiatry* 146: 182–86 (1989); and R. D. Miller and P. B. Fiddleman, "Emergency Involuntary Commitment: A Look at the Decision-making Process," *Hospital and Community Psychiatry* 34: 239–54 (1983).

108. S. G. Mestrovic and J. A. Cook, "The Dangerousness Standard: What Is It and How Is It Used?" *International Journal of Law and Psychiatry* 8: 443–69 (1986).

109. Conn. Gen. Stat. Ann. 17-183.

110. The classic review is John Monahan, *The Clinical Prediction of Violent Behavior* (Rockville, Md.: NIMH, 1981).

111. California Welfare and Institutions Code, Sec. 5150.

112. Cleveland et al., *supra* note 92.

113. See, e.g., M. L. Durham and J. Q. LaFond, "The Empirical Consequences and Policy Implications of Broadening the Statutory Criteria for Civil Commitment," *Yale Law and Policy Review* 3: 395–446 (1985); S. K. Hoge, P. S. Appelbaum, and A. Greer, "An Empirical Comparison of the Stone and Dangerousness Criteria for Civil Commitment," *American Journal of Psychiatry* 146: 170–75 (1989); S. K. Hoge, G. Sachs, P. S. Appelbaum, A. Greer, and C. Gordon, "Limitations on Psychiatrists' Discretionary Civil Commitment Authority by the Stone and Dangerousness Criteria," *Archives of General Psychiatry* 45: 764–69 (1988); J. Monahan, M. Ruggeriero, and H. D. Friedlander, "Stone-Roth Model of Civil Commitment and the California Dangerousness Standard," *Archives of General Psychiatry* 39: 1267–71 (1982); M. R. Munetz, K. R. Kaufman, and C. L. Rich, "Modernization of a Mental Health Act: I. Commitment Patterns," *Bulletin of the American Academy of Psychiatry and the Law* 8: 83–93 (1980); and S. P. Segal, M. A. Watson, S. M. Goldfinger et al., "Civil Commitment in the Psychiatric Emergency Room: I. The Assessment of Dangerousness by Emergency Room Clinicians," *Archives of General Psychiatry* 45: 748–52 (1988).

The numbers may be even greater at recommitment hearings. See C. H. D. Parry, E. Turkheimer, P. Hundley, and E. Creskoff, "A Comparison of Respondents in Commitment and Recommitment Hearings," *Law and Human Behavior* 15: 315–24 (1991). For an analysis similar to the one offered here, see E. Turkheimer and C. D. H. Parry, "Why the Gap? Practice and Policy in Civil Commitment Hearings," *American Psychologist* 47: 646–55 (1992).

114. P. D. Lipsett, "Emergency Admissions of Civil Involuntary Patients to Mental Hospitals Following Statutory Modification," in P. D. Lipsett and B. D. Sales, eds., *New Directions in Psycholegal Research* (New York: Van Nostrand Reinhold, 1980), pp. 247–64; J. McCready and H. Merskey, "Compliance by Physicians with the 1978 Ontario Mental Health Act," *Canadian Medical Association Journal* 24: 719–24 (1981); S. Page and E. Yates, "Civil Commitment and the Danger Mandate," *Canadian Journal of Psychiatry* 18: 267–71 (1973).

115. P. S. Appelbaum and R. M. Hamm, "Decision to Seek Commitment: Psychiatric Decision Making in a Legal Context," *Archives of General Psychiatry* 39: 447–51 (1982); H. I. Schwartz, P. S. Appelbaum, and R. D. Kaplan, "Clinical Judgments in the Decision to Commit: Psychiatric Discretion and the Law," *Archives of General Psychiatry* 41: 811–15 (1984).

116. J. S. Thompson and J. W. Ager, "An Experimental Analysis of Civil Commitment Recommendations of Psychologists and Psychiatrists," *Behavioral Sciences and the Law* 6: 119–29 (1988); R. M. Bagby, J. S. Thompson, S. E. Dickens, and M. Nohara, "Decision Making in Psychiatric Civil Commitment: An Experimental Analysis," *American Journal of Psychiatry* 148: 28–33 (1991).

117. See ENKI Research Institute, *supra* note 42; Munetz et al., *supra* note 89; and Peters et al., *supra* note 81.

118. J. I. Marx and R. M. Levinson, "Statutory Change and 'Street-level' Implementation of Psychiatric Commitment," *Social Science and Medicine* 27: 1247–56 (1988).

119. In the state being studied, the person could be detained for 24 hours initially, and for an additional 5 days at the request of the examining clinicians, without further judicial review.

120. Initially the law allowed involuntary commitment of people found dangerous to others, dangerous to self, or "incapable for caring for self"—the last a grave disability equivalent. The judge who heard these petitions in the county in question, however, considered the incapacity provision too vague and refused to commit people under its provisions. Thus, the county operated effectively with only the dangerous to others and dangerous to self criteria. When the statute was amended, the grave disability provision was tightened to define a committable person as someone "who is so unable to care for his own physical health and safety as to create an imminently life endangering crisis." Following the adoption of this language, the judge allowed grave disability commitments to proceed.

121. Unfortunately, Marx and Levinson do not indicate the proportion of their subjects who were identified as dangerous to others, as opposed to dangerous to self. Rather, they assume in both their report of results and their discussion that all patients who fit their dangerous category were portrayed as assaultive. This cannot be the case. Still, this problem does not negate their overall findings, which rest on the significant drop in the proportion of subjects portrayed as dangerous either to others or to self.

122. When petitioners came to the county's probate court, the judge routinely referred them to an emergency mental health service for consultation with the clinicians there to assess whether their relatives met commitment criteria. His decisions about signing the orders to apprehend were based in large part on whether the mental health professionals believed that the subjects were committable. The way petitioners filled out the required forms was guided, probably to a significant extent, by the advice they received from the consulting clinicians.

123. Marx and Levinson, *supra* note 118, p. 1253. Even with a presiding judge who was apparently firmly committed to narrow commitment criteria that emphasized dangerousness, the Marx and Levinson data show that almost 20 percent of petitions approved presented no evidence of either behavior or threats indicating dangerousness, even before the statutory change. The judge may have "fudged" on his expressed criteria for commitment to hospitalize patients in other situations where such action seemed warranted.

Further, the Marx and Levinson study may provide an explanation for one of the findings of the Peters et al. study of changes in Florida's commitment law discussed earlier (*supra* note 81). The observational data from the court observed by Peters's research group showed no decrease (in fact, an increase) in the number of commitments when a more restrictive statute was implemented, although respondents were characterized as more dangerous by the petitioning clinicians. In light of the Marx and Levinson findings, one might ask whether the apparent change in the degree of dangerousness of the patients was an artifact of clinicians' continuing to do what they needed to do to get their patients committed.

124. California Welfare and Institutions Code, Sec. 5250.

125. Stone, *supra* note 64.

126. See Alan Stone's critique of *Lessard* in ibid.

127. Even in California, through a process that should be familiar by now, all parties in the commitment system manage to circumvent the limits of the statute. Suicidal patients are not discharged after 31 days, nor are patients who are dangerous to others released at the end of their maximum periods of commitment. Instead, they are reclassified as gravely disabled and thereby made subject to California's conservatorship proceedings. Once they are found incapable of managing their affairs, a conservator is appointed with authority to consent to hospitalization for as long as necessary. See Warren's discussion in *Court of Last Resort, supra* note 42, pp. 27–29; and G. H. Morris, "Conservatorship for the 'Gravely Disabled': California's Nondeclaration of Nonindependence," *San Diego Law Review* 15: 201–37 (1978).

128. Samuel Jan Brakel's review of provisions in the commitment statutes of the fifty states illustrates the far from universal endorsement of the *Lessard* requirements. See Brakel, *supra* note 54 (especially Tables 2.4–2.7). One of the most complete judicial repudiations of *Lessard* is embodied in the Second Circuit Court of Appeals' decisions in *Project Release v. Prevost,* 722 F.2d 960 (2d Cir. 1983).

129. Washington Revised Code Annotated, Sec. 71.05.020(1) (commitment permissible if person "manifests severe deterioration in routine functioning evidenced by repeated and escalating loss of cognitive or volitional control over his or her actions and is not receiving such care as is essential for his or her health or safety").

130. N.C. General Statutes, Sec. 122-58.2.

131. Alaska Statutes, Sec. 47.30.915(7)(B); Arizona Revised Statutes Annotated, Chap. 36-501; Colorado Revised Statutes, Art. 27-10-101; Hawaii Revised Statutes, Sec. 334-60.2; Kansas Statutes Annotated, Art. 29, Sec. 59-2902; Rhode Island General Laws, Sec. 40.1-5-2; Texas Mental Health Code Annotated, Sec. 5547-50.

132. American Psychiatric Association, "Task Force Report on Involuntary Outpatient Treatment," (Washington, D.C.: APA, 1988); R. D. Miller, "Outpatient Civil Commitment of the Mentally Ill: An Overview and an Update," *Behavioral Sciences and the Law* 6: 99–118 (1988).

133. "Hospitalization of Mentally Ill Made Easier Under New Colorado Law," *Psychiatric News* 24(19): 7 (1989); Colorado Revised Statutes 27-10-102(5).

134. Pierce et al., *supra* note 78.
135. P. S. Appelbaum, "Crazy in the Streets," *Commentary* 83(5): 34–39 (May 1987); Isaac and Arnot, *supra* note 46; A. B. Johnson, *Out of Bedlam: The Truth About Deinstitutionalization* (New York: Basic Books, 1990); J. Morrissey, "Deinstitutionalizing the Mentally Ill," in W. P. Gove, ed., *Deviance and Mental Illness* (Beverly Hills, Calif.: Sage, 1982), pp. 147–76. Torrey, *supra* note 44.
136. See the state-by-state breakdown of this figure in Torrey, *supra* note 44, Appendix A.
137. One of the most remarkable efforts in this regard occurred in Vermont. See C. M. Harding, G. W. Brooks, T. Ashikaga, J. S. Strauss, and A. Breier, "The Vermont Longitudinal Study of Persons with Severe Mental Illness: I. Methodology, Study Sample, and Overall Status 32 Years Later," *American Journal of Psychiatry* 144: 718–26 (1987).
138. C. J. Smith and R. Q. Hanham, "Deinstitutionalization of the Mentally Ill: A Time Path Analysis of the American States, 1955–1975." *Social Science and Medicine* 15D: 361–78 (1981); Morrissey, *supra* note 135.
139. "California to Phase out Mental Hospitals by 1982," *Psychiatric News* 8(8): 1, 18 (April 18, 1973). The proposal to eliminate the state hospitals entirely was withdrawn a short time later, although the policy of severe reduction in in-patient beds continued. See "California Shelves Plan for Abolishing Hospitals," *Psychiatric News* 8(24): 1 (December 19, 1973).
140. H. H. Goldman, N. H. Adams, and C. A Taube, "Deinstitutionalization: The Data Demythologized," *Hospital and Community Psychiatry* 34: 129–34 (1983). The current figure is an unpublished NIMH estimate.
141. Torrey, *supra* note 44.
142. J. A. Clausen, "Stigma and Mental Disorder: Phenomena and Terminology," *Psychiatry* 44: 287–96 (1981); E. C. Johnstone, D. G. Cunningham-Owens, A. Gold, T. J. Crow, and J. F. MacMillan, "Institutionalization and the Defects of Schizophrenia," *British Journal of Psychiatry* 139: 195–203 (1981).
143. H. H. Goldman, "Epidemiology," in J. Talbott, ed., *The Chronic Mental Patient—Five Years Later* (New York: Grune & Stratton, 1984), pp. 15–31; Lamb, *supra* note 73.
144. *Outcasts on Main Street: Report of the Federal Task Force on Homelessness and Severe Mental Illness* (Washington, D.C.: Interagency Council on the Homeless, 1992).
145. H. R. Lamb and R. Shaner, "When There Are Almost No State Hospital Beds Left," *Hospital and Community Psychiatry* 44: 973–76 (1993). How does this hypothesis fit with the data that suggest that patients who need treatment are not being refused admission in large numbers? One must keep in mind that, in most of the studies of clinicians' admitting practices, the ratings of patients' need for treatment come from the same clinicians whose behavior is being observed. The virtual nonexistence of patients rated as in need of treatment who are turned away (in the few studies performed to date) could reflect clinicians' efforts to deal with tension created by the shortage of hospital beds. Clinicians' definitions of who is in need of hospitalization may change as beds become less available, if only as a mechanism to avoid the guilt associated with believing that patients need care but being unable to provide it. This unconscious "racheting up" of the threshold at which patients are defined as needing hospitalization may make it difficult for researchers to identify the very effects (namely, refusing treatment to those in need) of which the rising threshold is a manifestation. Similar problems, of course,

afflict other efforts to define the effects of commitment law changes. Subsequent research would do well to employ objective appraisals of patients' status, including their need for hospitalization.

146. The irony of this situation should not be overlooked. If beds had not acted as the primary limiting factor on admissions of patients in many areas, restrictive commitment laws indeed might have had a more salient effect. As it is, probably more people are legally committable in many jurisdictions under either narrow or broad standards than can be accommodated in public facilities. Thus, the potentially limiting effect of new commitment laws has been nullified by a contracting mental health system. If bed capacity is expanded in the future, we may well have to deal with the question of whether any restrictive standards that remain should be broadened to reach the groups in need.

147. National Center for State Courts, "Guidelines for Involuntary Civil Commitment," *Mental and Physical Disability Law Reporter* 10: 409–514 (1986).

148. The latest supporting evidence for this proposition comes from the celebrated New York City case of Larry Hogue, a crack cocaine abuser who terrorized an Upper West Side neighborhood. Committed numerous times for threatening, assaultive, and destructive behavior, he was released repeatedly from mental hospitals because his crack-induced psychosis remitted rapidly once he was off the drug. Although his history suggested that he would return to drug use as soon as he hit the streets, in the hospital he was neither "mentally ill" nor "dangerous." When sufficient community concern was expressed, however, a New York appellate court overruled a lower court's opinion that long-term hospitalization would contravene the state's dangerousness statute. See J. P. Fried, "Court Orders Confinement of Drug User: Larry Hogue Is Called Threat to Neighborhood," *New York Times,* March 2, 1993, pp. B1, 6.

149. J. Monahan, "Risk Assessment of Violence Among the Mentally Disordered: Generating Useful Knowledge," *International Journal of Law and Psychiatry* 11: 249–57 (1988).

150. Bagby and Atkinson, *supra* note 86.

151. But see Miller, *supra* note 87.

152. Colorado Revised Statutes, *supra* note 133.

153. J. L. Geller, "In Again, Out Again: Preliminary Evaluation of a State Hospital's Worst Recidivists," *Hospital and Community Psychiatry* 37: 386–90 (1986).

154. Washington Revised Code Annotated, *supra* note 129.

155. Georgia Code Annotated, Sec. 37; Hawaii Revised Statutes, Sec. 334; North Carolina General Statutes, Sec. 122C; Tennessee Code Annotated, Sec. 33.

156. E. P. Mulvey, J. L. Geller, and L. H. Roth. "The Promise and Peril of Involuntary Outpatient Commitment," *American Psychologist* 42: 571–84 (1987).

157. M. J. Fine and C. Acker, "Hoping the Law Will Find an Answer," *Philadelphia Inquirer,* September 13, 1989, p. 1-Aff; L. H. Roth, "Mental Health Commitment: The State of the Debate, 1980," *Hospital and Community Psychiatry* 31: 385–96 (1980).

158. Munetz et al. *supra* note 89.

159. The work of social psychologist Tom Tyler presents a model that could be used in such investigations. See T. R. Tyler, *Why People Obey the Law* (New Haven, Conn.: Yale University Press, 1990).

160. Stone, *supra* note 64; Stromberg and Stone, *supra* note 66; Roth, *supra* note 67; Treffert, *supra* note 68.

3

Duty to Protect Potential Victims of Patients' Violence: Public Peril vs. Protective Privilege

The pink message slip in my box had an unfamiliar name and a local number. "Please call back. Urgent. Dr. Thomas." I punched the number and got a secretary, who put me through. Doug Thomas introduced himself. He was a local psychotherapist, sorry to take my time, sure we had not met. Could he consult with me about a very difficult case? One of his patients seemed to be on the verge of losing control. Murder was not out of the question. We agreed that he would come to see me the following day.

Dr. Thomas was younger than I expected, thin, in a cardigan, no tie. Something about him told me his patients probably called him by his first name. In another setting, he might have come across as warm and empowering. Today, however, he looked as though he could use some help himself. He spoke quickly, evidently relieved at having another person with whom to discuss the situation. As his words poured out, I stopped him on occasion to clarify a point. He shifted nervously as I spoke, only looking comfortable again when I let him continue presenting the case.

As he related the story, the outlines became clear. His patient, George, had been coming to see him weekly for almost eight years. Now in his mid-40s, George worked as a mechanic in a neighborhood auto shop. The work they did together was "supportive," "problem-solving." George was not the kind of patient who wanted to get at the root of his problems. He wanted to know what he should do tomorrow. When they first began therapy, they talked a lot about George's anger, which got in his way at work and in social settings. Dr. Thomas hoped that, if George could vent his feelings in the office, he would not feel impelled to act on them outside. More recently, the therapy had focused on marital difficulties between the patient and his wife, but it was clear that George's anger was never far below the surface.

Until the last two months, the therapy had seemed to be working well. George had never acted out his anger, never been violent. True, he had bought a pistol for "target practice" two years ago, and he had recently obtained a permit to carry a concealed weapon; and there had been times when Dr. Thomas feared that George might lose control and strike someone who had upset him; but the feared breakthrough of rage had never occurred. Nonetheless, Dr. Thomas had told George that, as a psychotherapist, he felt he had a responsibility to take some action to prevent violence, if he ever believed it was imminent.

About six months before, George's unmarried sister-in-law, who lived in the house, began dating a former priest. The man, an alcoholic, had been active in the anti-war movement during the 1960s and 1970s. George disliked everything about him: that he had left the priesthood, that he had opposed his own government, that he drank to excess—as George's father had. Nevertheless, the two were married a few months later, much to George's distress.

The tense and deteriorating relationship between the men culminated in a fistfight at a family Christmas party at George's house. Dr. Thomas had never determined the exact precipitants of the fight, although George's new brother-in-law had clearly been drinking at the time, which had not helped matters any. The brother-in-law got the worst of it but apparently was not hurt badly; and though he talked about filing charges, he never followed through.

In the ensuing two months, George told Dr. Thomas often about the fury he felt toward his brother-in-law, and sometimes he asserted his intention to kill the man, if he ever set foot in George's house again. Other times, George backed away from his threat, but Dr. Thomas thought that this might only reflect a grudging concession to social conventions. Keeping the two of them separated was complicated by the fact that George's in-laws lived upstairs, in an apartment they rented from him, and by the fact that his sister-in-law, naturally enough, wanted to visit her parents and bring her husband along. She and her husband had kept their distance since the fight, but it was only a matter of time before they turned up. At that point, Dr. Thomas feared—particularly if the brother-in-law was inebriated—George might not be able to control himself, a fight would ensue, and somebody, probably the brother-in-law, would get hurt or worse.

With this concern gnawing at him, Dr. Thomas decided he had to do something, though he wasn't sure what. Finally, he settled on calling George's wife, asking her to pass a message through her sister to the brother-in-law that it might be advisable for him to stay away from the property. If Dr. Thomas had imagined that this would settle the matter, he was wrong. The brother-in-law called Dr. Thomas the next day to ask what was going on. Why should he stay away from his in-laws' house? And if George was a dangerous mental patient, why wasn't Dr. Thomas doing something to protect the public—like hospitalizing George or calling the police? A sticky discussion ensued. Dr. Thomas decided that he had gotten in over his head. He called me the next day. His questions: Had he done the right thing so far? What should he do now?

As much as Dr. Thomas genuinely wanted to protect both the brother-in-law and his own patient, he had other motives in coming to see me. He made it plain that he wanted to get out of this situation without being sued by one unhappy party or the other: by the brother-in-law, because he had not done enough to keep George from harming him; or by George himself, for breaking the confidentiality that ordinarily attends the psychotherapist–patient relationship. His fears were not without foundation. Although he had started practice at a time when therapists worried little about obligations to nonpatients and when confidentiality was often considered to be absolute, things had changed over the years. Dr. Thomas now found himself confused and frightened by a new legal world that seemed to demand extraordinary efforts on his part to control patients' behavior, and to threaten ruin if those efforts failed.

Traditional Approaches to Mental Health Professionals' Liability for Their Patient's Violent Acts

Until the mid-1970s, psychiatrists and other psychotherapists had little to fear from lawsuits initiated by third parties who had been harmed by their patients. The courts had defined a limited area of risk, generally involving instances where hospitalized patients were negligently discharged or allowed to escape from psychiatric facilities and then caused harm to other people.[1] Plaintiffs in these suits sought to hold psychiatrists[2] liable for the allegedly improper manner in which decisions were made about release, granting of passes, or placement on open wards. Although the rationale for psychiatrists' liability in these cases was often unstated, it appeared to derive from the maxim in tort law that "[o]ne who takes charge of a third person whom he knows or should know to be likely to cause bodily harm to others if not controlled is under a duty to exercise reasonable care to control the third person to prevent him from doing such harm."[3]

Whether reasonable care was exercised by an in-patient psychiatrist was ordinarily judged by whether the actions that led to release or escape were in compliance with generally accepted medical and psychiatric standards.[4] That is, as in most malpractice cases, psychiatrists were held liable not simply because an unfortunate outcome ensued, but because their professional conduct preceding the outcome deviated from the professional standard of care.

A major obstacle encountered by third parties who wanted to bring cases against psychiatrists for harms suffered when patients were released or allowed to escape was the fact that most psychiatric patients were hospitalized in state facilities. Until well into this century, the great majority of states adhered to the doctrine of sovereign immunity, which precluded the state or its employees from being sued for negligent acts.[5] "Release and escape cases," therefore, were quite uncommon until the 1950s. Even then, they shared several characteristics that limited the degree of concern they aroused among psychiatrists.

First, liability was only imposed when psychiatrists had actual physical custody of the person who later committed an injurious act. Thus, it was clear to members of the profession which patients they were expected to control. Second, the duty of psychiatrists in most of these cases was well-defined and circumscribed: they were required to make reasonable efforts to retain in the hospital any patient who was still dangerous and in need of care. No additional obligations, beyond the usual practice of in-patient psychiatry, were placed on clinicians. Third, the courts emphasized that only deviations from the professional standard of care would induce liability, not "an honest error of professional judgment made by qualified and competent persons."[6] The "honest error" doctrine had long been a part of malpractice law, and the courts enforced it rigorously. Fourth, the courts also recognized that release was "one of the medical and public risks which must be taken on balance" in pursuit of "the hope of recovery and rehabilitation of a vast number of patients [which otherwise] would be impeded and frustrated."[7] Trial discharges and placement on open wards, even of patients with past histories of violence, were seen as important components of a psychiatric treatment system designed to return patients to community living.[8]

Finally, the courts in these cases typically predicated liability on the question of whether the patient's violent act was "foreseeable."[9] This usually meant that the patient must have had a history of violent threats or behavior. Otherwise, the courts were willing to

> recognize as a matter of law that mental disorders are elusive and difficult to analyze and evaluate [and that] modern psychiatric medicine would be unable to predict within any degree of medical probability that [if a patient suffered a relapse] such a psychotic episode would be violent, dangerous to the patient or to others, or homicidal or suicidal.[10]

Given these attitudes, it was uncommon for psychiatrists to be held liable in release and escape cases, barring unusual circumstances, such as a negligent failure of the treatment staff to share important information among themselves regarding patients' care.[11]

The traditional attitude of the courts toward psychiatric liability for patients' violent or destructive acts is best exemplified by a pair of cases from New York.[12] The cases both dealt with fires set by a teenage boy, Robert Brown, who was a resident at a state school for the mentally retarded.[13] While working on a nearby farm as part of the school's program, Brown slipped off and set a series of fires, including one that destroyed a building on adjacent property. After Brown, who had not been known as a fire-setter before, confessed to starting the fires, the sheriff sent him back to the institution rather than pressing charges. The school was told that Brown was "suspected" of setting fires.

On returning to the institution, Brown was restricted to working inside the school buildings. Before long, chafing at his confinement, he pleaded to be permitted to work outdoors again. Three months later, permission for outside work was given by the medical director of the facility. The following day, Brown escaped from an outdoor work detail, broke into a house belonging to the chief of dental services at the state school, found matches, and set a fire that burned it to the ground. The owners of both buildings destroyed by Brown—the farm building he set fire to before his restriction indoors and the house he ignited afterward—sued the state. Each set of owners charged that the staff of the institution had been negligent in not supervising Brown more closely. The cases were joined for purposes of review by the court.

With regard to the first claim, by the owners of the property adjoining the farm where Brown had worked, the general reluctance of the courts to find treatment staff negligent when patients harmed others was evident. The court cited an earlier case, which had held:

> A balance must be struck between contending interests—(1) the State's duty to treat and care for its mental defective wards, with an eye toward returning them to society more useful citizens, and (2) the State's concern that the inmates of its institutions cause no injury or damage to the property of those in the vicinity. That balance may be hard to achieve. We keep within settled legal principles, however, if the State is held only to a duty of taking precautions against those risks "reasonably to be perceived" [citation omitted] and if the community assumes the risk of accidental loss or damage to property by an inmate of an open institution . . .[14]

Since Brown had never before set fires, and since the state school therefore had no reason to suspect him of such a proclivity, the claim of the owners of the building was denied.

With regard to the claim by the dentist employed at the school, however, the court found that the situation had changed. The fire that destroyed his house was "attributable to the negligence of the State in its failure to keep a close watch on Robert Brown, having been previously warned of his fire setting tendencies" (p. 911). Thus, the state was held liable for the damage that ensued.

The resolution of these two claims, based on similar facts, yet decided differently, illustrates how difficult it was to persuade a court to impose liability on individuals (and the state) responsible for the treatment of mentally ill or retarded persons in the absence of clear indications that harm was likely. But it also demonstrates that neglect of a known risk could, in rare cases, lead to a finding of liability. Had these rules been in place when Dr. Thomas learned of George's anger toward his brother-in-law—although Dr. Thomas might still have wondered about his ethical obligations to prevent violence from occurring—he would have had much less serious legal concerns. As an out-patient clinician, Dr. Thomas would have been assumed by the courts to have no duty to control George's behavior and no liability for George's acts. A good deal, however, has changed in the law since Robert Brown set his string of fires in upstate New York and the process of change began just a few years after the embers from those fires died out.

The Genesis of a Broader "Duty to Protect"

The innovation in law that lay behind Dr. Thomas' urgent call grew out of a tragedy that occurred on the other side of the continent. In 1969, an Indian graduate student at the University of California, Berkeley, Prosenjit Poddar, entered psychotherapy with a psychologist at the university health service. Poddar had done poorly after his romantic attentions had been rebuffed by an American girl, Tatiana Tarasoff, whom he had dated for several months the previous year. He had become depressed and withdrawn, neglecting his appearance, his studies, and his health. Obsessed with the woman who had spurned him, Poddar met with her several times in the months before entering therapy and tape-recorded their conversations, trying to ascertain why she did not love him.[15]

Soon after the start of psychotherapy, the treating psychologist became concerned about Poddar's potential for harming Tatiana Tarasoff. Whether Poddar told the psychologist directly about his intent to kill her (as her parents later alleged)[16] or whether he merely manifested his obsession with her and the psychologist learned from a friend of Poddar that he had purchased a gun[17] is unclear. Whatever the basis for the psychologist's concern, he consulted with two supervising psychiatrists and then notified the campus police that he would be requesting commitment of the patient. He asked them to detain Poddar while the necessary paperwork was completed.

The police picked up Poddar, but after talking with him, finding him "rational," and eliciting his promise that he would stay away from Tatiana Tarasoff, who was then out of the country on vacation, they let him go. No further action was taken by the therapists, apparently because they felt uncomfortable about having breached Poddar's confidentiality by informing the university police of their intention to commit him. Poddar never returned to therapy, but he did seek out Tatiana's brother, whose roommate he became and from whom he learned of her return to the country. Roughly two months after the attempt had been made to commit him, Poddar went to the Tarasoff house, armed with a pellet gun and a kitchen knife, and found Tatiana alone. She refused to speak with him and began screaming, at which point Poddar shot her, chased her as she attempted to flee, and stabbed her to death. He then returned to her house and called the police.

Faced with this horrifying crime, Tatiana's parents sought to hold the therapists and the campus police responsible for what had occurred. They filed suit alleging negligence on the therapists' part for failing effectively to detain Poddar and for failing to warn them (Tatiana being unreachable) of the threat to their daughter's life. Clearly, they were striking out across uncharted legal territory. Poddar never had been hospitalized, and thus the linchpin of all previous decisions in which psychiatrists had been found liable was missing in this case. If the courts agreed with the family that the therapists (setting aside any duties the police may have had) had a duty to protect Tatiana Tarasoff, they would have to base their decision on a new theory of psychiatric liability.

In the event, that is exactly what happened. The California Supreme Court, ruling that the suit could proceed to trial, held that a therapist who "determines, or pursuant to the standards of his profession should determine, that his patient presents a serious danger of violence to another" has a duty to take whatever steps are "reasonably necessary" to protect the intended victim.[18] The source of this duty was the "special relationship" that the court concluded existed between a therapist and a patient, and the additional obligations such a relationship imposed.

Invocation of "special relationships" has served as a mechanism by which courts can bypass the law's deeply rooted hesitancy about imposing affirmative duties on one person to protect or rescue another.[19] In Anglo-American law in general, no sanctions are applied to persons who fail to assist their fellows, even when assistance may be life-saving and may require only minimal effort. Thus, a person who knowingly walks past a toddler drowning in a wading pool—a situation in which a moment's intervention would have saved the child's life—bears no civil or criminal responsibility for the toddler's demise. Were the child's parents or babysitter to behave similarly, however, they would be held culpable, since they had a legally cognizable "special relationship" with the child.

There is no touchstone to determine when a special relationship exists. Indeed, the determination is often driven by the desired outcome: when courts believe, on whatever grounds, that a duty to rescue should be imposed, they proclaim a special relationship; when they feel otherwise, they solemnly declare its absence. Among the relationships deemed special have been common carrier–passenger, innkeeper–guest, employer–employee, shopkeeper–business visitor, host–social guest, and school–pupil.[20] Courts have justified each of these exceptions to the general rule by pointing to some characteristic of the relationship that warrants imposing a special, heightened duty.

In the case of the psychotherapist–patient relationship, the *Tarasoff* court's analysis of why a duty to rescue or protect should be imposed was skeletal. The court referred to several lines of cases that it apparently considered analogous. One was the release and escape decisions discussed earlier. The implication here seemed to be that, although Poddar's therapists did not exercise physical control over him, they had the opportunity to do so, given the commitment laws of the state of California. Thus, a duty arose comparable to the one that would have applied if he had been in their custody. A second line of cited cases dealt with physicians who had failed to warn patients' family members that the patients' conditions were infectious. The rationale here appeared to be that, just as physicians have specialized knowledge of the dangers of transmission of communicable diseases, so Poddar's therapists had knowledge of his dangerousness that was not available to the public at large. Along with this knowledge came an obligation to act.

Two additional facets of the *Tarasoff* decision are worthy of comment. First, the court restricted the ambit of obligation owed by therapists to identifiable victims of their patients. As explicitly affirmed in a later case,[21] this limitation excludes liability for patients whom therapists might only know to be dangerous to the public at large. Second, in contrast to this limiting of the persons to whom a duty was owed, the extent of therapists' duties to protect qualified individuals was quite broad. In this regard, it is important to note that there were actually two decisions by the California Supreme Court in this case; the second and definitive decision in 1976 displaced its predecessor of two years earlier.[22] The first decision had imposed only a duty to *warn* potential victims. When the case was reheard, in part at the request of a number of psychiatric and mental health organizations, the court apparently was persuaded that warnings alone often would be inadequate to protect victims. In place of a duty to warn, the court imposed a broader, less precise duty to protect—that is, to take "whatever other steps are reasonably necessary under the circumstances."[23]

Pushing aside the narrow requirements of the earlier release and escape cases, *Tarasoff* imposed a sweeping duty on all classes of therapists to protect identifiable potential victims of their patients. Since California was often a bellwether state, particularly where new developments in tort law were concerned, many observers assumed that the ruling would be adopted elsewhere. For the psychotherapeutic professions, this was a matter of urgent concern.

Clinicians' Reactions to *Tarasoff*

Most psychiatrists and other mental health professionals were upset by the *Tarasoff* court's imposition of a duty to protect third parties. Alan Stone, whose comments often typified the reaction of his colleagues, was vice-president of the American Psychiatric Association when the final opinion in *Tarasoff* appeared. He called the decision "extremely irrational"; and looking beyond the reasoning of the opinion itself to what he presumed was the court's underlying motivation, he declared it "one of the most extreme examples" of California's "effort to compensate everyone for everything."[24] Stone also found a connection between California's recent reform of its civil commitment statute—which was designed to make it more difficult to hospitalize patients—and the newly proclaimed duty to protect.[25] According to Stone, the California Supreme Court, compelled by the new statute to find other mechanisms than hospitalization to protect the public from the risk of harm at the hands of the mentally ill, shifted the burden of providing for public safety from the state hospital system to psychotherapists.

Stone's suspicions were shared by some lawyers, including William Curran, whose column on law and medicine appeared regularly in the *New England Journal of Medicine*. With the decision in *Tarasoff,* he wrote, the California Supreme Court had "made the physician a guarantor against harm to [a third party], here not even a patient, on the basis of its own concept of monetary justice."[26] Bernard Diamond, psychiatrist and professor of criminology and law at the University of California, Berkeley, described the state's psychiatrists as "going around bemoaning their fate and cursing under their breath this judicial intervention in what they regard as their private affairs with their patients."[27]

What caused this intense reaction by mental health professionals and their sympathizers? Unlike new restrictions on civil commitment, whose perceived effects were limited to clinicians' professional lives and only became apparent over time, the threat posed by *Tarasoff* and similar cases was immediate and much more direct. Psychiatrists and other mental health professionals suddenly found themselves at risk for costly, embarrassing, and painful court proceedings if their patients committed violent acts. And they suspected that the deck was stacked against them.

The *Tarasoff* court had required psychotherapists to anticipate their patients' violence "pursuant to the standards of [their] profession." Until roughly the time of the *Tarasoff* litigation, this was something that most psychiatrists thought themselves fully capable of doing. For decades forensic psychiatrists had assisted the courts in sentencing, release, and other decisions by offering their conclusions concerning defendants' and prisoners' propensities for violence. Indeed, some influential psychiatrists considered themselves so accomplished at this task that they argued for the abolition of prisons, with wrongdoers instead turned over to psychiatrists for treatment.[28] This proposal contained the implicit assumption that psychiatrists would also know when treatment had been effective—that is, when further violence was not likely to occur—at which point those confined would be freed to rejoin society. Transition to this form of therapeutic criminology was accomplished in part through the adoption of statutes in some states permitting indefinite sentences to forensic facilities for selected classes of defendants, often termed "defective delinquents" or "sexually dangerous persons."[29]

By the 1960s and early 1970s, however, faith in psychiatrists' predictive abilities had begun to crumble; indeed, several studies that appeared during this period suggested that psychiatrists performed relatively poorly at the task. Most of these studies involved follow-ups of defendants or prisoners who were predicted to be dangerous, but who were released from custody because of some legal imperfection in their detention or because a judge disagreed with the psychiatric prognostication.[30] All of the studies showed that only a small fraction of those released were later arrested for violent acts, inviting the conclusion that psychiatrists vastly overpredicted future violence.[31] Thus, by 1974, opinion among experts in dealing with violent patients had swung so far in the other direction that the American Psychiatric Association's Task Force on Clinical Aspects of the Violent Individual could reach the following conclusion: "Neither psychiatrists nor anyone else [has] reliably demonstrated an ability to predict future violence or 'dangerousness.' Neither has any special psychiatric 'expertise' in this area been established."[32]

Psychiatrists and other psychotherapists, still assimilating the data on their deficiencies as predictors of violence, were stunned to be thrust back into this role by the courts and to face the risk of liability for failure at what the experts said was an impossible task. The *amicus curiae* brief of the American Psychiatric Association and other mental health groups supporting the request for a rehearing of the original *Tarasoff* decision argued that "[t]his Court's newly formulated duty to warn directly conflicts with this growing body of scientific evidence."[33] To many commentators, it made no sense to charge psychotherapists with negligence for failing to do what even their most diligent peers could not accomplish.[34]

But it was more than concern over personal liability that led to the vociferous reaction to *Tarasoff*. Many therapists believed that the decision challenged the integrity of the psychotherapeutic process. Beginning with Freud, therapists had argued that the confidentiality of the information conveyed by patients had to be protected stringently if psychotherapy were to succeed.[35] How else could they persuade patients to confide their dreams, fears, and fantasies, all of which was essential if they were to obey the psychodynamic psychotherapist's dictum that whatever came to mind must be shared?[36] If families, friends, or the public at large were to learn what patients said in therapy, the treatment of these patients whose confidentiality had been abrogated would end, and other patients would be deterred from seeking treatment in the first place. Once one agreed that psychotherapy made important contributions to the functioning and well-being of thousands of patients—and most clinicians averred that it did—one had to conclude that mechanisms were needed to ensure that information provided by patients did not leave the confines of the consulting room.

Surveys of therapists and their patients, many undertaken in the wake of the *Tarasoff* decisions, confirmed that these views were widely held. In one study, 98 percent of a sample of mental health professionals said that they believed confidentiality was essential for therapy.[37] In a California study of psychiatrists and psychologists, 79 percent of respondents believed that patients would divulge less information if they knew there was a risk of disclosure.[38] Studies of patients seemed to confirm these beliefs. In a New Jersey study of patients in therapy, 22 percent said that they had hesitated to seek treatment because of fears concerning disclosure of confidential information; since the sample came entirely from people who had overcome their concerns and entered therapy, the percentage of potential patients with such fears was presumably even higher.[39] Similarly, 67 percent of psychiatric in-patients in a Pennsylvania survey said that they would be angry or upset if they discovered that hospital staff members had revealed their communications to other people without their consent.[40]

The premise underlying these views of both therapists and patients—that confidentiality is crucial to psychotherapy and deserves societal recognition—was accepted in the majority of states at the time of the *Tarasoff* decision, as reflected in statutes affording special protection to psychotherapeutic communications.[41] These laws created a testimonial "privilege" that enabled patients to prevent their therapists from revealing in court or other legal proceedings information communicated in therapy sessions, in contravention of the ordinary powers of the courts to subpoena all relevant information.[42] Although frequently riddled with exceptions,[43] these privilege statutes conveyed to psychotherapists and their patients a sense of the special confidential nature of things said in the therapist's office, and they acknowledged the special and presumably valuable character of the therapist–patient relationship.

Tarasoff seemed to threaten all that. The California Supreme Court explicitly considered whether California's privilege statute and another law on confidentiality of mental health records should be read as indicating a statutory preference for sheltering patients' confidences over protecting third parties. But in the end, the court ruled to the contrary: "The protective privilege ends where the public peril begins."[44] In one sense, the psychotherapeutic professions had come to the same conclusion on their own. The American Medical Association's Principles of Medical Ethics, which governed psychiatrists as well as other physicians, had already made it clear, as the *Tarasoff* court noted, that confidentiality could be breached when "it becomes necessary in order to protect the welfare of the individual or of the community."[45] But *allowing* psychotherapists to reveal confidential communications in the (presumably rare) circumstances when they thought that such action was required differed considerably from *demanding* that they do so under ill-defined circumstances of "serious danger" to other people.[46] Concern about the loss of professional discretion to the courts undoubtedly played a role here. Beyond that, however, commentators voiced the fear that potential liability, combined with the difficulties of predicting violent behavior and the already demonstrated tendency of mental health professionals to overpredict dangerousness, would lead to far more breaches of confidentiality than might otherwise take place.[47]

As skeptical as psychiatrists were learning to be about their abilities to predict patients' future violence, they had little hesitation in offering forecasts of the effects that the anticipated abrogation of the principle of confidentiality would have on psychotherapeutic practice. The chairman of the APA's Committee on Confidentiality declared that the *Tarasoff* decision "wipes out" the doctor-patient relationship.[48] Psychiatrists offered a litany of projected problems:

- Psychotherapists, caught between concerns over liability for failing to predict violence and liability for needlessly breaching patients' confidences, would be deterred from attempting to treat potentially violent patients.[49]
- Assuming that therapists were willing to continue to treat patients with suspected potential for violence, the patients themselves would be discouraged from seeking treatment by their knowledge of therapists' duty to protect. This tendency would be magnified by the warning about the duty that conscientious therapists would feel obliged to offer at the initiation of therapy. Among those dissuaded from crossing the thresholds of therapists' offices would be persons who unrealistically feared that they might be violent (a common fantasy, even in high-functioning groups), as well as members of groups with the greatest propensity for violence—juvenile delinquents, prisoners, and parolees—in whose successful treatment society had a particular interest.[50]
- Patients who overcame such inhibitions and entered therapy would nonetheless be hesitant to share violent fantasies out of concern that these might provoke a warning. This would render therapy ineffective and result in a net increase in the amount of violence with which society had to contend.[51]

- Therapists themselves, concerned about the risks of malpractice suits, might distort the course of therapy, either to focus inappropriately on patients' passing thoughts of violence or to avoid listening to such fantasies—a "hear no evil, have no duty" approach. Alternatively, psychotherapists might be so unnerved by the obligation to detect violence potential that the whole process of therapy could go awry.[52]

- Once a warning was issued, therapy would essentially end. As in the case of Prosenjit Poddar, dangerous persons would be released to prey on their victims without the treatment that alone could alter the anticipated outcome. Not only would the breach of confidence itself ensure this end, but the patient's perception that the therapist was allied with the victim, rather than with the patient, would seal the therapy's doom.[53]

- Beyond the negative effects of warnings on therapy, their presumed benefits would not accrue. Since many potential victims are intimates of patients, they either are already prepared for the dangers they face or are helpless or unwilling to remove themselves from the situation.[54] Battered wives are a classic example.[55]

- Warnings would induce considerable anxiety in potential victims and might not aid them greatly, given the difficulties involved in protecting themselves from an assault without complete disruption of their lives.[56] Indeed, potential victims might sue therapists for the emotional distress caused by warnings that turned out to be unnecessary.[57]

- Third parties who received warnings and were not inclined toward strictly passive measures of defense might undertake preemptive strikes on patients. Warnings might therefore place patients in danger, even when the patient would probably never have harmed the prospective victim.[58]

- Therapists—psychiatrists, in particular—who have the power to initiate involuntary commitment in their jurisdictions, would solve their dilemma at a stroke by hospitalizing any patient about whom they had the slightest concerns regarding violence.[59] This would lead to overuse of scarce and expensive hospital beds and would needlessly deprive patients of their liberty. Indeed, one psychiatrist-lawyer actually urged mental health professionals to follow this course, leaving all release decisions to judges, since the latter—unlike psychiatrists—are immune from suit. This massive display of civil disobedience, she believed, would force the legal system to its senses, leading to a repudiation of the duty to protect.[60]

Psychiatrists' responses to the duty to protect varied, however, and particularly as time passed, voices endorsing the duty—although not always in the form crafted by the *Tarasoff* court—began to emerge. From the start, many psychiatrists acknowledged a moral duty to protect potential victims, even as they resisted its codification in law.[61] Others accepted versions of the legal duty that held therapists to clearer and less demanding standards for the difficult tasks of predicting and preventing violence.[62] The American Medical Association endorsed taking "reasonable precautions for the protection of intended victims, including notification of law enforcement authorities" when there is a "reasonable probability" that a patient may carry out a threat to "inflict serious bodily harm to another person."[63] Some clinicians claimed there was no conflict between a duty to protect and the duties incumbent in ordinary clinical care.[64] Indeed, it could only benefit patients themselves to avert acts of violence.[65] A therapeutically oriented law professor suggested that the duty to protect might even encourage more appropriate choices of treatment, especially if it led to incorporation of the potential victim—often an intimate—into joint therapy with the patient.[66]

Most of the more positive reactions came a decade or more after *Tarasoff* appeared. In the meantime, no other court decision had induced a similar wave of dread among psychotherapists. The dread, of course, was predicated on the assumption that *Tarasoff* would set the pattern for other courts around the country. For a few years, this seemed not to be happening. By the early 1980s, however, the floodgates opened.

Evolution of the Duty to Protect

Courts asked to consider questions of therapists' liability after *Tarasoff* invariably looked to the analysis in that case as their starting point. Some courts were content merely to apply the California doctrine to the facts before them, without substantial modification.[67] As with most new legal doctrines, however, a fair amount of experimentation by the courts took place, producing both expanded and restricted versions of the duty to protect.

As radical as *Tarasoff* seemed when it was decided, the duty created by the California Supreme Court was circumscribed in several ways. The first of these limitations to be rejected by another court was the requirement that the victim be "identifiable" before a duty to protect could be invoked. It is difficult to know just how carefully the *Tarasoff* court considered the implications of this identifiability rule in the first place. Since Tatiana Tarasoff was easily recognized as the target of Poddar's threats, it may be that the court's opinion was shaped to fit the peculiarities of the case, with the judges' being reluctant to define a duty that was not required by the facts at hand. Or perhaps the specification that the victim be known is an anachronism left over from the initial decision in the case, in which the duty enunciated consisted of an obligation to warn potential victims. One cannot easily warn someone whose identity is obscure.

Whatever the case, the identifiability requirement had a major flaw. Accepted at face value, it suggested that a psychotherapist had no duty to protect the victims of a patient who proclaimed his intention to shoot the first three people he saw on the street after leaving the therapist's office, whereas it would apply if the patient specified a single intended victim. Given this inconsistency, it was only a matter of time before the identifiability requirement was challenged.

The challenge came in a Nebraska case, *Lipari v. Sears, Roebuck and*

Co.[68] Mrs. Lipari and her husband, who were unknown to the patient/assailant, were sitting in a nightclub when the patient entered and sprayed the room with bullets. Mrs. Lipari was wounded and her husband was killed. She claimed that the Veterans Administration, which had been treating the patient in an out-patient clinic, should have known that he was dangerous and should have taken steps to prevent the shooting. When the defendants objected that the Liparis were not identifiable victims, the federal district court hearing the case refused to limit the duty to protect in that way. As long as victims were part of a class of persons to whom ''an unreasonable risk of harm'' could be ''reasonably foreseen,'' the therapists had a duty to protect them. Other cases since *Lipari* have held similarly.[69]

Another limitation of the ruling in *Tarasoff* was that it applied the duty to protect only to cases involving persons physically endangered by a patient. Nothing was said about a therapist's responsibility to prevent damage to property. The Vermont Supreme Court, however, faced with a case in which a patient burned down his parents' barn, held that the same rationale applied to protecting victims' possessions as well.[70] Moreover, that court also extended the duty to protect beyond the doctoral-level mental health professionals (psychiatrists and psychologists) who were the target of the suit in *Tarasoff*. A master's-level counselor, who was the patient's primary therapist in the Vermont case, was held liable for his purported negligence. The court's language suggested that all mental health professionals were now at risk if they failed to protect potential victims.

Other courts have extended the reach of possible liability for violating the *Tarasoff* duty to protect in a variety of ways. It has been applied to emergency settings, where there was no preexisting relationship between the psychiatrist and the patient, and to a situation in which the victim had been warned previously, appeared to be aware of the patient's potential for violence, and failed to protect herself.[71] Therapists have also been held liable for harm to the child of a victim, who witnessed the attack by a patient, on the theory that, if the victim herself were identifiable, it was foreseeable that her son might be in her presence and might be traumatized by the event.[72]

Perhaps most troubling to clinicians are the small number of cases in which the duty to protect has been invoked despite the fact that none of the prerequisites of the *Tarasoff* ruling seem to have been met. The prototypical case is *Davis v. Lhim,* in which a psychiatrist was held responsible for a patient's murder of his mother in Alabama several months after his discharge from a Michigan state hospital.[73] An expert witness for the plaintiff testified that the patient's act was foreseeable and that the victim was identifiable because a hospital emergency room record several years earlier had noted that the patient had threatened his mother with harm unless she gave him money. Despite this testimony, the trial record suggests that the in-

patient psychiatrist had no reason to anticipate that the patient was dangerous or that the mother would be at any significant risk (she died as she was
struggling with her son to take away a shotgun he was brandishing, perhaps
for the purpose of harming himself); nor is it at all clear that meaningful
steps could have been taken to protect her. The only plausible justification
for the decision holding the psychiatrist liable is a desire on the part of the
court to compensate the survivors without regard to fault on the part of the
psychiatrist. Cases such as *Davis* struck fear into the hearts of psychotherapists around the country.[74]

In contrast to cases that have interpreted *Tarasoff* broadly, a number
of courts have taken a narrow view of its scope. Several decisions have
turned down opportunities to extend the duty to protect to cover nonidenti-
fiable (but perhaps foreseeable) victims, electing instead to cling tightly to
the original California formulation of the duty.[75] Other courts have restricted the application of the duty to protect, in two major ways: by requiring that the patient must make a specific threat of violence before a
duty is invoked; and by limiting the duty to circumstances in which actual
control of the patient is possible.

Applying Colorado law, the federal district and appellate courts in *Brady
v. Hopper,* a case growing out of John Hinckley's attempted assassination
of President Reagan, adopted the first of these approaches. Both courts
ruled that Hinckley's psychiatrist could not be held liable for his patient's
acts because Hinckley had made no specific threat of violence.[76] Uncertain
as the prediction of violence was, both courts held, it was reasonable from
a public policy perspective to impose a duty to protect only when an explicit threat was made.[77]

The second limitation on the *Tarasoff* rule can be seen in *Hasenei v.
U.S.,* another federal court decision, which dealt with injuries inflicted by
a Veterans Administration out-patient who was driving a car while intoxi-
cated.[78] It was apparently clear that the patient was not committable, and
thus that the VA did not have the ability to exercise physical control over
his behavior. Since, without an identifiable victim, this left the VA psychiatric staff powerless to prevent the accident, the court concluded that there
was no basis for the imposition of liability.[79]

Peculiar fact situations have led other courts to reject application of a
Tarasoff-like duty to protect. In Iowa, the state supreme court turned aside
an effort by a woman who had killed her husband to impose liability on her
psychiatrist for failing to predict and prevent the act.[80] The court's rationale
was that allowing persons to benefit from their own criminal acts was contrary to public policy. A second Iowa case arose when a patient tried to run
down her husband's lover with her automobile.[81] Given that the patient had
tried this before—without the knowledge of her psychiatrist—the Iowa court
held that the victim was well aware of the threat and the psychiatrist had
no further duty.[82]

Finally, some courts have simply refused to adopt *Tarasoff* or rejected the duty to protect on its face. The doctrine of sovereign immunity has been revived and applied to decisions, especially those regarding discharge, in some states, precluding imposition of liability for later violence by patients.[83] A more direct assault on *Tarasoff* can be seen in *Shaw v. Glickman,* in which a Maryland court refused to adopt a duty to protect when a patient shot his wife's lover, having found the pair *in flagrante delicto.*[84] The trio had all been in group therapy together, and the victim alleged that the group's leader should have known of the danger he (the victim) was in. Perhaps believing that he who seduces another man's wife does so at his own risk (although rejecting the trial court's explicit statement of this principle), the court found that Maryland's rules on confidentiality—precluding the issuance of a warning—took precedence over whatever duty the therapists may have owed to the victim. *Tarasoff,* the court concluded, is simply not good law in Maryland.

Within a decade of the *Tarasoff* decision, almost a score of states had their own related court opinions on the books, and almost all of these had endorsed some version of the duty to protect. The duty even went full circle, being applied to release and escape cases in a manner that extended clinicians' duty beyond confinement to providing warnings and other protective measures.[85] Across jurisdictions, though, the dimensions of the duty varied strikingly, contributing to widespread confusion among patients, clinicians, and lawyers about what obligations might accrue, particularly in jurisdictions where no definitive statement on the duty had yet been made by the courts. Nonetheless, the duty to protect had clearly grown from a California-specific doctrine to a national rule, albeit one whose dimensions were subject to considerable variation from state to state. Given its widespread adoption, one might ask how realistic the many initial concerns of clinicians turned out to be. The answer is complex, intriguing, and more than a little surprising.

Consequences of Adopting a Duty to Protect

The projected consequences of the duty to protect were premised on two assumptions: that psychotherapists would behave differently in the wake of the decision in *Tarasoff,* specifically that they would much more often break confidentiality to protect potential victims; and that patients, learning of this new threat to the privacy of their communications, would react adversely, avoiding therapy entirely or using it in unproductive ways. Each of these premises, however, turned out to be flawed.

Perhaps most surprising were the results of two major surveys of psychotherapists, undertaken shortly after *Tarasoff* was decided, that examined changes in therapists' behavior when their patients endangered others. The first study surveyed psychiatrists and psychologists in California within one year of the final ruling in *Tarasoff*.[86] The study found that 50 percent of respondents said they had issued warnings about patients' potential violence *prior* to the final decision in *Tarasoff*, while 38 percent had done so in the year since the decision. Although the data do not permit conclusions to be drawn about the extent of changes in behavior—since responding therapists had been practicing for an average of 13 years prior to the decision, so the time periods contrasted were by no means comparable—they do indicate an unexpected prevalence of protective behavior by the study sample before the *Tarasoff* litigation ended.[87] This finding suggested that the impact of *Tarasoff* would be more limited than had been anticipated, since therapists already had been breaching confidentiality to protect potential victims. Thus, many of the purported harms, including discouraging patients from pursuing therapy, presumably had been accruing even before *Tarasoff* came along.

Why were therapists behaving in this way in the absence of legal compulsion? The answer to this question came from a second study that took a different approach to measuring the impact of *Tarasoff*. This national survey, conducted in 1980, looked at a stratified random sample of 2,875 psychiatrists, psychologists, and social workers.[88] Respondents were queried about the most recent case they had treated involving a dangerous patient. As expected, clinicians who were aware of *Tarasoff* and believed that the duty to protect was legally or ethically binding on them were more likely to have warned potential victims than were therapists who were unaware of or who rejected the duty.[89] The differences were even greater when an actual threat had been made.[90] On the other hand, there were no significant differences in the rates of warning victims, the police, or other authorities between therapists who accepted a duty to protect on an ethical basis and therapists who felt themselves legally bound to act on victims' behalf. Among respondents outside California, 60 to 71 percent believed that they had a professional ethical duty to protect, while 78 to 83 percent believed that they had a personal ethical duty to do so. The widespread acceptance of an ethical duty to protect made the additional impact of the *Tarasoff* ruling on therapists' conduct marginal.[91]

Although we cannot conclude that promulgation of a legal duty to protect had no impact on therapists' behavior, the differences, if they exist, appear to have been quantitative rather than qualitative. Warnings or other protective actions may have been taken more frequently after *Tarasoff* than before, but most therapists had already accepted an ethical obligation to protect potential victims and were willing to act on it. How long prior to *Tarasoff* such attitudes were prevalent is difficult to say, but a 1956 survey of psychiatrists revealed that 34 of 37 respondents would have reported a patient who revealed acts of "disloyalty and sabotage against the United States."[92] Similarly, 64 percent of 369 psychologists questioned in 1958 would have released confidential information to prevent a homicide.[93] The *Tarasoff* ruling undoubtedly would have increased these figures, but they show that the underlying values were already in place.

If, prior to *Tarasoff,* psychotherapists were already acting frequently to protect victims, the anticipated increase in one set of negative consequences for patients and victims—disruption of therapy, with consequent increased risk to potential targets of patients' violence—was unlikely to be substantial. But greater public awareness of psychotherapists' obligations to breach confidentiality—now transmuted into a legal rule—still might discourage persons in distress from seeking treatment or from fully disclosing their feelings. For these consequences, public perception of a change in psychotherapists' behavior might be more important than reality.

Surveys of patients and the general public, however, have not revealed such an effect. Indeed, patients in a wide variety of jurisdictions seem remarkably unaware of the legal rules governing confidentiality in psychotherapeutic treatment.[94] Studies have shown consistently that most persons in or out of therapy believe that their communications will be kept confidential, even when actual legal protections are lacking. Most respondents say that they rely on the ethics of the psychotherapy professions, rather than any legal provision, to protect their confidences.

If patients were made aware of the possibility that their communications might have to be disclosed, would it affect their disclosures in therapy? The evidence here is conflicting. One set of studies indicated that, when told that there was no legal privilege for their comments, nonpatients believed that they would speak less freely were they to enter therapy[95]—a finding confirmed elsewhere.[96] Among respondents in the California survey of psychotherapists after *Tarasoff,* 25 percent said that they thought they had seen at least one patient who became less willing to discuss violent tendencies after learning of the duty to protect.[97] But several studies of actual disclosure in therapy and evaluation situations in which assurances of confidentiality were manipulated experimentally have found no significant differences in subjects' revelations.[98] Moreover, most lay respondents in the small number of studies that have examined the issue have endorsed mental health professionals' breaching confidentiality when such conduct is necessary to protect endangered persons.[99] In sum, it has been difficult to demonstrate that the two major mechanisms thought likely to mediate the negative effects of a legal duty to protect have had important consequences for the conduct of psychotherapy.

Although the impact of the duty to protect has not been studied as commonly as, for example, the outcome of civil commitment reform, some data allow us to look more directly at some of the predictions of dire consequences that were made following recognition of the duty. Were psychotherapists, for example, deterred from treating potentially violent patients?

The nationwide study of therapists mentioned earlier, which was led by Daniel Givelber, a law professor, offers the best data on this issue. Respondents who reported feeling themselves bound by a duty to protect on either a legal or an ethical basis were no more likely than others to have stopped treating dangerous patients.[100] This suggests that no large-scale aversion to continuing to see violent patients arose after *Tarasoff*, although anecdotal data indicate that at least some therapists have shied away from violent patients,[101] and this is in keeping with my experience. The exact proportion, however, remains uncertain.

The impact of the duty to protect on therapists' behavior in the consulting room has been examined, too. Soon after *Tarasoff*, 27 percent of the respondents to the California survey said that they now focused more on patients' potential dangerousness, and 19 percent said that they had lowered their threshold for what constituted a threat serious enough to warrant concern.[102] Moreover, 54 percent reported increased anxiety about handling such cases, and a nearly identical percentage said that they had a greater fear of lawsuits. Whether these anxieties actually affected treatment can only be conjectured.

A number of small-scale surveys and case reports address another concern of many clinicians about the duty to protect: the possibility that warnings or their protective actions would have a devastating impact on potentially violent patients. Beck's survey of thirty-eight Massachusetts psychiatrists found that sixteen of them had warned potential victims or the police in twenty-six cases.[103] Four warnings were followed by unfortunate outcomes, including three cases in which violence occurred, and at least one in which the course of therapy was severely disrupted. (Of course, violence might have resulted even if no action had been taken by the therapist.) In every case in which a bad outcome occurred, the psychiatrist had breached confidentiality without first discussing the matter with the patient. A second, similar effort by Beck, examining the responses of thirty-four other psychiatrists in private practice, showed fourteen respondents who had warned in fifteen cases.[104] Violence occurred in two cases, and in one additional case there was a negative impact on treatment. At least one other author has reported a case in which a patient left treatment after a warning was issued, although the case appears to have been handled badly and the warning was probably unnecessary.[105]

Balancing these reports, however, are an even larger number of instances in which warnings or other protective action seem to have had neutral or even positive effects on therapy. The latter included lessened anxiety for the patient[106] and for the potential victim.[107] The theory that bringing potential victims into treatment with threatening patients would have beneficial consequences for their relationship as a whole was borne out in at least some cases.[108] As clinicians adjusted to the new requirements—a development to which we will return—they reported using clinically appropriate means to protect victims while intruding minimally on the process of therapy.[109]

An assortment of negative effects have been reported in a handful of cases. Some potential victims who have been warned have reported overwhelming anxiety and helplessness,[110] but I know of no suits filed against psychotherapists for needlessly inducing anxiety. A few suits against therapists have been brought by patients who felt that their confidentiality should not have been breached; but the only judgment rendered against a psychiatrist came in unusual circumstances in which the legitimacy of the warning was dubious.[111] One psychologist reported being threatened by a patient after issuing a warning,[112] though it would not be surprising if similar threats were made in other cases as well.

The major unresolved empirical issue involves the degree to which the increased risk of liability for patients' violence has led mental health professionals to admit patients to psychiatric facilities, or to retain them there, when they would otherwise have been released. There are data supporting each side of the debate. As one of the first to express concern about the problem, I offered case examples in which patients who would generally be considered inappropriate for hospitalization were detained because of a commingled desire to protect the public and fear of liability.[113] Others have since reported similar cases,[114] but—since an anecdote can be found to support almost any proposition—more systematic data are needed to address the issue definitively.

Such data exist, but they give conflicting views of practice. For example a study of psychologists' decision making showed that, when presented with hypothetical cases in which the potential for liability varied, clinicians were less likely to say (other factors being equal) they would release the patients who presented high liability risks.[115] In the real world, commitments to New York City hospitals skyrocketed after much-publicized murders perpetrated by a patient who had been released from an emergency room; although protection of the public might, in theory, have been the sole motive, fear of liability seems to have played an important role.[116] And a Pittsburgh study showed that emergency room clinicians were unwilling to release persons sent with commitment papers from another emergency room, even when they disagreed with the previous assessment of the patient's dangerousness.[117] The authors concluded that fear of liability was the motivating factor, if a patient whom someone else thought was dangerous should subsequently commit a violent act.

The most detailed look at the effects of liability concerns on clinicians' hospitalization practices came in a study of an Alabama hospital that was going through protracted and highly publicized litigation resulting from a murder committed by a released patient.[118] Staff members reported high levels of concern about being sued in similar cases, and rates of release of patients to the community dropped significantly during the trial and in the months thereafter.[119]

On the other hand, an extensive study of practices in five California emergency rooms revealed that, in the aggregate, patients who were committed ranked high on indicators of need for treatment and of dangerousness.[120] This suggested to the researchers that inappropriate commitments were not occurring—at least not frequently.[121] A study from another California hospital yielded similar results.[122] It seems clear that dramatic or celebrated local incidents can temporarily (at least) affect admitting decisions. The extent to which systems are affected in the aggregate in the absence of such special factors is not yet settled.

Taken as a whole, the data on the consequences of the duty to protect show many fewer effects, especially negative effects, than were anticipated. The most devastating outcomes (including the destruction of psychotherapy) have clearly not occurred. We have seen some of the reasons for this—in particular, the acceptance of an obligation to protect potential victims in advance of the court's ruling in *Tarasoff,* and the widespread public unawareness of the potential consequences of this new legal duty. But other factors, in both mental health and law, also contributed to this unanticipated set of outcomes. They bear closer scrutiny.

Factors Affecting the Impact of the Duty to Protect

Legal innovation, like other social policy initiatives, sometimes hits its target perfectly, often misses completely, and usually falls somewhere in between, in a gray zone of partial success and unanticipated complications. Given the inertia inherent in a system that depends as much on precedent as does the common law, doctrinal reforms often are motivated only by the most extreme cases, which alone provide the impetus to break the shackles of the status quo. Extreme cases, however, often evoke problematic remedies, unnecessary or unworkable in most circumstances.

Such was the case with *Tarasoff.* It is disturbing that therapists aware of an explicit threat to an innocent young woman should elect not to reveal it to her, while taking no other measures to reduce the risk she faced.[123] Indeed, as we have seen, behavior of this sort appears not to have been in keeping with the emerging ethical consensus of the therapeutic professions, whether embodied in the AMA's code, therapists' responses to hypothetical cases posed in surveys, or the actual conduct of mental health professionals. It is therefore not surprising that the *Tarasoff* court—unaware that therapists typically accepted the responsibility to protect potential victims—reacted by imposing sweeping and ambiguous obligations on psychotherapists. Courts are surely not alone in being tempted to move more aggressively and to write more broadly when they sense a moral vacuum, and that must have been precisely the impression Justice Tobriner and his colleagues had of the situation in *Tarasoff*.[124]

The major problem with the decision was not that it imposed unheard-of demands on psychotherapists, but that it fashioned a rule so ambiguous as to arouse enormous anxiety among those at whom it was directed. Since the predicted negative consequences of the decision, if they were to occur, would be mediated by the fears of therapists and patients alike, this was no small problem. In retrospect, it appears that two ambiguities lay at the heart of the concern induced by *Tarasoff*: therapists were left uncertain about when their obligations arose under the duty to protect, and they had little guidance on how to discharge them.

With regard to when the duty would be invoked, the court imposed an obligation to protect intended victims "[w]hen a therapist determines, or pursuant to the standards of his profession should determine, that his patient presents a serious danger of violence to another . . ." (p. 340). It seems clear that the professions were already willing to act when they believed a patient might be dangerous. But given the difficulty in specifying when violence might occur, holding therapists to normative standards of prediction is a different matter. In elaborating on its ruling, the *Tarasoff* court recited the mantra of malpractice law: "[T]he therapist [in making a prediction] need only exercise 'that reasonable degree of skill, knowledge, and care ordinarily possessed and exercised by members of (that professional specialty) under similar circumstances.' " (p. 345) But what did such a guideline mean in the absence of clear standards for predicting dangerousness?

Justice Mosk, in his concurring opinion in *Tarasoff*, argued that this guideline made no sense at all. Extending the duty to situations in which a therapist "should have known" that a patient would be violent, he maintained, "will take us from the world of reality into the wonderland of clairvoyance." (p. 354) He anticipated the farce that would result when expert witnesses took the stand to testify that, according to professional standards that existed only in their imaginations, the defendant should have known that his or her patient would be violent. His words echoed the fears of members of the mental health professions.

The second major area of ambiguity lay in the methods identified by the revised opinion in *Tarasoff II* to discharge the duty. Requiring therapists to take "whatever means are reasonably necessary" to protect the potential victim left them uncertain as to precisely what they had to do. After all, they were not trained as experts in protecting possible victims of assault. The standard seemed designed more to ensure that victims would receive compensation than to set out a realistic requirement to be met by psychotherapists. After the fact, when violence had already occurred, it would always seem that the means that were reasonably necessary to prevent it had *not* been taken; otherwise, the assault would have been prevented. Ironically, the mental health professions are at least partly responsible for this situation. It was their furious attack on the duty to warn in *Tarasoff I* that led to this broader formulation of the rule.

Many of the predictions of doom that attended the decision in *Tarasoff II* were responses to these problems with the duty to protect. It took little imagination, given the difficult situation in which the California Supreme Court's conception of the duty seemed to place therapists, to anticipate large numbers of lawsuits, with consequent defensive practices involving frequent breaches of confidentiality and with patients discouraged from seeking therapy. Given the breadth and ambiguity of the decision, the parade of horribles unfolded logically before one's eyes.

But when an extreme case creates an extreme—and problematic—remedy and induces panic among those affected by the decision, the law provides mechanisms for correcting the situation. Part of the reason the duty to protect has not led to the extinction of psychotherapy as a form of treatment is that the rules laid out in *Tarasoff II* are not the only (or even the dominant) formulations of the law today. To be sure, these corrective changes occur slowly—usually over decades rather than years—and one is always better off with a sound rule at the inception. Nevertheless, mental health law has shown a reassuring ability to refashion itself in response to the perceived errors of earlier reforms.

Judicial Responses

Some of the judicial responses, which took place in the common law courts, we have already examined. The circumstances under which a duty arises were narrowed by a few courts to encompass only patients who made explicit threats or who were committable under state law.[125] Sovereign immunity seemed to find new life in several states, as psychiatrists' decisions to discharge patients were accepted as constituting a class of discretionary behavior—as opposed to what the courts referred to as "ministerial acts," which did not involve discretion—which traditionally had been exempt from liability.[126]

In addition, a more subtle shift occurred in many cases in which courts were not seeking to cut back on the reach of the duty to protect, but merely sought to apply the existing duty in reasonable ways. As more typical fact situations appeared, the courts grew less extreme in their judgments. Thus, for every case like *Davis v. Lihm,* in which the basis for a finding of foreseeable dangerousness appeared to be manufactured out of whole cloth, many more cases like *Ross v. Central Louisiana State Hospital* appeared.[127]

Ross dealt with a situation in which a woman discharged from a state hospital shot her two children seven months later, killing her daughter and wounding her son. At the civil trial, the court heard uncontroverted testimony that the patient had "never exhibited any propensity toward violence" (p. 699). The plaintiffs' contention that the hospital should have warned the family that the patient would be dangerous if she neglected to take her medication was rejected by the court, which concluded that "[a] hospital cannot be expected to warn third persons of possible dangers which it could not foresee" (p. 700).

Similarly, courts began to look more closely and more sympathetically at the behavior of the defendant psychotherapists. In a case stemming from the discharge of a patient from St. Elizabeths Hospital in Washington, D.C., who later stabbed his wife 55 times with a pair of scissors, the court distinguished between the responsibilities of the therapist and those of the hospital.[128] The therapist had known of the patient's fantasies of violence against his wife, had evaluated them, and had decided that they would not be acted on. Although she was wrong, she had conformed to her profession's standard of care in performing the evaluation, and nothing more could be asked of her. The hospital, however, could be held negligent for having allowed the patient, who had been found not guilty of a previous offence by reason of insanity, to leave the grounds of the facility repeatedly.[129]

All this is not to say that, after the lapse of a decade or so, liability was no longer imposed on therapists for failing to protect third parties. Juries still found for plaintiffs in such cases, and their verdicts were still upheld by appellate courts. Indeed, such opinions continued to be rendered occasionally in cases in which they seemed plainly unfair.[130] And an untold number of other cases were settled before reaching trial, for bad reasons as well as good.

But by the mid-1980s the courts were clearly making good-faith efforts to apply the rules that had been developed in *Tarasoff* in a fashion that did not impose an unfair burden on the psychotherapeutic professions. Although few courts were ready to dispense with the duty altogether,[131] many were willing to limit it, and many more to be less liberal about finding liability, even when presented with plaintiffs who had suffered great misfortune and naturally aroused intense sympathy. The assumption made by many psychotherapists that courts would interpret the duty to protect in specific cases as broadly as possible—and as much to their profession's detriment as had the *Tarasoff* court—was simply wrong.

Legislative Responses

Another equally important element of the corrective response came not from the courts, but from legislatures. Soon after the final decision in *Tarasoff*,

California psychiatrists began to lobby to have the decision modified by statute. After nearly a decade of effort, they were ultimately successful. By now, nearly a score of states have adopted statutes regulating liability in duty to protect situations.[132] Although they differ among themselves in their particulars, these statutes generally address the two major ambiguities in the *Tarasoff* court's formulation of the duty—when it arises, and how it can be discharged—in similar ways.

The statutes, for the most part, follow the lead of the court in *Brady v. Hopper*,[133] limiting the duty to situations in which an actual threat has been made. This is plainly an underinclusive strategy; there certainly will be instances in which all signs point to incipient violence and a psychotherapist should act to protect potential victims, even though threatening words have not passed the patient's lips. As we have seen, however, therapists tend to take protective action when they believe someone is endangered. The question here is when is failure to act so clear-cut a dereliction of duty that liability should be imposed? The actual threat standard is a reasonable one for this purpose.

Almost all of the statutes require that the threats that trigger the duty to protect be made against identifiable victims, harkening back to the formulation in *Tarasoff* itself. As noted earlier, however, such a rule is problematic in that it suggests that threats of violence against unnamed or unidentifiable victims fall outside the duty. Kentucky seems to have found a reasonable compromise here. Its statute invokes the duty when "the patient has communicated . . . an actual threat of some specific violent act."[134] Thus, if the patient threatens to spray Main Street with bullets, even if the specific potential victims remain unidentifiable, a duty to protect exists.

The other major accomplishment of the statutes is their clarification of the means by which the duty can be discharged. As a group, the statutes specify that any one of a small number of actions will, if taken, be considered to have discharged the therapists' obligations in full: warning the victim or the police (some states require that both be warned), hospitalizing the patient voluntarily, or seeking involuntary commitment. This new standard combines the original "duty to warn" approach of *Tarasoff I* with the option of hospitalization in lieu of breaching confidentiality. Presumably, therapists can take other measures if they prefer, but they must then defend their reasonableness after the fact, whereas selecting one of the specified ways of discharging the duty should provide absolute protection.

The statutes are new enough that appellate decisions construing them have not yet begun to appear.[135] But they clearly represent the trend for the future. The duty to protect has not been abandoned (the Ohio statute appears to be exceptional in abrogating the duty[136]), but the objections of mental health professionals have been acknowledged and an accommodation has been reached. Fairness and clarity have been balanced against the twin goals of tort law: encouraging greater care in decision making and providing just compensation to victims. Insofar as the statutes create a system in which required breaches of confidence are fewer, defensive actions are less common, and the overall impact of the duty to protect is more limited, the negative effects of the duty on the behavior of therapists and patients alike are less likely to occur.

Clinicians' Responses

While the law was moving away from the most radical expressions of the duty to protect, mental health professionals were finding ways to live with its requirements. In part, this involved recognizing that the mental health professions had been acting to protect potential victims long before the courts told them they had to. In practice, they had developed means of fulfilling their perceived responsibilities to the general public, while minimizing the adverse impact of such action on their patients and on the therapeutic process.

Psychiatrist Loren Roth and attorney Alan Meisel, in the first of what was to become a genre of papers explaining to psychotherapists how to live with the duty to protect, pointed out that "alternatives are often available that permit continuing management of the violent or potentially violent patient without compromising treatment." [137] They offered an example in which treatment staff had taken custody of a threatening patient's weapon, and another in which staff had restricted access to a phone and to visitors of a patient who had threatened to have her lover killed, until it was clear that she did not intend to act on her threats. Moreover, they indicated that they had never found it necessary to warn a potential victim without first obtaining the patient's permission, a precaution that Beck found minimized the disruption of the therapeutic relationship. [138]

Perhaps the most important insight of Roth and Meisel (and other writers) was that a patient's expression of violent ideation did not necessarily imply that an adversarial relationship must thenceforth exist between the patient and the therapist. Most people are ambivalent about their aggressive desires, and that is particularly likely to be true when they reveal their violent fantasies to another person—perhaps especially to their therapist. Although it may be an exaggeration to classify every instance of such disclosure as a "cry for help," there is nonetheless some truth to the general belief that patients who talk about their fantasies (rather than simply acting on them) have at least a conflicted desire to be stopped.

Thus, therapists recognized that they could reach out to the part of their patients' personalities that resisted the idea of violence, in an attempt to form an alliance that would prevent the act from occurring. After all, it would usually benefit the patient, as well as the potential victim, to avoid violence. Many patients could then be enlisted in designing a plan to preclude violence—including warning potential victims. Indeed, some patients might even find therapists' revelation of their fantasies to be the safest and most effective means of communicating their anger and perhaps achieving their interpersonal goals.[139]

Above all, many psychotherapists came to recognize that they need not abandon their clinical instincts when a patient threatened violence. Rather than calling an attorney for advice, they learned to consult their clinical colleagues for suggestions on how to manage the patient. Nor did they find themselves limited to warnings or hospitalization. The literature provides ample evidence of an array of interventions that may be employed, including a focus in therapy on the violent fantasies, a judicious use of medication, involvement of third parties (such as family members) in monitoring the patient, and bringing potential victims into therapy.[140]

A good example of how clinical judgment triumphed over early fears with regard to the duty to protect can be seen in the evolution of a standard regarding disclosure to patients of the need to protect potential victims. Early critics had assumed that, for ethical reasons, all patients would need to be told of therapists' duties to break confidentiality, which would then have a chilling effect on the course of psychotherapy.[141] It became clear over time, however, that the risk that communications would have to be revealed was minuscule for most patients and that, even under a strict interpretation of informed consent, the risk (if they were apprised of it) could hardly be considered material to their decision as to whether or not to participate in treatment. (The doctrine of informed consent is discussed at greater length in Chapter 4.) Thus, cooler heads began to suggest that only "high-risk" patients—perhaps those with a previous history of violence—needed to be given notice of therapists' duty to protect possible victims, and that other patients could be kept uninformed of this duty until a situation actually arose in which it might be relevant.[142]

Many of these factors mitigating the impact of the duty to protect were evident in the resolution of Dr. Thomas's concerns about George. The case had not been going well when Dr. Thomas first consulted me. Feeling the panic common to many clinicians when threats of violence and fears of liability mix, Dr. Thomas had acted unwisely. If he had really believed that George was a serious threat to his brother-in-law, communicating a warning indirectly, through what amounted to a high-stakes game of "telephone"— he called his patient's wife, who told her sister, who warned the potential victim—would have been inappropriate; the warning should have been made directly to the victim. On the other hand, if the risk was small, confidentiality should have been maintained, and other means should have been found to manage the patient. In any event, the action should have been discussed with George before it was taken.

But Dr. Thomas did one important thing right: he sought consultation when he felt that things had gone awry. I suggested that he talk directly with the patient about his concerns and explain to him exactly what he would like to discuss with George's brother-in-law. Since Dr. Thomas was uncertain about the real risk his patient presented, I offered to see the patient in consultation to give him an independent view of the situation. As we talked for some time, he grew perceptibly calmer.

Dr. Thomas returned to his patient to talk over the situation. George did not want any further information to be disclosed, fearing that the police might get involved and that this would jeopardize his son's criminal justice career. Nor did he agree to see me. But he apparently was impressed by the degree of Dr. Thomas' concern and convincingly downplayed the seriousness of his earlier threats. Dr. Thomas decided that no further action was necessary.

I talked with Dr. Thomas a few months later. The patient had left therapy with him to seek treatment at a nearby mental health center. The initial breach of confidentiality, made without George's knowledge, seems to have been too great a blow to his trust in Dr. Thomas to enable them to continue. But George's wife, who still saw Dr. Thomas, told him that George was much more relaxed and no longer talked of harming his brother-in-law. Confronting him with the consequences of his fantasies, it seemed, had enabled the more mature and reality-oriented side of his character to take control. On balance, the clinical management of the case was successful in preventing violence, although the early missteps by Dr. Thomas probably forced the patient to continue treatment elsewhere.

We are left, then, with a complicated and interrelated set of explanations for why the duty to protect failed to produce the catastrophe that was predicted. At the outset, critics miscalculated the degree to which the *Tarasoff* court and those that followed it required psychotherapists to do something they were not already doing. Similarly, the extent to which patients would pay attention to these issues was considerably overestimated. But we ought not neglect the homeostatic mechanisms within the law itself that came into play, as courts faced with more typical fact situations modified the California version of the duty to protect to pay greater heed to the worries of clinicians. Concerned clinicians also had access to statutory revisions of the duty, which have been enacted in more than one-third of the states. Finally, when the panic died down a bit, clinicians realized that they had in their quiver clinical approaches to managing situations of potential violence that could be employed in lieu of breaking patients' confidentiality. The duty to protect has complicated life for some clinicians, but it may have made life safer for some potential victims; and it has by no means been the disaster some authorities feared.

Future of the Duty to Protect

What is the future of the duty to protect? This question moves us beyond the realm of mental health law into one of the most controversial areas of tort law in general: the expansion of the duty to rescue. *Tarasoff,* however exceptional it seemed to psychotherapists, is part of a broader trend in tort law toward expanding the duties that citizens owe each other when one is in danger and a second can provide assistance. Although Anglo-American common law historically has avoided imposing duties to aid others, that diffidence began to be overcome before *Tarasoff* and has continued to wane—fueled in part by the *Tarasoff* decision—since.

In many concrete cases, the gradual modification of the ancient rule has been masked by an adherence, as in *Tarasoff,* to customary conventions. As exceptions are carved out, they are carefully construed as situations involving "special relationships," which have always been set apart from the general rule. But it was never clear what aspect of the relationship between Prosenjit Poddar and his psychologist was sufficiently special to warrant imposition of a major duty toward third parties, and the California Supreme Court paid little attention to explaining this point. Instead, as many critics complained, the relationship was deemed special because the court desired to impose liability, rather than the reverse.

However weak the case for recognizing a special relationship between psychotherapists and their patients may be, the ostensible rationale—based on the therapist's predictive powers and ability to control the patient—seems compelling compared to the grounds for finding special relationships in other cases in which liability has been imposed. Does an employer who sends a worker home from work early because the person is sick or inebriated have a special relationship that warrants liability if the employee injures others in an auto accident on the way? Would that same relationship exist if the worker had completed the shift before heading home? Several courts have concluded that the answer to the first question is yes, even if the answer to the second is no.[143] But is the conclusion that liability should be imposed in the first class of cases really based on a special relationship that evaporates when the shift bell rings? Or do the decisions to penalize the employers really represent a rejection of the limitations of special relationship analysis in favor of broader duties to prevent harm?[144]

Some legal commentators now argue openly that the latter is the case. The rationales they offer for abandoning the limitations of the special relationship approach vary strikingly, but the bottom line is the same. Some base their arguments on the currently dominant economic approach to tort law, maintaining that we now have the doctrinal tools necessary to create efficient mechanisms for rewarding rescuers and sanctioning those who could protect third parties but do not. Saul Levmore, for example, reads the new

"special relationship" cases as embodying three elements: a single nonrescuer, with unique access to information about the danger or a unique ability
to prevent it; a situation in which the nonrescuer could have prevented a
serious loss with little effort; and the absence of any legitimate reason for
the nonrescuer to believe that someone else would save the day.[145] He
argues that, given these circumstances (which fit the *Tarasoff* situation to a
tee), it may be reasonable to impose liability for failure to protect, since
protective actions buffer large gains at relatively low cost. Moreover, he
suggests that we may soon go beyond single nonrescuer cases to more difficult multiple nonrescuer cases (for instance, who should be held liable if
fifty people on a beach watch a swimmer drown and none acts to save
her?).

Kim Lane Scheppele, a political scientist drawn to these and related
conundrums, rejects the economic rationale in favor of a fairness-based approach.[146] Utilizing a contractarian theory of justice similar to that popular-
ized by John Rawls,[147] Scheppele suggests that courts should and generally
do compel information disclosure when one party has a "deep secret," the
existence of which the other party cannot even suspect, that may lead to
harm to the latter.[148] Scheppele's analysis suggests that a psychotherapist
aware of a threat made by a patient, or perhaps of other evidence of danger,
acts unfairly when he or she fails to reveal that information to the intended
victim. But the rationale is more broadly applicable to any person, regardless of relationship to the perpetrator or the victim, who becomes aware of
the existence of a threat.

A third line of analysis supporting a duty to rescue not based on special relationships looks to the psychological literature on altruism to identify
characteristics of situations in which most people would feel some obligation toward a victim, and which therefore justify imposition of a legal duty—
special relationship or no.[149] These include cases in which the victim depends for assistance on the potential rescuer; the victim has not induced the
peril by his or her own action; and only one potential source of assistance
exists (analogous to Levmore's single nonrescuer).

Perhaps the most straightforward and radical approach to this problem
calls for the simple rejection of any pretence that duty to rescue or protect
cases differ at all from other tort cases. J. M. Adler, making this claim,
has argued that the duty to behave reasonably, which in general may be
violated only at the risk of liability in tort, should apply to these cases as
well.[150] Thus, we should ask whether any person—not just a psychotherapist—who withheld knowledge of a threat would thereby have acted unrea-
sonably; and if the answer is yes, we should impose liability.[151]

That so many doctrinal roads lead to a similar endpoint is impressive.
The classical special relationship rule appears to be an endangered species.
Not only is there little likelihood that psychotherapists will be completely

freed from a duty to protect third parties, but it seems probable that related duties will continue to be imposed on ever broader segments of the population. This is not to suggest that general duties to rescue are likely to be imposed in the near future in American law, especially given the difficulties inherent in fashioning such duties. But a continued extension of duties to situations where potential rescuers have either unique knowledge of harm or a unique ability to intervene seems to me quite probable.

Indeed, psychotherapists themselves have seen the *Tarasoff* rationale expanded to cover a growing number of related situations. Several *Tarasoff*-like cases involved patients whose erratic driving, due either to their mental disorders or to substance abuse, led to serious injury or death to third parties.[152] This line of cases obliges therapists to protect victims from their patients' negligent behavior, when the patients' lack of care behind the wheel is foreseeable. In contrast, *Tarasoff* itself and its earliest offspring focused on protecting victims from patients' intentionally harmful acts. Predicting negligence is a daunting task (few people, after all, threaten to be negligent)—particularly when it involves a behavior, like driving, that cannot be assessed reliably in the usual clinical situation.

Holding clinicians responsible for patients' actions behind the wheel, moreover, raises the difficult question of how they should deal with alcohol- and drug-abusing patients. Despite extensive public campaigns against drinking and driving, the behavior remains common. Must clinicians—including general physicians—take measures to prevent such actions by their patients? If so, what actions are required? Patients who drink and drive cannot be hospitalized against their will on that basis alone. Nor can state motor vehicle departments impose sanctions on them unless they are caught in the act. Driving is so important a liberty interest in our society that a physician or psychotherapist who threatens a patient's continued freedom to engage in it, on the basis of speculative information obtained during an office visit, may well not see that person again. How the case law will resolve these issues remains to be seen.[153]

Another circumstance in which therapists may have duties to protect third parties—although to date no cases address the issues—is when a patient who tests positive for the human immunodeficiency virus (HIV) engages in sexual or other behavior that places third parties at risk.[154] The American Psychiatric Association has adopted the position that breaching confidentiality is acceptable when required to protect third parties,[155] while the American Medical Association has gone even farther, suggesting in its position statement that physicians have an obligation to do so.[156] This matter is complicated by variations in state statutes, with some jurisdictions prohibiting any disclosure of persons' HIV status,[157] and others permitting disclosure only to limited categories of persons (such as spouses).[158]

The duty to protect has become so much a part of clinical practice that some writers have stretched the limits of the existing duty to include new circumstances in which it might be invoked. One author speculated on the existence of a duty arising from forensic evaluations[159]—perhaps a reasonable extrapolation from the clinical setting in which the duty originated.[160] Another set of authors proposed that therapists might be liable for failing to protect patients of other clinicians, when they are treating those clinicians and have knowledge that they may have engaged in improper sexual conduct with their patients.[161] Given the complexities of the situation, it may be premature for clinicians to embrace this duty, especially since the courts have not yet recognized any such obligation. Indeed, the very real possibility that such a duty would dissuade sexually errant therapists from seeking help for their problems raises questions about whether it would constitute sound policy.[162] But one hardly can blame psychotherapists, steeped in almost two decades of concern about the duty to protect, for perceiving new duties wherever they turn.

Accepting that the duty to protect is here to stay and that other social actors may soon be faced with expanded duties of a similar sort, how ought we to react to these developments? In principle, the duty to protect is difficult to reject, especially for members of professions dedicated to assisting others in need.[163] Indeed, I suspect that—just as mental health professionals anticipated the formal promulgation of a duty to protect, well before *Tarasoff,* by seeking to guard potential victims of their patients from harm— clinicians as a group would endorse the trend toward broader duties to rescue. In the absence of clearly detrimental effects, and with courts and legislatures muting the more problematic forms that the duty has taken, the duty to protect now looks like a reasonable step in the evolution of mental health law.

References

1. "Annotation: Liability of One Releasing Institutionalized Mental Patient for Harm He Causes," 38 ALR 3d 699.
2. Since, until recently, hospitalization for mental disorders was entirely a psychiatric function, the other mental health disciplines were spared the effects of these suits.
3. *Restatement (Second) of Torts,* Section 319.
4. *Leverett v. Ohio,* 399 N.E.2d 106 (Ohio Ct. App. 1978).
5. New York was one of the first states to abrogate the doctrine of sovereign immunity and allow itself to be sued. Thus, a disproportionate number of the early cases come from New York.
6. *St. George v. State,* 127 N.Y.S.2d 147 (N.Y. App. Div. 1954), p. 150.
7. *Taig v. State,* 241 N.Y.S. 2d 495 (N.Y. App. Div. 1963).
8. There is no small irony in the fact that, during a period when long-term hospitalization was the rule, the courts were more aware than were many psychiatrists of the desirability of returning patients to the community. Moreover, they were willing to clear the way of legal barriers, offering a fair degree of immunity to psychiatrists

who were preparing patients for discharge. As will be seen, more recent times have borne witness to a reversal of these roles.

9. "Annotation," *supra* note 1.

10. *Ellis v. U.S.*, 484 F. Supp. 4 (D.S.C. 1978), p. 12.

11. *Underwood v. U.S.*, 356 F.2d 92 (5th Cir. 1966).

12. Consolidated as *Hilscher v. State*, 314 N.Y.S.2d 904 (Ct. Claims 1970).

13. "State school" was one of a series of euphemisms for institutions in which mentally retarded people were housed, ostensibly for training and habilitation, but often with little attention of any sort. For an overview, see A. Deutsch, *The Mentally Ill in America: A History of Their Care and Treatment from Colonial Times*, 2d ed. (New York: Columbia University Press, 1949).

14. The quote is from *Excelsior Insurance Co. v. State*, 296 N.E.2d 553 (N.Y. 1946). The internal citation omitted is to the famous case of *Palsgraf v. Long Island Railroad Co.*, 162 N.E. 99 (N.Y. 1928), which offers the classic statement of foreseeability as the determinant of whether a legal duty to protect others exists.

15. The facts of the *Tarasoff* case can be found in *Tarasoff v. Regents of the University of California*, 551 P.2d 334 (Cal. 1976) [subsequently cited as *Tarasoff II*]; in the appeal of the criminal case brought against Poddar, *People v. Poddar*, 518 P.2d 342 (Cal. 1974); and in A. A. Stone, *Law, Psychiatry and Morality* (Washington, D.C.: American Psychiatric Press, 1984), chapter 7. Each source provides a slightly different view of the facts, and none is comprehensive.

16. *Tarasoff II, supra* note 15.

17. Stone, *supra* note 15.

18. *Tarasoff II, supra* note 15, p. 340.

19. S. Levmore, "Waiting for Rescue: An Essay on the Evolution and Incentive Structure of the Law of Affirmative Obligations," *Virginia Law Review* 72: 879–941 (1986).

20. Ibid., pp. 899–900.

21. *Thompson v. County of Alameda*, 614 P.2d 728 (Cal. 1980).

22. *Tarasoff v. Regents of the University of California*. 529 P.2d 553 (Cal. 1974) [subsequently cited as *Tarasoff I*].

23. It is not clear to what extent the rehearing by the California Supreme Court was a response to the anguished cries of mental health professionals about the 1974 opinion. The earlier decision had found that the police, too, could be held liable for their actions. Police groups were outraged, claiming that they could not perform their complex functions if they always had to be concerned about the possibility of being sued for their decisions. The revised *Tarasoff II* opinion executed a 180-degree turn on this question, holding that, as a matter of public policy, the police should continue to be shielded—as they had been historically—from liability for their negligent acts. Second thoughts by the justices about the propriety of imposing liability on the police may well have been their primary motivation for rehearing the case.

24. M. McDonald, "Court Reaffirms 'Warning' Decision," *Psychiatric News* 11(1): 1ff (August 6, 1976).

25. Stone, *supra* note 15.

26. W. J. Curran, "Confidentiality and the Prediction of Dangerousness in Psychiatry," *New England Journal of Medicine* 293: 285–86 (1975).

27. M. McDonald, "The Tarasoff Warning Decision," *Psychiatric News* 11(24): 1ff (December 17, 1976).

28. K. Menninger, *The Crime of Punishment* (New York: Viking Press, 1968).

29. Group for the Advancement of Psychiatry, *Psychiatry and Sex Psychopath Legislation: The 30s to the 80s* (New York: GAP, 1977).

30. The studies are nicely summarized in J. Monahan, *Clinical Prediction of Violent Behavior* (Rockville, Md.: NIMH, 1981).

31. The studies, as a group, are problematic with regard to their methods and the scope of the conclusions that can be drawn from them. See the critique by T. R. Litwack and L. B. Schlesinger, "Assessing and Predicting Violence: Research, Law, and Applications," in I. Weiner and A. Hess, eds., *Handbook of Forensic Psychology* (New York: Wiley, 1987), pp. 205–49. Among the difficulties with the studies are deficiencies in the ascertainment of violence during the follow-up period (most studies relied on arrest records, which are always inadequate as a reflection of actual behavior); biases in the selection of the study groups (many studies were "experiments of nature," in which persons released because of legal decisions were followed to ascertain subsequent violence; the most dangerous of these people were undoubtedly *not* released, lowering the rate of true positive predictions); and many of the "predictions" on which the designations of "dangerous" persons were based were probably made on a *pro forma* basis and do not reflect genuine efforts at prediction.

32. American Psychiatric Association, "Report of the Task Force on Clinical Aspects of the Violent Individual" (Washington, D.C.: APA, July 1974), p. 28.

33. Brief *amicus curiae* of American Psychiatric Association et al., *Tarasoff v. Regents of the University of California,* 551 P.2d 334 (Cal. 1976), p. 9. In one of those amusing peculiarities of life, the lawyer who signed the brief on behalf of the mental health coalition was named Freud.

34. A. A. Stone, "The *Tarasoff* Decisions: Suing Psychotherapists to Safeguard Society," *Harvard Law Review* 90: 358–78 (1976).

35. For a classic statement of the importance of confidentiality in psychotherapy, see R. Slovenko, *Psychotherapy, Confidentiality, and Privileged Communication* (Springfield, Ill.: Charles C. Thomas, 1966), chapter 6; see also American Psychiatric Association, "Model Law on Confidentiality of Health and Social Service Records. *American Journal of Psychiatry* 136: 137–48 (1979).

36. Although the necessity of revealing potentially compromising information is most evident in traditional psychodynamic psychotherapy, it exists in other forms of psychotherapy as well, including structural, behavioral, interpersonal, cognitive, and gestalt approaches. The ethical codes of all the psychotherapeutic professions require adherence to the principle of confidentiality in the treatment setting, albeit with some exceptions. See the codes compiled in Gorlin, R. A. ed., *Codes of Professional Responsibility,* 2d ed. (Washington, D.C.: BNA Books, 1990).

37. R. D. Jagim, W. D. Wittman, and J. O. Noll, "Mental Health Professionals' Attitude Toward Confidentiality, Privilege, and Third-party Disclosure," *Professional Psychology* 9: 458–66 (1978).

38. T. P. Wise, "Where the Public Peril Begins: A Survey of Psychotherapists to Determine the Effects of *Tarasoff,*" *Stanford Law Review* 135: 165–90 (1978).

39. J. J. Lindenthal and C. S. Thomas, "Psychiatrists, the Public and Confidentiality," *Journal of Nervous and Mental Disease* 170: 319–23 (1982).

40. D. Schmid, P. S. Appelbaum, L. H. Roth, and C. W. Lidz, "Confidentiality in Psychiatry: A Study of the Patient's View," *Hospital and Community Psychiatry* 34: 353–55 (1983).

41. Some of these statutes covered only communications with psychiatrists (by means of a physician–patient privilege), but many were extended to psychologists and other classes of psychotherapists. See D. Woodman, "Protection of 'Privileged Communications' in Civil Cases," *National Law Journal,* August 20, 1979, pp. 22–23.

42. Privilege statutes relating to psychotherapy fall into several categories. Some states

afford privilege to all communications of patients to their physicians, including psychiatrists. Separate statutes may cover other classes of psychotherapists. In other jurisdictions, a distinct psychotherapist–patient privilege statute exists, which excludes nonpsychiatric physicians. As new groups of psychotherapists (for example, social workers) have gained prominence and political clout, they have often been added to existing statutes or covered by laws that apply specifically to them.

43. R. Slovenko, "On Testimonial Privilege," *Contemporary Psychoanalysis* 11: 188–205 (1975).

44. *Tarasoff II, supra* note 15, p. 347.

45. American Medical Association, *Principles of Medical Ethics* (Chicago: AMA, 1957), Section 9. Two small-scale studies in the 1950s indicated that a majority of the psychiatrists and psychologists surveyed supported this principle. See R. B. Little and E. A. Strecker, "Moot Questions in Psychiatric Ethics," *American Journal of Psychiatry* 113: 455–60 (1956); M. Wiskoff, "Ethical Standards and Divided Loyalties," *American Psychologist* 15: 656–60 (1960).

46. This objection was mounted with particular force to the initial opinion in *Tarasoff,* which appeared to limit the therapist's options to warning the potential victim, even if other actions more protective of confidentiality could be taken. See A. A. Stone, "APA and 'Tarasoff,' " *Psychiatric News* 10(11): 2 (June 4, 1975).

47. Stone, *supra* note 34.

48. McDonald, *supra* note 24.

49. Stone, *supra* note 34.

50. Stone, *supra* note 34.

51. H. Gurevitz, "*Tarasoff:* Protective Privilege versus Public Peril," *American Journal of Psychiatry* 134: 289–92 (1977); Stone, *supra* note 34.

52. Wise, *supra* note 38.

53. Stone, *supra* note 34.

54. P. S. Appelbaum, "Rethinking the Duty to Protect," in J. C. Beck, ed., *The Potentially Violent Patient and the* Tarasoff *Decision in Psychiatric Practice* (Washington, D.C.: American Psychiatric Press, 1985), pp. 110–30.

55. E. Walker, *The Battered Woman* (New York: Harper & Row, 1979).

56. S. L. Halleck, *Law in the Practice of Psychiatry* (New York: Plenum Medical Book Co., 1980); J. C. Beck, "Violent Patients and the *Tarasoff* Duty in Private Psychiatric Practice," *Journal of Psychiatry and Law* 13: 361–78 (1985).

57. E. J. Griffith and E. E. H. Griffith, "Duty to Third Parties, Dangerousness, and the Right to Refuse Treatment: Problematic Concepts for Psychiatrist and Lawyer," *California Western Law Review* 14: 241–74 (1978).

58. APA et al. *amicus* brief, *supra* note 33.

59. P. S. Appelbaum, "The New Preventive Detention: Psychiatry's Problematic Responsibility for the Control of Violence," *American Journal of Psychiatry* 145: 779–85 (1988).

60. L. T. Greenberg, "The Psychiatrist's Dilemma," *Journal of Psychiatry and Law* 17: 381–411 (1989).

61. Stone, *supra* note 34.

62. Appelbaum, *supra* note 54; M. J. Mills, "The So-called Duty to Warn: The Psychotherapeutic Duty to Protect Third Parties from Patients' Violent Acts," *Behavioral Sciences and the Law.* 2: 237–57 (1985).

63. "Recent Opinions of the Judicial Council of the American Medical Association," *Journal of the American Medical Association* 251: 2078–79 (1984).

64. J. C. Beck, "The Potentially Violent Patient: Legal Duties, Clinical Practice, and Risk Management," *Psychiatric Annals* 17: 695–99 (1987).

65. S. Rachlin, "Psychiatric Liability for Patient Violence," in H. Van Praag, R. Plutchik, and A. Apter, eds., *Violence and Suicidality: Perspectives in Clinical and Psychobiological Research*, (New York: Brunner-Mazel, 1990), pp. 19–33.

66. D. B. Wexler, "Patients, Therapists and Third Parties: The Victimological Virtues of *Tarasoff*" *International Journal of Law and Psychiatry* 2: 1–28 (1979).

67. See, e.g., the first case outside of California to follow the *Tarasoff* doctrine: *McIntosh v. Milano*, 403 A.2d 500 (N.J. Super. Ct., 1979).

68. *Lipari v. Sears, Roebuck and Co.*, 497 F. Supp. 185 (D. Neb. 1980).

69. See, e.g., *Peterson v. Washington*, 671 P.2d 230 (Wash. 1983); and *Schuster v. Altenberg*, 424 N.W.2d 159 (Wis. 1988). Both of these cases involved harm inflicted by a patient behind the wheel of an automobile, a fact situation in which it would seem unlikely that the victim could be identified in advance. See also *Hamman v. County of Maricopa*, 775 P.2d 1352 (Ariz. 1989).

70. *Peck v. Addison County Counseling Service*, 499 A.2d 422 (Vt. 1985). Arson, it should be noted, is the property crime that comes closest to constituting violence against persons, since the likelihood that people will injured by the fire or as a result of attempting to control it is relatively great. The Vermont court suggested as much in its opinion. Whether the decision would have been the same if, for instance, the issue had been malicious destruction of a tractor is unclear. No other court, to my knowledge, has applied *Tarasoff* to a case exclusively involving damage to property.

71. Both of these circumstances were presented in the facts underlying the 9th Circuit Court of Appeals' decision in *Jablonski v. U.S.*, 712 F.2d 391 (9th Cir. 1983).

72. *Hedlund v. Superior Court of Orange County*, 669 P.2d 41 (Cal. 1983).

73. *Davis v. Lhim*, 335 N.W.2d 481 (Mich. Ct. App. 1983). The decision was later overruled on other grounds—namely, that the state was immune to suit for the discretionary behavior of its employees, which included decisions about whether to discharge patients. See *Canon v. Thumundo*, 422 N.W.2d 688 (Mich. 1988).

74. The facts in *Rotman v. Mirin,* a Massachusetts case that was settled out-of-court after a jury found for the plaintiff, are similarly incongruent with the *Tarasoff* doctrine. Dr. Mirin had for several years been treating a man who was obsessed with a former girlfriend. The patient had been hospitalized at times, and the girlfriend and her family were well aware of the possible danger he posed. Outside the hospital, however, he had been stable, with no indication of any increase in risk over time. Dr. Mirin had instructed the patient's mother to call him at the first sign of the patient's decompensation. Nonetheless, when the patient began to decompensate over a weekend, shortly after he had been seen by Mirin, the mother did not call, and he murdered his former girlfriend before the next appointment was to take place. It is difficult to see in what way Dr. Mirin's behavior fell below the professional standard of care. Indeed, one cannot readily identify what step (other than keeping the patient indefinitely hospitalized) Dr. Mirin could have taken, but did not take. Nonetheless, a jury was persuaded to impose a multimillion dollar judgment against Dr. Mirin, on the grounds that he had been negligent. See *Rotman v. Mirin*, No. 88-1562 (Mass. Super. Ct. 1988).

75. See, e.g., *Furr v. Spring Grove State Hospital*, 454 A.2d 414 (Md. Ct. Spec. App. 1983); *Leedy v. Hartnett*, 510 F. Supp. 1125 (M.D. Pa. 1981); and *Leonard v. Iowa*, No.247/91-270 (Iowa Sup. Ct., Sept. 23, 1992).

76. *Brady v. Hopper*, 751 F.2d 329 (10th Cir. 1984); see also *Cooke v. Berlin*, 735 P.2d 830 (Ariz. Ct. App. 1987); *Rogers v. South Carolina Dept. of Mental Health*, 377 S.E.2d 125 (S.C. Ct. App. 1989); and *Eckhardt v. Kirts*, 534 N.E.2d 1339 (Ill. App. Ct. 1989).

77. This interpretation of Colorado law was rejected by the state's supreme court in *Perreira v. State*, 768 P.2d 1198 (Colo. 1989), where the court adopted a foreseeability approach, at least with regard to the release of an involuntarily committed in-patient who later caused harm.

78. *Hasenei v. U.S.*, 541 F. Supp. 999 (D. Md. 1982).

79. A federal appeals court in *Currie v. U.S.*, interpreting North Carolina law, went even further, holding that psychiatrists have no obligation to seek confinement of a dangerous patient. The court implied, however, that they could be required to take other protective measures, such as warning identifiable potential victims, which was done in this case. See *Currie v. U.S.*, 836 F.2d 209 (4th Cir. 1987).

80. *Cole v. Taylor*, 301 N.W.2d 766 (Iowa 1981).

81. *Estate of Vottler*, 327 N.W.2d 759 (Iowa 1982).

82. A similar result was obtained in *Wagshall v. Wagshall*, 538 N.Y.S.2d 597 (App. Div. 1989), a case in which a wife shot her husband eight months after leaving outpatient treatment. In addition to noting the time lapse since her treatment, the court justified dismissing the complaint, on grounds that the husband had actual notice of his wife's intentions based on a previous attempt.

83. *Canon v. Thumundo, supra* note 73.

84. *Shaw v. Glickman*, 415 A.2d 625 (Md. Ct. Spec. App. 1980).

85. In a merging of the two lines of cases, many release and escape decisions, rather than relying exclusively on the older body of law that gave rise to *Tarasoff*, now began their analysis with a consideration of the duty to protect. Among these cases were *Petersen v. Washington, supra* note 69; *Bradley Center v. Wessner*, 296 S.E.2d 693 (Ga. 1982); *Cain v. Rijken*, 700 P.2d 1061 (Or. App. 1985); *Naidu v. Laird*, 539 A.2d 1064 (Del. 1988).

86. Wise, *supra* note 38. In a random sample of 530 licensed psychologists and all 3,155 psychiatrists belonging to the California Psychiatric Association, only 34 percent and 35 percent, respectively, returned the questionnaire. This is a low rate of return even for mail surveys of this type (in which it is always difficult to motivate subjects to participate). The absence of responses from almost two-thirds of the sample introduces biases of unknown type and dimensions into the results. For example, if therapists who had previously warned potential victims were more interested in the issue and more likely to respond, the resulting data concerning psychotherapists' behavior are likely to be seriously skewed. There is no way of knowing how representative the reported data are.

87. Further complicating any attempt to interpret the study is the author's framing of time periods of interest. By labeling only the behavior of therapists after the issuance of the final (1976) opinion as "post-*Tarasoff*," she neglects the potential impact on clinicians' behavior of the publicity surrounding the murder, the criminal trial and its appeal, the filing of the civil suit against Poddar's therapists, and the initial (1974) much-discussed decision in the case. At a minimum, it would have been interesting to know what percentage of the therapists who reported issuing warnings before 1976 had done so only after the 1974 opinion.

88. D. J. Givelber, W. J. Bowers, C. L. Blitch, "*Tarasoff*, Myth and Reality: An Empirical Study of Private Law in Action," *Wisconsin Law Review* 443–97 (1984). This study had a better response rate—60 percent—although only 48 percent of psychiatrists returned the questionnaire.

89. Only the difference for psychiatrists reached statistical significance.

90. The differences were significant for all three groups.

91. It is, of course, possible that *Tarasoff* and the ensuing discussion helped to shape these ethical norms.

92. Little and Strecker, *supra* note 45.

93. Wiskoff, *supra* note 55.

94. D. Shuman and M. Weiner, *The Psychotherapist-Patient Privilege: A Critical Examination* (Springfield, Ill.: Charles C. Thomas, 1987).

95. Ibid.

96. D. J. Miller and M. H. Thelen, "Knowledge and Beliefs About Confidentiality in Psychotherapy," *Professional Psychology: Research and Practice* 17: 15–19 (1986); W. O. Faustman and D. J. Miller, "Considerations in Prewarning Clients of the Limitations of Confidentiality," *Psychological Reports* 60: 195–98 (1987).

97. Wise, *supra* note 38.

98. J. M. McGuire, S. Graves, and B. Burton, "Depth of Self-disclosure as a Function of Assured Confidentiality and Videotape Recording," *Journal of Counseling and Development* 64: 259–63 (1985); T. Muehleman, B. Pickens, and F. Robinson, "Informing Clients About the Limits to Confidentiality, Risks, and Their Rights: Is Self-disclosure Inhibited?" *Professional Psychology: Research and Practice.* 16: 385–97 (1985); M. W. Haut and T. Muehleman, "Informed Consent: The Effects of Clarity and Specificity of Disclosure in a Clinical Interview," *Psychotherapy* 23: 93–101 (1986). For a study that did show some effect, see D. O. Taube and A. Elwork, "Researching the Effects of Confidentiality Law on Patients' Self-disclosure," *Professional Psychology: Research and Practice* 21: 72–75 (1990). Effects on disclosure regarding thoughts of harm to self or others were significant only for the subgroup with higher levels of psychopathology—the group believed more likely to have such thoughts.

99. D. E. Rubanowitz, "Public Attitudes Toward Psychotherapist-Client Confidentiality." *Professional Psychology: Research and Practice* 18: 613–18 (1987); Faustman and Miller, *supra* note 96.

100. Givelber et al., *supra* note 88. The interpretation of these data is complicated by the odd way in which the respondents seem to have been surveyed. They were asked independently whether they had treated dangerous patients before the study year (1979–1980) and during the study year. Respondents who felt bound by a duty to protect showed no higher a rate of having treated dangerous patients in the past than currently. But since the year chosen as the basis for comparison (1979–1980) is not particularly meaningful in the evolution of the duty to protect, one cannot rely very much on this finding. For example, therapists may have been dissuaded from treating dangerous patients at the inception of their careers in 1974 (or even earlier) as a result of the publicity surrounding the *Tarasoff* case. Clearly, a more direct query on this point would be useful in future studies. Nonetheless, it is noteworthy that some 45 to 60 percent of therapists who felt themselves bound by *Tarasoff* were still treating dangerous patients.

101. J. C. Beck, "Violent Patients and the *Tarasoff* Duty in Private Psychiatric Practice," *Journal of Psychiatry and Law* 13: 361–76 (1985).

102. Wise, *supra* note 38.

103. J. C. Beck, "When the Patient Threatens Violence: An Empirical Study of Clinical Practice After *Tarasoff*," *Bulletin of the American Academy of Psychiatry and the Law* 10: 189–99 (1982).

104. Beck, *supra* note 101. The discussion here follows one set of numbers offered by Beck. Unfortunately, there appear to be discrepancies among the figures given at different times in the paper and between the presentation of the numerical summaries and the case examples.

105. R. Weinstock, "Confidentiality and the New Duty to Protect: The Therapist's Dilemma," *Hospital and Community Psychiatry* 39: 607–8 (1988).

106. R. J. Carlson, L. C. Friedman, and S. C. Riggert, "The Duty to Warn/Protect: Issues in Clinical Practice," *Bulletin of the American Academy of Psychiatry and the Law* 15: 179–86 (1987).
107. J. Treadway, *"Tarasoff* in the Therapeutic Setting," *Hospital and Community Psychiatry* 41: 88–89 (1990).
108. Ibid.; L. R. Wulsin, H. Bursztajn, and T. G. Gutheil, "Unexpected Clinical Features of the *Tarasoff* Decision: The Therapeutic Alliance and the 'Duty to Warn,' " *American Journal of Psychiatry* 140: 601–3 (1983).
109. Beck, *supra* notes 101 and 103; Carlson et al., *supra* note 106; L. H. Roth and A. Meisel, "Dangerousness, Confidentiality, and the Duty to Warn," *American Journal of Psychiatry* 134: 508–11 (1977).
110. Beck, *supra* note 101.
111. *Hopewell v. Adibempe,* No. GD 78-28756, Civil Division, Court of Common Pleas of Allegheny County, Pennsylvania, June 1, 1981; see also J. G. Pasalis, "Why I Went Public with a Patient's Secret," *Medical Economics,* September 17, 1990, pp. 69–80.
112. K. Fisher, "Duty to Warn: Where Does It End?" *APA Monitor,* November 1985, p. 24.
113. Appelbaum, *supra* note 59; P. S. Appelbaum, "Hospitalization of the Dangerous Patient: Legal Pressures and Clinical Responses," *Bulletin of the American Academy of Psychiatry and the Law* 12: 323–29 (1984).
114. J. Brown and J. T. Rayne, "Some Ethical Considerations in Defensive Psychiatry: A Case Study," *American Journal of Orthopsychiatry* 59: 534–41 (1989).
115. C. Turkington, "Litigaphobia: Practitioners Exaggerated Fear of Lawsuits Cripples Them and Does Patients a Disservice," *APA Monitor,* November, 1986, pp. 1ff. To the best of my knowledge, this study has never been published in a scientific journal.
116. Brown and Rayne, *supra* note 114.
117. C. W. Lidz, E. P. Mulvey, P. S. Appelbaum, and S. Cleveland, "Commitment: The Consistency of Clinicians and the Use of Legal Standards," *American Journal of Psychiatry* 146: 176–81 (1989).
118. N. G. Poythress and S. L. Brodsky, "In the Wake of a Negligent Release Law Suit: An Investigation of Professional Consequences and Institutional Impact on a State Psychiatric Hospital." *Law and Human Behavior* 16: 155–73 (1992).
119. The case study reported here involved negligent release litigation of the sort that was possible even before the decision in *Tarasoff.* Nonetheless, I think the evidence may fairly be taken as suggesting the general impact of litigation resulting from the adverse consequences of patients' behavior.
120. S. P. Segal, M. A. Watson, S. M. Goldfinger, and D. A. Averbuck, "Civil Commitment in the Psychiatric Emergency Room: III. Disposition as a Function of Mental Disorder and Dangerousness Indicators," *Archives of General Psychiatry* 45: 759–63 (1988).
121. Aggregate data, of course, do not allow one to determine whether, in at least some cases, persons are being admitted not because they need treatment, but to avoid liability.
122. D. E. McNiel, R. S. Myers, H. K. Zeiner, H. Wolfe, and C. Hatcher, "The Role of Violence in Decisions About Hospitalization from the Emergency Room," *American Journal of Psychiatry* 149: 207–12 (1992). Again, this study was based on aggregate data, and it clearly does not exclude the possibility that decisions in a small but meaningful number of cases are affected by fear of liability.
123. This conclusion, of course, depends on the therapists' believing that the threat will be acted on. We have no way of entering the thought processes of Poddar's ther-

apist or his supervisors, but their initial willingness to seek Poddar's hospitalization suggests that they believed his expressed desire for revenge was more than empty posturing.

124. The mental health professions are not free of responsibility for creating this impression. Although they did not enter the case until after the initial decision by the California Supreme Court, which laid out the basic principles that would be followed in the subsequent (and binding) decision, their role may have exacerbated the perception of moral failure. The collaborative *amicus* brief, after all, emphasized the overarching importance of confidentiality, seemingly even when lives could be saved by its breach. *Amici* did not alert the court to the reality that therapists routinely breached confidentiality when third parties were endangered, and that what they were requesting was not permission to stand idly by while innocent victims were killed, but the ability to exercise some measure of clinical discretion in fulfilling their responsibilities. By taking an extreme "proconfidentiality" position, the mental health professions may have ensured the very outcome they sought to avoid.

125. See the cases cited *supra* note 76.

126. *Canon v. Thumundo, supra* note 73; *Cairl v. State,* 323 N.W.2d 20 (Minn. 1982); *Darling v. Augusta Mental Health Institute,* 535 A.2d 421 (Me. 1987); *Sherrill v. Wilson,* 653 S.W.2d 661 (Mo. 1983).

127. *Ross v. Central Louisiana State Hospital,* 392 So.2d 698 (La. App., 1980). For additional examples, see *Soutear v. U.S.,* 646 F. Supp. 524 (D. Mich. 1986); *Cooke v. Berlin,* 735 P.2d 830 (Ariz. Ct. App. 1987).

128. *White v. U.S.,* 780 F.2d 97 (D.C. Cir. 1986).

129. For another careful examination of a therapist's performance, which concluded that no duty had been breached, see *Schrempf v. New York,* 66 N.Y.2d 289 (1985).

130. See *supra* note 74; and S. Rachlin and H. I. Schwartz, "Unforeseeable Liability for Patients' Violent Acts," *Hospital and Community Psychiatry* 37: 725–31 (1986).

131. For an exception, see *Boynton v. Burglass,* 16 Fla. L.W. D2499 (September 24, 1991), in which an intermediate appellate court in Florida, focusing on difficulties in predicting dangerousness and on harm from violating patients' confidentiality, rejected the duty to protect on its face.

132. P. S. Appelbaum, H. Zonana, R. Bonnie, and L. H. Roth, "Statutory Approaches to Limiting Psychiatrists' Liability for Their Patients' Violent Acts," *American Journal of Psychiatry* 146: 821–28 (1989).

133. *Brady v. Hopper, supra* note 76.

134. Kentucky Revised Statutes, Section 202A.400.

135. Violent acts that result in litigation must occur after the effective date of the statutes that govern them. Given the number of years that it takes for a case to wind its way through the system and reach the appellate courts, it is not surprising that we have yet to see such decisions. They may, however, begin appearing soon.

136. Ohio Revised Code Annotated, Section 5122.34.

137. Roth and Meisel, *supra.* note 109, p. 510.

138. Beck, *supra* notes 101 and 103.

139. P. S. Appelbaum, "Tarasoff and the Clinician: Problems in Fulfilling the Duty to Protect," *American Journal of Psychiatry* 142: 425–29 (1985); Carlson et al., *supra* note 106.

140. Appelbaum, *supra* note 139; J. C. Beck, ed., *The Potentially Violent Patient and the Tarasoff Decision in Psychiatric Practice* (Washington, D.C.: American Psychiatric Press, 1985); Carlson, et al., *supra* note 106; Roth and Meisel, *supra* note 109.

141. See, e.g., Stone, *supra* note 34.

142. P. S. Appelbaum and A. Rosenbaum, "Tarasoff and the Researcher: Does the Duty to Protect Apply in the Research Setting? *American Psychologist* 44: 885–94 (1989); Roth and Meisel, *supra* note 109; F. Shane, "Position Paper: Confidentiality and Dangerousness in the Doctor-Patient Relationship: The Position of the Canadian Psychiatric Association," *Canadian Journal of Psychiatry* 30: 293–96 (1985).

143. See *Otis Engineering Corp. v. Clark,* 668 S.W.2d 307 (Tex. 1983) and the cases cited therein.

144. A Pennsylvania court in *Coath v. Jones* went so far as to hold an employer liable for the criminal behavior of a *former* employee, when that person used his company identification to gain access to the victim's residence. The opinion stated that it considered a special relationship to exist between the company and victim because—and only because—the violence was foreseeable. This transmutes the special relationship into a simple foreseeability test, in which the employer is held liable for failing to prevent violence even in the absence of a relationship that could be considered "special" in the legal sense.

145. Levmore, *supra* note 19.

146. K. L. Scheppele, *Legal Secrets: Equality and Efficiency in the Common Law* (Chicago: University of Chicago Press, 1988).

147. J. Rawls, *A Theory of Justice.* (Cambridge, Mass.: Harvard University Press, 1971).

148. Scheppele makes this argument in her analysis of the law of fraud (in both contract and tort cases) but fails to utilize it in her analysis of *Tarasoff,* which is somewhat superficial and unsatisfying. Nonetheless, the implications of her earlier argument for the duty to protect are too plain for me to resist extending them here.

149. V. C. Brady, "The Duty to Rescue in Tort Law: Implications of Research on Altruism," *Indiana Law Journal* 55: 551–61 (1980).

150. J. M. Adler, "Relying upon the Reasonableness of Strangers: Some Observations About the Current State of Common Law Affirmative Duties to Aid or Protect Others," *Wisconsin law Review* 867–928 (1991).

151. For suggestions that this may already be occurring, see *Mathes v. Ireland,* 419 N.E. 2d 782 (Ind. Ct. App. 1981), and "Judge Refuses to End Suit Against Killer's Parents." *New York Times,* November 10, 1989, p. A-25. One court, however, has rejected the possibility of liability for lay people in a duty-to-protect case. See *Megeff v. Doland,* 176 Cal. Rptr. 467 (Ct. App. 1981).

152. "Annotation: Liability of Physicians, for Injury to or Death of Third Party, Due to Failure to Disclose Driving-related Impairment," 43 ALR 4th 153; S. L. Godard and J. D. Bloom, "Driving, Mental Illness, and the Duty to Protect," in J. C. Beck, ed., *Confidentiality Versus the Duty to Protect: Foreseeable Harm in the Practice of Psychiatry* (Washington, D.C.: American Psychiatric Press, 1990), pp. 191–204.

153. By no means does this exhaust the list of patients whose mental states may render them unsafe behind the wheel and hence expose their physicians to liability for the accidents they cause. Among the diagnostic groups that raise similar problems are the elderly (especially those with dementia), persons with epilepsy, and diabetics. See D. W. Gilley, R. S. Wilson, D. A. Bennett, G. T. Stebbins, B. A. Bernard, M. E. Whalen, and J. H. Fox, "Cessation of Driving and Unsafe Motor Vehicle Operation by Dementia Patients," *Archives of Internal Medicine* 151: 941–46 (1991); and P. Hansotia and S. K. Broste, "The Effect of Epilepsy or Diabetes Mellitus on the Risk of Automobile Accidents," *New England Journal of Medicine* 324: 22–26 (1991). Persons taking commonly prescribed psychoactive

medications, such as sedative/hypnotics, may also be at greater risk of traffic accidents. See E. H. Ellinwood and D. G. Heatherly, "Benzodiazepines, the Popular Minor Tranquilizers: Dynamics of Effect on Driving Skills," *Accident Analysis and Prevention* 17: 283–90 (1985).

154. K. Appelbaum and P. S. Appelbaum, "The HIV-antibody Positive Patient," in J. C. Beck, ed., *Confidentiality Versus the Duty to Protect: Foreseeable Harm in the Practice of Psychiatry* (Washington, D.C.: American Psychiatric Press, 1990), pp. 121–40.

155. American Psychiatric Association, "AIDS Policy: Confidentiality and Disclosure," *Psychiatric News,* January 15, 1988, p. 27.

156. Council on Ethical and Judicial Affairs, "Ethical Issues Involved in the Growing AIDS Crisis," *Journal of the American Medical Association* 259: 1360–61 (1988).

157. See, e.g., Massachusetts General Laws, Chap. 111, Sec. 70F.

158. See, e.g., California Health and Safety Code, Sec. 199.25 (1988).

159. K. H. Rothenburg, "The Application of the *Tarasoff* Duty to Forensic Psychiatry," *Virginia Law Review* 66: 715–26 (1980).

160. P. S. Appelbaum, "Confidentiality in the Forensic Evaluation," *International Journal of Law and Psychiatry* 7: 67–82 (1984).

161. S. Eth and G. B. Leong, "Therapist Sexual Misconduct and the Duty to Protect," in J. C. Beck, ed., *Confidentiality Versus the Duty to Protect: Foreseeable Harm in the Practice of Psychiatry* (Washington, D.C.: American Psychiatric Press, 1990), pp. 107–20.

162. Unlike most classes of patients, other therapists are quite likely to be informed regarding the obligations their psychotherapists may have to breach confidentiality to protect third parties.

163. Professor Richard Bonnie of the University of Virginia Law School has challenged the necessity of relying on tort law to accomplish these ends. He writes, "I could envision a combination of regulatory duties to report . . . and some form of victim compensation through the public purse. In this way, we could serve both the deterrent and compensatory objectives of tort law, but without all of the undesirable consequences of imposing tort liability and administering the tort system" (Ltr. to author, July 21, 1992). Whether regulatory requirements would provide sufficient incentive to encourage clinicians to conform to a reasonable standard of care and whether a no-fault compensation pool for crime victims is likely to be established are both open questions. In the meantime, reliance on tort remedies does not seem unreasonable.

4

Right to Refuse Treatment with Medication: Consent, Coercion, and the Courts

When Michael Nelson came to Boston State Hospital (BSH) in 1971 as a psychiatrist on its chronic service, he could see the sad history of state hospitals for the mentally ill etched on its stained facades. The historic facility, which first opened in 1839 as a municipal lunatic hospital, was transplanted to the fields of Mattapan in 1893. In those years, the growing city of Boston had not yet engulfed the farms that surrounded the hospital's 232 acres of rolling grounds. Like its sister institutions of the era, BSH was designed to be as self-sufficient as possible, its patients employed as laborers in the farm fields, barns, and orchards developed on the property.[1]

As immigrants poured into Boston, and Yankee farmers' sons and daughters migrated there from the countryside, BSH was expanded repeatedly to house the rising numbers of the indigent insane. Sadly, though, the hospital was typical of state facilities: providing treatment or even humane care often took second place to crowding more mentally ill persons into its buildings.[2] Patients often were "warehoused" rather than actively treated, particularly on the chronic wards reserved for those thought unlikely ever to recover.

To be sure, there were exceptions to this downhill slide. BSH was one of the first state hospitals to spin off its own receiving facility, the famous Boston Psychopathic Hospital.[3] And in the 1950s, an innovative (if quixotic) effort was made by a team of psychoanalysts to use intensive talking therapy to help chronic schizophrenic patients. But the general trajectory was clear.

Following decades of relative neglect and underfunding, deinstitutionalization and the community psychiatry movement hit BSH hard in the 1960s.

The hospital was carved up into fiefdoms, each controlled by a different community mental health center. Administrators of these programs were loath to allocate resources to the patients housed in the mammoth old buildings, preferring instead to use them for community-based care. Staff morale and the physical plant deteriorated in parallel, as plans were discussed to phase out the facility altogether.

This was the situation into which psychiatrist Michael Nelson stepped as the institution's new superintendent in 1973. He had few resources for repairing the antiquated plumbing, which sent the stench of sewage through one of the most heavily used buildings, or for combatting the cockroaches that infested the wards. There was little he could do to turn to more productive uses the largely abandoned, weed-choked campus, now surrounded by a lower-class neighborhood that was not quite yet a slum. But even if he was powerless to change the physical reality with which patients had to deal, he thought there might be something he could do to help them leave BSH, and to survive more effectively in the outside world.

A civil libertarian himself, Nelson saw patients being denied entitlements—welfare, housing, Social Security benefits—that might have helped them stabilize their lives. Many did not have the sophistication necessary to navigate the application and appeal processes, and almost all lacked the resources to hire attorneys to guide them. Thus, Nelson invited Greater Boston Legal Services to open a legal aid office on the hospital grounds. Richard Cole, a third-year law student from Boston University, soon arrived to staff the office, and in short order he was appointed head of the institution's civil rights committee.

Nelson's idea had been that Cole would help patients fight bureaucracies outside the mental health system, but Cole had a different conception of his role. As he roamed the sparsely furnished hospital wards, Cole solicited patients' complaints and, he said, heard one objection voiced time and again. Patients were upset at being compelled to take antipsychotic medications against their will. These medications, first introduced in the mid-1950s, had revolutionized the care of the most severely ill patients. They often suppressed difficult-to-control symptoms such as delusions and hallucinations, and they restored patients' abilities to think and communicate clearly. The effectiveness of the antipsychotics made massive deinstitutionalization possible and helped to create a new style of hospital-based treatment, which featured rapid stabilization and return to the community in days or weeks. As a matter of policy, when patients refused to take the prescribed doses by mouth, they might be compelled to take them—sometimes by injection.

Unfortunately, the medications did not work equally well for all patients, and indeed for some they helped not at all. The drugs' sedative properties tempted staff members to administer them even to patients who lacked the target symptoms for which antipsychotics were designed. More-over, the medications commonly had unpleasant side-effects, including a sense of restlessness, muscle spasms, and a state called akinesia, in which movement and thought itself might be slowed to a crawl. More frightening still was a syndrome called "tardive dyskinesia," which only appeared after months or years of treatment and was characterized by uncontrollable (and frequently irreversible) muscular contractions in the face, limbs, and trunk. It seemed wrong to Cole that the state—through its agents, the psychiatric staff of BSH—could compel people to accept these drugs.[4]

As he listened to patients' complaints, Cole began to identify patients who might serve as plaintiffs in a lawsuit challenging the practice. One of them was Rubie Rogers, a 36-year-old black woman, who had been in BSH continuously for three years as a voluntary patient. She had a history of thought disorder, hallucinations, and delusions—just the symptoms against which antipsychotic medications are most effective—with episodes of self-destructive and violent behavior. But Cole claimed that Rogers had become so upset by the recurrent muscle spasms that she experienced after she re-ceived doses of one of the most commonly prescribed of the antipsychotic medications, Haldol, that on one occasion she had set herself on fire. This, she had thought, would ensure her transfer to a medical hospital where she would not be given Haldol against her will.

By April 1975, Cole's case was ready. He filed suit in federal district court in Boston on behalf of Rubie Rogers, six other named plaintiffs, and all other hospitalized patients at the May and Austin units of BSH. The suit alleged that involuntary medication, even of committed patients, violated patients' constitutional rights to freedom of speech and association, due process, freedom from cruel and unusual punishment, treatment in the least restrictive alternative, and equal protection of the laws. Cole and his fellow attorneys representing the plaintiffs asked the court for an injunction pro-hibiting further use of medication without patients' consent, and for mone-tary damages from a group of fifteen named defendants, all but one of whom—the commissioner of mental health—worked at BSH.[5]

Shortly after the suit (which is generally known by the name of its lead plaintiff, *Rogers*) was filed, the court issued a temporary restraining order forbidding involuntary medication except in emergencies ("a serious threat of, or as a result of, extreme violence, personal injury or attempted suicide") while the case was pending. The process of litigation dragged on for years before the verdict was returned. But when the opinion was finally issued, the world of psychiatry was stunned by its contents. Judge Joseph Tauro had concluded that voluntary and involuntarily committed patient's rights to privacy and freedom of speech (specifically, freedom to generate ideas and thoughts) meant that patients, if competent, had the right to refuse treatment with medication.

Treatment of Mental Illness and Informed Consent

The premise underlying the opinion in *Rogers*—that mentally ill patients should have the right to refuse treatment—marked a break in judicial reluctance to interfere with administrative policy in American mental hospitals. Lacking truly effective treatments for severe mental illness, and faced with the ravaging effects of the disorders themselves, psychiatrists had long sought cures by extreme (and sometimes desperate) means. But even when treatment consisted of bleeding, purging, and "whirling chairs," as it did in many mental hospitals in the early and mid-nineteenth century,[6] or when a primitive form of psychosurgery performed with modified ice-picks gained popularity in 1940s and 1950s,[7] hospital administrators simply assumed that patients could be compelled to accept whatever treatment their doctors thought was appropriate. Even voluntary patients (like Rubie Rogers) who had the right to leave the facility if they desired were often treated over their objections.

Mental hospitals were singularly different from general medical hospitals in this respect. In the Anglo-American legal tradition, patients' consent has always been required before physicians could lawfully proceed with medical treatment—particularly in instances of invasive (usually surgical) treatments.[8] The oldest reported case affirming this proposition is *Slater v. Baker and Stapleton,* an English case decided in 1767.[9] The failure of Dr. Baker, a surgeon, to obtain Slater's consent before refracturing and resetting his broken leg was held by the court to be a clear transgression of existing rules:

> [I]t appears from the evidence of the surgeons that it was improper to disunite the callous without consent; this is the usage and law of surgeons: then it was ignorance and unskillfulness in that very particular, to do contrary to the rule of the profession, what no surgeon ought to have done; and indeed it is reasonable that a patient should be told what is about to be done to him, that he may take courage and put himself in such a situation as to enable him to undergo the operation.

The principles embodied in *Slater* were assimilated by American law, a process reflected most clearly in the much-cited dictum of Judge Benjamin Cardozo in 1914 in *Schloendorff v. Society of New York Hospital:*

> Every human being of adult years and sound mind has a right to determine what shall be done with his own body; and a surgeon who performs an operation without his patient's consent commits an assault, for which he is liable in damages.[10]

Just after the middle of this century, consent law in the United States, as typified by *Schloendorff,* underwent a historic transition. Cardozo's "right to determine what shall be done with his own body" had not granted the patient the right to very much information on which to base a decision. In a growing wave of opinions that crested in the early 1970s, American courts replaced Cardozo's doctrine of simple consent with a requirement that physicians must obtain patients' "informed consent." [11] The new rules, seeking to offer patients more meaningful choices about their treatment, stated that physicians must disclose the nature and purpose of treatment, along with a summary of relevant risks, benefits, and treatment alternatives, to render the consent they obtained legally effective.

The courts' expansion of physicians' duties represented an attempt to achieve the degree of patient control over medical decision making suggested, but not effected, by *Schloendorff* and similar cases. At its core, the new line of cases reflected a desire to alter the essential nature of the doctor–patient relationship, bringing the patient closer to an equal footing with the doctor as a participant in shaping treatment decisions, rather than granting the patient only the option of accepting no treatment (by exercising an ill-informed veto). [12] Patients in mental hospitals became increasingly conspicuous exceptions to the norm of enhanced patient roles in making treatment decisions.

There seem to have been two principal reasons why psychiatric patients were always exempted from the coverage of legal consent requirement: the assumption that mentally ill people were uniformly incompetent to make decisions for themselves, and thus stood outside the reach of the rule of consent; and in the case of involuntary patients, the belief that the power to treat the mentally ill was inherent in the power to commit them. But by the 1970s, as informed consent law was flowering, both of these rationales were being called into question.

Exceptional Status of the Treatment of Mental Illness: The Presumptions Crumble

As dedicated as our society is to protecting the rights of persons to make their own decisions, it requires a person to possess a modicum of decision-making abilities before it will honor that person's individual choices—including choices about signing a contract, writing a will, and even marrying. The basis for this requirement lies deep in two different strands of the Western philosophical tradition. From the point of view of deontologic thinkers (like Immanuel Kant) who endorse ethical principles independent of their consequences, autonomy is a good in its own right. But this status as a good depends on the ability of persons to pursue a coherent set of principles in which their behavior is grounded. [13] In contrast, utilitarian thinkers such as John Stuart Mill posit that autonomy serves to maximize individual happiness, since every person is presumed best able to determine how his or her own happiness can be achieved.[14] But utilitarians, too, point to a loss of rationality as undermining the basis for honoring individual choice, since irrational persons are unlikely to know how to achieve their desires.

Thus, inherent in the philosophical grounding of Western respect for individual choice is the condition that persons be able to function rationally in making that choice. This rule applies to choices of medical treatment, as well. Even Cardozo, in his formulation in *Schloendorff*, limited the application of his dictum to persons of "adult years and sound mind." Such people, in legal terms, are said to be "competent" to exercise their rights. Mental illness, by definition, calls the soundness of the mind—and therefore the legal competence—of the actor into question. In fact, nineteenth-century theorists believed that serious mental illness so impaired mental functioning as to render its victims thoroughly unable to make competent decisions of any kind.

This view was embodied in many states' laws, which deprived all persons committed to state institutions of their rights to make choices for themselves, including decisions about managing their financial affairs, disposing of their property after their demise, voting in public elections, and marrying.[15] Moreover, in many jurisdictions, former patients had to initiate a court proceeding at which they demonstrated their competence before these rights were restored. This perspective long delayed the adoption of statutes permitting mentally ill persons to hospitalize themselves voluntarily,[16] and it also accounts (in part) for the traditional presumption that consent for treatment need not be obtained from the mentally ill.[17]

The equation of committability with incompetence began to change in the years following World War II, as commentators, including the authors of the NIMH Draft Act Governing Hospitalization of the Mentally Ill, argued that mental conditions that might necessitate involuntary hospitalization did not necessarily render the person incapable of making decisions about other aspects of his or her life. Momentum for change grew as a more refined view of incompetence began to develop, spurred, in particular, by advocates for the mentally retarded.[18] They argued that mental retardation typically affects some functions more than others. For example, a mentally retarded person might not be able to manage his finances very well, but he could be perfectly capable of deciding where he wanted to live, who his personal physician should be, and with whom he desired to associate. Persons should not be deprived of their power to make decisions, these advocates argued, unless they were demonstrably unable to make the precise decisions in question. In essence, this was an argument for a transformation of the law of competence and guardianship from a global to a specific focus.

Advocates for the mentally ill realized that similar arguments could be

applied to persons affected by mental disorders. Mental illness is a hetero-
geneous category that covers a wide range of conditions. Even within single
diagnostic groups, differences in functional impairment are vast. Some
schizophrenics can barely dress and feed themselves, while others hold down
jobs and are fiercely independent. If needless deprivation of rights is to be
avoided, some distinction has to be made among members of these groups.
As this argument gained credence, the law began to change. States no longer
considered commitment to a mental facility to be equivalent to a finding of
incompetence.[19] Guardianship laws were altered in many jurisdictions to
require specific findings of incompetence, with limitations on decisionmaking authority specifically tailored to each person's impairments.[20]

Commentators began to recognize the implications of this shift with
regard to the rights of committed patients to consent to or refuse treatment.
In arguing that competent patients should have the right to reject treatment,
Michael Shapiro, a law professor at the University of Southern California,
framed the issue this way:

> [A]s a matter of empirical observation, it seems far too simplistic to regard
> someone who is mentally ill or disordered as being wholly unable to make
> rational decisions about the conduct of his life. The mind is just too complex
> to permit such an inference; it is a *non sequitur* to infer from a lack of aptitude
> or a dysfunction in one kind of mentation a similar lack or dysfunction in
> another.[21]

The distinction between mental patients (many of whom were treated
without their consent) and patients hospitalized for medical problems (who
had always been assumed, unless specifically determined to be incompetent, to have the right to refuse care) rested on an assumption of global
incompetence on the part of the former. To the extent that the new ways of
understanding competence challenged the conclusion that mental illness invariably led to incompetent decision making, the justification for a blanket
denial of mentally ill persons' right to decide about treatment was called
into question. Instead, it was argued, the mentally ill should be dealt with
in the same way as were the physically ill: they should be presumed to have
the competence to consent to or refuse treatment, and rebutting that presumption should require an individualized assessment.

The obvious retort to this postulated equivalence between medically ill
and mentally ill patients is that the state has an unusually strong interest in
the treatment of the mentally ill, exemplified by its power to commit them
against their will. According to this view, while informed consent might be
applicable to the voluntary psychiatric patient, it remained irrelevant to the
committed patient. Yet, even as this counterargument was being formulated, the ground on which it rested was shifting.

By the early 1970s, the momentous reorientation in commitment standards described in Chapter 2 was in full swing. In place of standards based on the perceived need of mentally ill people for care and treatment came statutes restricting commitment to those who were dangerous to themselves or others. This shift was justified, in part, on the basis that the proper reach of state power did not extend to all situations where it might benefit people over their objections (including nonconsensual treatment of their mental disorders), but only to a subgroup of such situations in which the prospective patients' behavior clearly endangered others or (it was agreed with some reluctance) themselves.

Thus, in 1971, the commitment statute in Massachusetts under which several of Ruby Rogers's fellow plaintiffs at Boston State Hospital were subsequently committed had been revised to limit commitment to those persons who presented a likelihood of serious physical harm to themselves or to others. The statute made no mention of patients' need for or amenability to treatment.[22]

A new argument now suggested itself with regard to the nature of the state's interest in overriding patients' rights to refuse medication. The purpose of civil commitment—at least as embodied explicitly in contemporary commitment statutes—was no longer to treat the mentally ill, but rather to protect them or others from the consequences of their behavior. If that was the case, the state's interest in commitment was limited to preventing harm—a goal that could be achieved in most cases by hospitalizing and carefully supervising patients. As in general medical settings, therefore, the state had no compelling interest sufficient to override the interest of competent mental patients in making their own treatment decisions. Patients should have the right to accept or refuse treatment, including treatment with medications, as they saw fit, unless found incompetent to do so by a court of law. Moreover, even when a compelling state interest in nonconsensual treatment could be established (as in the case of incompetent patients), it would have to be satisfied by means that were the least intrusive on patients' rights, which might mean applying other treatment techniques (such as psychotherapy) before resorting to medications.[23]

Paul Friedman, the managing attorney of the Mental Health Law Project, a major litigant on behalf of patients' rights, summed up this argument:

> While participation in a behavioral program [i.e., treatment] could eliminate a
> mental patient's dangerous propensities and permit his earlier release, a com-
> petent patient's choice to preserve the integrity of his fundamental rights [i.e.,
> to refuse treatment], the infringement of which is not absolutely necessary to
> the state's interest in protecting its citizens, should be respected.[24]

As the landscape of legal theory was changing in these two significant ways—the dissolution of the presumption of incompetence of the mentally

ill, and the reorientation of commitment law—small cracks began to appear
in the courts' previous support for unbridled physician discretion in the
treatment of mentally ill patients. The first breakthrough came in *Winters*
v. Miller, a case brought by a Christian Scientist, who sought damages
from psychiatrists who had treated her against her will at a public facility.[25]
Recognizing a legitimate basis for the patient's suit, the court held that her
first amendment right to freedom of religion overrode whatever interest the
state might have in promoting public health and welfare. As for the state's
argument that it was only acting to further the patient's best interests, the
court noted that the patient had never been declared incompetent and thus,
presumptively, was able to determine for herself how best to pursue her
interests.

Whereas *Winters* turned on the nature of the patient's objection to
treatment and on special protection afforded religious beliefs by the Constitution, a series of cases followed in quick succession that focused more
directly on the nature of the treatment that was being employed. Treatments
that were considered relatively "intrusive,"[26] and thus more susceptible to
abuse, were the first to be regulated. A major right to treatment case in
Alabama, *Wyatt v. Stickney,* resulted in a judicial order requiring, among
other remedies, that no behavior modification programs of competent patients be undertaken without the informed consent of these patients.[27] A
federal appellate court found that administering apomorphine (a drug that
induces vomiting) to patients in a prison hospital for the purpose of achieving behavior modification through aversive stimuli constituted cruel and unusual punishment.[28] Another federal court reversed the dismissal of a claim
by a prisoner-patient that his rights had been violated when he had been
treated with succinylcholine, a medication that paralyzes the breathing muscles for short periods of time, in what appears to have been yet another
instance of attempted aversive conditioning.[29] And the Minnesota Supreme
Court enjoined future use of electroconvulsive therapy or psychosurgery for
incompetent patients without a court hearing on the "necessity and reasonableness of the proposed treatment."[30]

Each of these decisions was limited to a particular class of treatments,
none of which involved standard medications. The rationale employed, when
identified at all, tended to be narrow: religious freedom in *Winters,* and the
right against cruel or unusual punishment in the prison hospital cases.[31] But
once the presumption that mental patients as a class could be treated without consent was abrogated, the broader constitutional arguments that could
be applied to routine medication—like antipsychotic drugs—inevitably began to be embraced by the courts as well. The legal stage was thus set for
the dramatic change in the law precipitated by the *Rogers* decision.

The Decisions in *Rogers:* A Right to Refuse Treatment

In October 1979, four-and-a-half years after the suit in *Rogers* was filed, following seventy-two days of testimony, the generation of more than 8,000 pages of transcripts, and the filing of over 2,300 pages of posttrial briefs, Judge Tauro's decision came in. Some attention was given to setting the scene. The conditions at BSH, which the judge had toured during the course of the trial, were portrayed starkly. Detailed descriptions were offered of many of the side-effects of antipsychotic medications, especially tardive dyskinesia. But the core of the opinion tracked the legal arguments that had been evolving slowly through the 1970s.

Mental patients, Judge Tauro concluded, were presumptively competent, a conclusion he found was recognized by Massachusetts law. Thus, their right to determine whether they should be treated was protected by their right of privacy under the federal constitution. In addition, patients' right to generate ideas, which was found to be impeded by the "mind-altering" medications they received, was protected by the first amendment:

> Whatever powers the Constitution has granted our government, involuntary mind control is not one of them, absent extraordinary circumstances. The fact that mind control takes place in a mental institution in the form of medically sound treatment of mental disease is not, itself, an extraordinary circumstance warranting an unsanctioned intrusion on the integrity of a human being.[32]

Voluntary patients were found to have the same right to refuse treatment as involuntary patients, and the state's argument that they had waived that right by agreeing to hospitalization was rejected. As for the countervailing interests of the state, treatment was permitted without consent in emergency situations (when there was "a substantial likelihood of physical harm to the patient or others"), but the use of nonconsensual treatment simply for the sake of helping the patient was proscribed:

> Given a non-emergency . . . it is an unreasonable invasion of privacy, and an affront to basic concepts of human dignity, to permit forced injection of a mind-altering drug into the buttocks of a competent patient unwilling to give informed consent . . . It takes a grave set of circumstances to abrogate [the right to be left alone]. That a non-emergency injection in the buttocks may be therapeutic does not constitute such a circumstance.[33]

The court refused to hold any of the fifteen defendants personally liable for harm to the plaintiffs, arguing that they had acted in good faith and in accord with what were then accepted practices regarding involuntary treatment. Moreover, their prescription of antipsychotic medications was in keeping with professional standards and had resulted in improvement for most of the plaintiffs.

As for the procedures that would be needed in the future if the state desired to overturn the nonemergency refusal of medication by a mentally ill patient, the court adopted a model similar to the one it believed was employed in other medical settings. The patient must be found incompetent by a court and have a guardian appointed to make the treatment decision. Physicians were no longer empowered to act as medical decision makers for their patients.[34]

Although the decision was in, the case was by no means over. An appeal by the state to the U.S. Court of Appeals for the First Circuit resulted in a decision upholding the main points of the lower court's opinion.[35] The U.S. Supreme Court, which agreed to hear the case, avoided rendering a definitive decision by suggesting that the constitutional basis on which the district court had rested its opinion might be unnecessary to the resolution of the case.[36] Rather, the Court questioned whether Massachusetts law, as embodied in a recent decision concerning the right of outpatients to refuse medication,[37] could provide adequate grounds to vindicate patients' right to refuse treatment. A remand to the First Circuit was followed by certification of the case to the Massachusetts Supreme Judicial Court for its opinion on the state law issues.

In the end, the outcome was much the same. Resting its holding on state law, the Massachusetts high court found in 1983 that competent patients had a right to refuse medication.[38] The procedures the Massachusetts court created, however, were a bit different from those outlined by Judge Tauro. Although a court hearing to adjudicate the question of a patient's incompetence was required, the decision as to treatment was to be made by the judge, not by a guardian. Only the judge was thought to be disinterested enough (unlike family members, who might have a stake in whether the patient were treated) to be able to apply the standard the court established: whether the patient, if competent, would have consented to the treatment. This "substituted judgment" standard was the ultimate attempt to respect individual choice, even after the person became incompetent.[39] The triumph in Massachusetts of the doctrine of informed consent, as applied to the mentally ill, and of a quarantine model of civil commitment appeared to be complete.

Psychiatry Responds to the New Right to Refuse

The reaction from psychiatric groups to the new right to refuse treatment was immediate and vitriolic. Alan Stone, then president of the American Psychiatric Association, called the federal district court opinion in *Rogers* "probably the most impossible, ill-considered judicial decision in the field of mental health law."[40] In its *amicus* brief supporting the state's appeal of the lower court opinion, the American Psychiatric Association claimed that the court "was setting into play a series of self-fulfilling prophecies likely to destroy the psychiatric hospital."[41]

What accounted for the anger and intensity of the response to *Rogers?* Part of the answer lies in psychiatrists' reaction to the language and style of Judge Tauro's opinion, rather than to its legal substance.[42] Judge Tauro characterized the actions of antipsychotic medications—and by implication the intent of the people who administered them—in terms that evoked the most sinister images of psychiatry. The medications were referred to as "mind-altering,"[43] and treatment itself was characterized as "involuntary mind control."[44] These are precisely the kind of stereotypes that set psychiatrists' teeth on edge. They believed that the stigma associated with such images discouraged adequate funding of psychiatric care and dissuaded persons in need of psychiatric assistance from seeking treatment. Moreover, the opinion offered an extensive list of medication side-effects, but made only a brief allusion to the therapeutic effects of the medications.[45] The decision provoked a substantial literature dedicated to correcting what psychiatrists perceived as mistaken legal notions of the effects of antipsychotic medications.[46]

Psychiatrists feared that misperceptions of the effects of antipsychotic medications might have played an important role in shaping the outcome of the case,[47] but they were concerned with more than simply the way in which their work was characterized. Psychiatrists worried that a ruling denying them the power to treat patients involuntarily—especially patients hospitalized against their will—would threaten the entire structure of the public mental health system.

The extent to which patients would refuse treatment was a matter of considerable concern. Major mental disorders often are accompanied by patients' denial of their illnesses—a phenomenon not usually seen in conjunction with physical disorders. Patients who are mentally ill are peculiarly likely either to disavow the signs and symptoms of their condition or to blame them on other factors.[48] Manic patients, for example, often feel euphoric and possessed of extraordinary powers; the suggestion that they may be suffering from a mental disorder is frequently met with disbelief. The most severely depressed patients are prone to attribute their symptoms to physical disorders. Patients with schizophrenia may blame their confused thinking or the hallucinatory voices they hear on devious plots hatched by sinister organizations.

Many commentators have speculated about the possible basis for this tendency of mentally ill persons to fail to acknowledge the existence of a disorder, but its foundation remains unclear. Nonetheless, the recognition that mentally ill persons—unlike people with fractured legs, for example— often do not seek care on their own was an important stimulus to the development of involuntary systems of psychiatric treatment. Now clinicians feared that giving the power to refuse treatment to committed patients—who by rejecting voluntary hospitalization in the first place had given notice of their resistance to the idea that they might need care—would result in an epidemic of treatment refusal in psychiatric facilities.[49]

Assuming that refusal would be rampant, psychiatrists offered predictions about the consequences of *Rogers* that had a distinctly apocalyptic tone. The APA characterized the right to refuse treatment as being likely to lead "to the restoration of the prison-like atmosphere that marked state mental hospitals before the 1950s"[50] as a result of uncontrolled violence committed by unmedicated patients.[51] As if to confirm these fears, Stephen Schultz, the attorney for the defendants (the hospital staff) in *Rogers,* catalogued the deterioration in patient behavior at BSH that accompanied the new rules imposed by the court: a higher rate of transfers of violent patients to a maximum security facility, skyrocketing use of seclusion to control disruptive patients, and termination of the psychiatric residency program on the May Unit at BSH, because "it was decided that it was too dangerous for a single resident to be assigned to a ward."[52] Many psychiatrists assumed that the situation would be the same in their facilities, as soon as a right to refuse treatment was decreed for their patients.

The projected effects of the right to refuse treatment on the staff in public hospitals also constituted an important concern. Psychiatric authorities expressed fears that the defection of psychiatrists from state hospitals would accelerate as the treatment setting became explicitly adversarial and as psychiatrists felt increasingly unappreciated and harassed:[53]

> Quality superintendents, psychiatrists, and other professionals of the mental health staff will be increasingly reluctant to seek employment in state mental hospitals when they assess the clinical and legal risks of working there. An adversarial atmosphere will be created in inpatient treatment units that will potentially inhibit the development of relationships between staff and patients and will thereby alienate and drive away competent clinical staff.[54]

Perhaps the most important concern psychiatrists had was that a right to refuse treatment might stifle the ability of psychiatric hospitals to ameliorate the conditions of patients who had been committed for care. Thomas Gutheil, a psychiatrist at the Massachusetts Mental Health Center, charged that the right to refuse treatment amounted to a "right to rot." Objecting to *Rogers'* characterization of treatment with antipsychotic medication as "involuntary mind control," he noted:

> [A] psychosis is *itself* involuntary mind control of the most extensive kind and itself represents the most severe "intrusion on the integrity of a human being."

The physician seeks to liberate the patient from the chains of illness; the judge from the chains of treatment. The way is paved for patients to "rot with their rights on."[55]

Among the problems predicted as treatment ground to a halt were an increased average length of stay; higher in-patient censuses, with patients who were too sick to be discharged accumulating in the hospital; greater chronicity of illness, as treatable patients went untreated; and poorer community functioning, resulting from patients being discharged while still highly impaired.[56] The image of an untreated patient—huddling in the corner of a ward, ignored by everyone else, bearing in solitude the burden of a personal psychosis—pervaded the clinical imagination. Indeed, one psychiatrist characterized the right to refuse treatment as a backdoor means of effectively abolishing involuntary commitment.[57]

Professional groups also expressed practical concerns. Recourse to the courts to override patients' refusals (when patients were found to be incompetent) was condemned as enormously costly.[58] Money would have to come from somewhere to pay for clinicians to evaluate and testify about refusing patients, for staff members required to accompany patients to and from hearings, for lawyers for each side, and for judges and judicial personnel. In addition, the delay inherent in accessing the already overcrowded courts would increase the costs of hospitalization, as length of stay grew markedly prolonged.

Although probably no other legal initiative in recent years has so aroused the ire of psychiatrists as a group, *Rogers* was not universally condemned. Some psychopharmacologists (although not the American College of Neuropsychopharmacology, which wrote a brief supporting the state's appeal against the district court's judgment in *Rogers*[59]) felt that medications were widely misused in state facilities and that closer supervision—by the courts, if need be—was warranted. One expert in psychopharmacology, who testified on behalf of a plaintiff in *Rogers,* said, "For every patient you can show me whose treatment is delayed by the need to have a court pass on his competency, I can show you more who were improperly medicated in the past and suffered needless side effects as a result."[60]

Other psychiatrists agreed with the *Rogers* court that involuntary treatment of competent patients was morally improper. Psychiatrist Seymour Halleck, for example, writing before the suit in *Rogers* was filed, argued that only patients who were dangerous and incompetent, and for whom the medications were likely to be effective, should be treated against their will. He advocated that treatment plans for this group of patients be presented to a review panel that included an attorney, and that the patient be permitted to hire his own psychiatrist and attorney to argue the case against treatment.

Halleck suggested that such a process would reassure patients, encourage doctors to be more precise and thoughtful in treatment planning, and help keep these cases out of the courts.[61]

Even Alan Stone, whose objections to *Rogers* helped set the tone for psychiatrists' responses to the decision, felt that psychiatrists "should and can" make the right to refuse treatment work.[62] "It would not only be politically unacceptable," he wrote, "it would be politically dangerous for the psychiatric profession to assume sole responsibility for determining competence and treating patients against their wishes." Stone also felt that it was improper for competent patients to be treated without their consent, urging instead that incompetence be made a requirement for civil commitment, so that only incompetent persons would be hospitalized involuntarily. Then, all committed patients could be treated appropriately, over their objections if necessary.

Finally, another mental health profession had its opinions to offer about the right to refuse treatment. The American Psychological Association consistently supported patients' rights to refuse treatment, filing multiple *amicus* briefs with the appellate courts. A paper appearing in *American Psychologist,* the official journal of the American Psychological Association, suggested some of the reasons for this divergence of opinion among the mental health professions.[63] Highlighting the economic losses that psychiatrists might sustain if patients refused the medications they prescribed, the authors proposed that psychology might be able to fill the void with nonmedical interventions, thus enhancing the psychological profession's role in the treatment of severely mentally ill persons.

Whatever other views might have surfaced in academic journals or among members of rival professions, however, the consensus among psychiatrists was clear:

> The law often appears to say to the patient, "You are mentally ill, dangerous, and need to be locked up," but on the other hand, "You may exercise your own judgment as to treatment or to refuse treatment."[64]

The situation made no sense to psychiatrists. Moreover, they thought that it was likely to lead to disaster in the psychiatric hospitals.

Other Jurisdictions Adopt a Right to Refuse Treatment: Rights-driven and Treatment-driven Models

As psychiatrists fretted about the impact of the right to refuse treatment promulgated in the initial *Rogers* opinion, other jurisdictions began to address the issue. By the time of the Massachusetts Supreme Judicial Court's final decision in *Rogers,* the right to refuse treatment was a major issue in mental health law and the subject of litigation around the country. Voluntary patients were quickly acknowledged to have the right to determine whether to accept medication, although not necessarily the right to remain in the hospital should they reject it. The focus of the litigation, therefore, was on the rights of involuntary patients. Although the resulting decisions were diverse in rationale and outcome, they can be divided into two groups, based on the extent to which the presiding court required adherence to the basic tenets of informed consent law for committed mental patients.

A large number of jurisdictions took what I have called a "rights-driven" approach to the issue.[65] Following the lead of the district court decision in *Rogers,* they held that patients—even those involuntarily committed—had a right to determine whether to receive treatment, unless they were determined to be incompetent to do so. The major differences among this set of decisions related to the procedures by which competence was to be assessed and (if the patient were found incompetent) by which a decision concerning treatment was to be made.

Some courts adhered closely to the *Rogers* model. They required that a determination of incompetence be made by a judge after an adversary hearing.[66] All but one of these courts assigned the decisionmaking power with regard to treatment, once a patient had been found incompetent, to the judge.[67] The rationale for this arrangement was that antipsychotic medication constituted a particularly intrusive form of treatment, and that only judges could be trusted with decisions of such magnitude.[68] Not every court followed the Massachusetts' court's rule that judges' decisions be made on the basis of what the patient would have preferred—the so-called "substituted judgment" approach. Some opted for decisions guided by the traditional "best interests" standard.[69] But as a group, the decisions that relied on judicial review were more alike than different.

In some cases, the process of determining patients' competence was not placed in judicial hands. Courts in a number of states refused to strike down systems in which nonjudicial review panels, often composed of clinicians and administrators, determined whether patients were competent and approved or rejected the medication proposed by the treating physician.[70] Typically, these panels followed relaxed rules of procedure and evidence that made for more informal proceedings than might take place in court.[71] Yet in these jurisdictions they were found to be adequate to protect patients' rights.

The second general approach to the right to refuse treatment—an approach antithetical to *Rogers* and the cases that followed it—can be termed "treatment-driven." Although courts following this approach acknowledged that committed patients had some right to refuse medication, they limited this to the right to refuse inappropriate medication. Thus, patients' treatment interests were given precedence over their interest in deciding whether treatment should take place.[72] Sometimes implicitly and sometimes directly, courts taking this approach viewed commitment as constituting an exception to the usual requirements for informed consent. The issue of patients' decisionmaking competence was irrelevant to courts that adopted this approach.

The treatment-driven view rejects the argument that the main underlying justification for dangerousness-based commitment statutes is quarantine, rather than treatment. And since treatment is considered the primary purpose of commitment, the initial determination that patients' rights should be abrogated for the purpose of commitment provides sufficient warrant for the subsequent administration of medication as well. In the words of one court, "Nonconsensual treatment is what involuntary commitment is all about."[73]

According to some courts that followed this reasoning, the traditional model of physician decision making adequately assures patients of appropriate care.[74] They afforded patients no external protection against forcible administration of medication; thus, patients had to rely on whatever persuasive power they might have with their psychiatrists to avoid being given unwanted medications. Other courts, given the magnitude of the interests involved, thought that patients were entitled to a review of the proposed treatment by an independent psychiatrist or panel.[75] Among the variations accepted by the courts were review by a consulting psychiatrist or the facility's medical director[76]; internal review followed by appeal to officials in the state department of mental health[77]; and physician discretion during the first fourteen days of hospitalization, after which patients' objections would trigger internal and external review.[78]

Despite the divergence in courts' approaches to this litigation—a difference also reflected in the legislation and rules enacted by states in response to or in anticipation of court decisions—the U.S. Supreme Court has never directly ruled on whether civilly committed mental patients have a right to refuse treatment. Twice the Court accepted cases that would have addressed the issue, but each time it sent the case back to the lower courts without a decision. The first such remand came in response to *Rogers,* with orders for the lower court to consider whether the case could be decided on the basis of Massachusetts law (which it was). But a second remand, in *Rennie v. Klein,*[79] may offer a clearer idea of the Court's perspective on this question.

Rennie, which raised many of the same constitutional issues as *Rogers,* was remanded for reconsideration in light of the Court's then-recent decision in *Youngberg v. Romeo.*[80] *Youngberg* dealt with the rights of a mentally retarded man committed to a state facility, where he had been assaulted by other patients and physically restrained by the staff. The Court acknowledged the patient's constitutional interests in freedom from harm and unnecessary restraint, but it held that these rights could be limited whenever, in the "professional judgment" of the treatment staff, they should be compromised for the benefit of the patient or of others in the facility.

Extrapolated to the treatment refusal context, *Youngberg*'s professional judgment rule resembles a treatment-driven model: as long as a well-trained professional determines that the treatment is appropriate, it can be administered, even over the objections of the patient. Thus, the remand of *Rennie* suggested that the Court might be endorsing a right to object to treatment, rather than a right to refuse it altogether, with the ultimate decision remaining in clinical hands. Once dissenting patients have had their objections considered by their treating physicians (or conceivably by second reviewers), the constitutional minima would be satisfied.

The only U.S. Supreme Court decision directly addressing the right to refuse treatment came in the prison context in *Washington v. Harper.*[81] Although the Court (surprisingly) did not cite *Youngberg* in its analysis, the *Harper* decision was consistent with the thrust of the *Youngberg* ruling. In it, Washington State's procedures for reviewing objections to treatment with antipsychotic medication were upheld as sufficient to protect prisoners' rights. The procedures called for administrative review of clinicians' requests to administer treatment over prisoners' objections; the review panel was composed of two clinicians (a psychiatrist and a psychologist) and a prison administrator. For treatment to be authorized, prisoners had to be found to meet Washington's dangerousness-based commitment criteria, but no determination of incompetence was required. Re-review took place every two weeks.

Since the Court's rationale in *Harper* relied largely on previous cases granting considerable discretion to prison administrators for other purposes, one cannot necessarily conclude that a case reaching the Court from a civil setting would be decided similarly. Nonetheless, the lower federal courts, following *Youngberg* and consistent with *Harper,* generally have declined to find a constitutional basis for committed patients' asserted right to informed consent or refusal.[82] They have accepted treatment-driven approaches, or nonjudicial rights-driven models, as adequate to protect patients' interests. But ironically, the Supreme Court's views may have little long-term impact on the issue. Whereas lawyers bringing patients' rights cases once struggled to find a basis for their being heard in federal court, many members of the mental health bar are now quite leery of that venue. A more conservative U.S. Supreme Court and, to a lesser extent, more conservative federal appellate and trial courts have made the federal system an unappealing setting for efforts to expand patients' rights.

In contrast, state courts have been much more receptive to rights-oriented arguments in the last decade, and they are now often the preferred locale for bringing cases that challenge mental health practices.[83] Moreover, these courts, by basing their decisions on state law, can insulate them effectively from review by the federal courts, since the latter cannot override a state supreme court's opinions on state law issues, unless the rights they recognize fall below those guaranteed in the federal constitution or contravene federal statutes.[84] State courts often have been willing, as was the Massachusetts Supreme Judicial Court, to identify independent state grounds— common law, statutory, or constitutional—on which to require a judicially controlled, rights-driven model.[85] In fact, in several instances, by applying state law, state courts have effectively overturned pro-treatment decisions of federal courts, substituting a judicial review process for the clinical or administrative review that the federal courts had found acceptable under the U.S. Constitution.[86]

The mistake of the Washington Supreme Court in *Harper* in striking down the state's review process on federal constitutional grounds opened the door for judicial review (and reversal) of the decision by the U.S. Supreme Court. Since the U.S. Supreme Court has declined to find a substantial right to refuse in federal law, state courts desirous of identifying such a right must locate it in their own state's laws, if anywhere; thus, the Washington Supreme Court's attempt to rest its decision on federal law is not likely to be repeated elsewhere.[87] State courts will be the primary decision makers about the extent of patients' rights to refuse treatment. Current trends suggest that rights-driven models, which bring the rules of informed consent law to the treatment of committed patients, are likely to predominate.

Consequences of a Right to Refuse Treatment

The spread of the right to refuse treatment offers us an opportunity to examine how prescient both its advocates and its critics were. Proponents urged that judicial recognition of a broad right to refuse treatment would protect the rights of patients to autonomous decision making, without materially impairing the functioning of the mental health system. Opponents predicted that the incidence of refusals would reach epidemic levels, leading to widespread violence, impaired care for large numbers of patients, and enormous costs for both mental health and judicial systems. A substantial number of studies (albeit of varying quality) now exist, allowing us to test these propositions. Moreover, the variations from state to state in the extent of the rights recognized and in the systems for overriding refusals might permit some comparisons to be made among alternative approaches.

To what extent have patients taken advantage of the right to refuse treatment? There was good reason to anticipate, as many critics did, huge increase in refusals of antipsychotic medications by hospitalized psychiatric patients. The early reports from Boston State Hospital and several studies conducted in jurisdictions that had not yet acknowledged a right to refuse treatment suggested that a large proportion of psychiatric patients would refuse medication when allowed to do so. In two studies conducted at a California Veterans Affairs hospital, where patients were asked whether they would be willing to accept medication if they had a choice, 28 percent and 48 percent of patients, respectively, replied that they would decline treatment with antipsychotic drugs.[88] A similar study performed in a military hospital, where again patients had no real option to reject treatment, found that 44 percent of schizophrenic patients said they would refuse the drugs.[89] These figures appeared to confirm fears of an impending surge of treatment refusal.

Studies of actual patient behavior in jurisdictions that have adopted a right to refuse treatment, however, yield somewhat different conclusions. When researchers in more than a dozen studies tallied up the numbers of patients in ordinary psychiatric facilities whose objections to treatment were subject to formal review (judicial or administrative, depending on the jurisdiction), they reported incidence rates of refusal of between 0.4 and 15.6 percent of total admissions. More than half of the studies reported rates of below 5 percent, and all but a handful of reports recorded rates of below 10 percent.[90]

Do these figures settle the issue? It might be argued that data on cases that reach the level of formal review are the most relevant to consider because they reflect the number of patients whose refusal is a serious impediment to their treatment, as evidenced by the efforts made to overturn their choices. Other patients might refuse treatment for short periods or in ways that do not interfere with their treatment plans, but one could question the importance of including them in incidence studies.

On the other hand, little knowledge exists of the biases that may influence clinicians' decisions to petition for review of patients' refusals. It has been suggested that psychiatrists may avoid taking patients through the review process because of the time and effort involved,[91] and that they may simply discharge uncooperative patients prematurely.[92] If so, the true incidence of significant refusal would be underestimated by examining only cases that reach formal review.

One way around the problem of accurately estimating the incidence of refusal is to examine patients' behavior on the hospital wards themselves. Understandably, few investigators have pursued this more costly approach to data gathering; but when they have, their results have pointed to a higher overall incidence of refusal. Incidence of refusal at any point during hospitalization was 24 percent in one study on an acute psychiatric unit (although most refusals were resolved within 24 hours)[93] and 17 percent among geriatric patients on a general hospital unit.[94] The largest study of this sort, reported by psychiatrist Steven K. Hoge and colleagues, prospectively identified all refusals that lasted more than 24 hours on acute wards in four public psychiatric facilities in Massachusetts.[95] The investigators found that 7.2 percent of patients refused antipsychotic medications. In contrast, had refusal in this study been identified only by tracking the cases that reached the stage of judicial review, the incidence would have been reported as 1.3 percent.

Integrating the results from all available studies, regardless of methodology, the general conclusion appears to be that an average of less than 10 percent of patients refuse antipsychotic medication when given the opportunity to do so. Although this hardly represents the epidemic that was originally feared, it does constitute a substantial number of medication refusers. The contagion model of treatment refusal—which anticipated that rejection of medication would spread from patient to patient on a hospital ward—seems to have been exaggerated, but refusal is certainly not uncommon.

Interestingly, the variation in incidence figures across jurisdictions does not depend on the extent of refusal rights granted patients or on the mechanism (administrative vs. judicial) in place for reviewing their refusals. Fluctuation in the number of reported refusers undoubtedly relates to such factors as the nature of the patient population, the degree to which a "patients' rights" orientation is prevalent in the community, and (for the majority of studies, which are based on records of the review process itself) the pressures that deter treating psychiatrists from pursuing the review process or impel them to do so.[96]

In one class of psychiatric facilities, however, the incidence of treatment refusal comes closer to the epidemic levels predicted when the right to refuse antipsychotic medications was first announced: forensic hospitals. These facilities generally treat mentally ill persons who are involved in the criminal justice system. Patients may be pretrial detainees, whose competence to proceed to trial is impaired by mental illness; persons who are found not guilty by reason of insanity, but who are too dangerous to themselves or others to warrant release to the community; and prisoners who are transferred for evaluation and treatment from penitentiaries, where they have become seriously mentally impaired and disruptive.

Incidence of treatment refusal in the half-dozen studies of forensic hospitals published to date (based on those cases reaching formal review) ranges from a low end of 11 and 13 percent,[97] to midrange figures of 24, 35, and 36 percent,[98] to a high of 45 percent.[99] This last figure, reported from Wisconsin's forensic hospital by psychiatrist Robert Miller and colleagues, becomes even more striking when examined closely. Among patients already receiving medications when the Wisconsin Supreme Court recognized a right to refuse treatment, 29 percent refused antipsychotics at some point in the following six months. Among patients admitted after the court ruling, however, Miller and co-workers found a staggering rate of refusal of 75 percent.[100]

The reasons for the divergence in incidence of refusal in civil and forensic hospitals are probably related to the differing incentives for patients to refuse treatment. Pretrial detainees and prisoners may have a stronger "rights orientation" than civil patients, a more adversarial relationship with the hospital, and greater access to legal counsel, who can advise them of their rights. Moreover, although secondary gain from remaining ill is not entirely absent in civil settings (for example, homeless patients get a safe place to live, with decent food, clothing, and activities as long as they remain hospitalized), it is much greater in the forensic hospital. Defendants who want to avoid standing trial and prisoners who would rather stay in the hospital than be transferred back to the penitentiary have obvious incentives to refuse medications. In contrast, persons found not guilty by reason of insanity, who often get released when their disorders are brought under control, may have strong reasons to take medications. Unfortunately, none of the reports from the forensic facilities break down refusers by type (such as pretrial defendants vs. defendants acquitted by reason of insanity vs. sentenced prisoners) in a manner that would allow us to test this hypothesis.

Although the incidence of refusal of medication—at least in civil facilities—is lower than was expected, it is nonetheless substantial. What about the other predictions critics made regarding the promulgation of a right to refuse treatment? Did they, too, come to pass, albeit not on the scale originally feared? Fortunately, published data allow us to examine the other predictions directly.

Another major concern of psychiatrists was that the incidence of violence among patients who had refused medication would skyrocket, forcing changes in the organization of psychiatric hospitals that would turn them into prisons. Concerns about increased rates of violence appear, to some extent, to have been justified. Most studies addressing this issue use the incidence of seclusion and restraint of patients as a proxy (and given contemporary practices, probably a reasonable one) for actual violence. With rare exceptions,[101] studies comparing rates of seclusion and restraint in refusers and nonrefusers or on hospital wards before and after the introduction of a right to refuse treatment found increases among refusers or after refusal became possible.[102]

The differences in rates of violence and attempts to control it by means of seclusion or restraint were, in many cases, quite striking. Psychiatrist Paul Rodenhauser and colleagues, reporting from an Ohio forensic facility, found that 63 percent of refusing patients required restraint, as compared with 25 percent of nonrefusers.[103] In the civil hospitals they studied in Massachusetts, Hoge and coworkers found significantly higher rates of seclusion and restraint among refusers (47 percent versus 19 percent among control patients), as well as higher rates of assaults and threats of assault (49 incidents versus 15).[104] Comparable results were obtained in the Minnesota state forensic hospital, where 35 percent of refusers, but no control patients, required seclusion.[105]

Although the data do appear to validate the concerns of critics about increases in violence, it is more difficult to demonstrate that the predicted consequence—the transformation of the hospital environment into a penal setting—in fact has occurred. Although rates of assault are up, assaults remain relatively rare events. One California hospital, for example, reported that yearly rates of assaults increased from 5 to more than 20 after the state adopted a rights-driven treatment refusal policy.[106] But even so, assaults occur roughly once every two weeks. Since refusing patients typically constitute a small minority of the in-patient population, the impact of their violence on the hospital milieu, although real, is limited.

Efforts to measure other negative effects of the right to refuse treatment on hospital wards have been infrequent. An Ohio study of two civil hospitals was probably the most ambitious of the type.[107] The authors found that most staff members who responded to their questionnaire believed that patients became increasingly agitated and dangerous without medications. Staff members reported increased use of seclusion and restraint, more stress on patients and staff, and a higher rate of injuries. Data from the hospitals, however, showed no change in the number of major incidents, and significant drops in the rates of patients' assaults on other patients and of self-inflicted harm. Observations of patients' behavior revealed no changes in the activities in which they engaged, or the percentages of time they spent on them. Both staff and patients reported positive changes in the atmosphere on the ward, including higher levels of perceived support and autonomy, although staff also reported more anger and aggression.

Not all studies reported such positive effects of introducing a right to refuse treatment. In California, one study documented a rise in the level of acuity—that is, the overall degree of symptomatology displayed by patients on the ward—presumably as a result of a larger number of untreated patients.[108] And Hoge et al.'s Massachusetts study found that clinicians reported negative effects on the ward milieu in 50 percent of the cases of refusal, caused by patients' reactions ranging from assaultiveness to withdrawn, psychotic behavior.[109]

Overall, life on psychiatric units, for both patients and staff members, has probably become more difficult following judicial recognition of a right to refuse treatment. The wards are more dangerous and probably less pleasant in other ways. But no one suggests that psychiatric hospitals—even state facilities—have become like prisons. There are no reports in the literature of open wards being locked, security personnel being added, or greater restrictions being placed on patients' privileges in the wake of a right to refuse treatment. And although one study reported that the "emotional drain on staff has increased tremendously" and "staff morale is at a real low" because of increased assaults,[110] there is no evidence of a mass outflow of staff members because a right to refuse treatment was adopted. Again, the results appear to justify some—but by no means all—of the fears of most psychiatrists.

Accepting that some disruption of the treatment milieu by unmedicated patients has occurred, what has been the impact on their treatment? Psychiatrists worried that patients whose refusals were upheld—particularly in systems where judges, rather than clinicians or administrators, made the decision—would deteriorate and languish indefinitely on the back wards of mental hospitals. The claim that thousands of patients would become permanent residents of our psychiatric wards, "rotting with their rights on," was a potent, emotionally charged argument for psychiatrists who opposed the right to refuse treatment. The likelihood that this would come to pass, however, seems to have been exaggerated.

The best evidence that it is not happening is derived from prospective studies of treatment refusal, which have failed to identify patients who need medication but do not receive it. In Hoge and colleagues' Massachusetts study of 103 patients who refused medication for longer than 24 hours, 18 percent ultimately were treated against their will.[111] What happened to the remainder? Did they "rot with their rights on"? In fact, the Hoge et al. data show that 54 percent of the refusing patients reaccepted medication voluntarily after a mean refusal time of seven days. An additional 23 percent of refusers were permitted by their treating psychiatrists to continue rejecting medication; in almost half of these cases, the physicians said that the patients' desire for a trial period without medications was not medically unreasonable. In most of the remaining cases for which data were available, the psychiatrists felt that it would be in the long-term interests of patients for the hospital to go along with their decisions for the time being. Most significantly of all, in no case was medication successfully refused when psychiatrists believed that it was needed urgently to prevent deterioration. Thus, the study did not identify any patients who were "rotting with their rights on."

To be sure, anecdotal reports describe patients who have been confined without treatment, ultimately inflicting harm on themselves or on other people.[112] But the psychiatric literature is devoid of studies suggesting that large numbers of patients in need of medication are going untreated because petitions for involuntary treatment have been rejected. It simply does not seem to be happening.

The final gloomy prediction made by opponents of a broad-based right to refuse treatment was that the review processes established to protect the right would be enormously costly, particularly when recourse to the courts was mandated. This prognostication appears to have been right on the mark. Available data address two categories of costs: costs related to the review process itself, and costs of delay while awaiting review.

It is easy to identify the types of costs associated with the review process, but few researchers have attempted to quantify them. Psychiatrists and other clinicians must complete the paperwork required to initiate the process, meet with attorneys, travel to hearings, and spend time waiting and testifying. A Massachusetts Department of Mental Health survey of 18 months of experience under *Rogers* estimated that 4,800 hours of clinical staff time was required for testimony at the 2,216 hearings, with at least another 2,200 hours needed to prepare affidavits and other documents.[113] Another estimate from the same state was that a total of 10.2 hours of a psychiatrist's time was required for each petition taken to judicial review.[114] At the Minnesota forensic hospital, researchers estimated that the costs incurred in processing sixteen refusing patients over two years totaled $150,000.[115]

Clinical staff, of course, are not the only people whose time is occupied in reviewing patients' objections to treatment. When judicial hearings are needed, the time of judges, court personnel, and attorneys for both parties must be taken into account. The Massachusetts Department of Mental Health found that, over the 18 months of the study, handling petitions required 10,500 hours of attorney time and 3,000 hours of paralegal time for the department alone.[116] To my knowledge, no one has attempted to quantify the time of independent evaluators, patients' attorneys, judges, and court personnel.

The second category of costs that arise in the course of reviewing patients' objections to treatment stems from the delay while a decision is awaited. Most hospitals that have utilized clinical/administrative review have been able to arrange for relatively prompt review, minimizing this effect.[117] Judicial review, however, has been plagued by delays. One year of statewide data in New York showed that the average time between filing a petition and the hearing itself was 38 days.[118] Multiplying that figure by the total number of refusers during that year yielded an estimate of 15,000 hospital days spent waiting for review, at an approximate cost of $3.4 million. Figures from one Minnesota hospital revealed that it took an average of 80 days for court review,[119] and Massachusetts data show delays averaging two to four months.[120] Results from other studies are consistent with these findings.[121] The expenses associated with delay are among the most formidable that have been documented to date.

Overall, the empirical data on the impact of the right to refuse treatment present a mixed picture. Refusal is not uncommon, but neither is it epidemic in most civil facilities. The wards are undoubtedly less pleasant and more unsafe, yet they have not come to resemble cell blocks. The costs of the review processes—particularly when they are run by the courts—are substantial, and they are especially onerous for a mental health system that is chronically strapped for funds. On the other hand, despite these effects, patients in need do not seem to go permanently untreated. Clearly, the predicted demise of in-patient (especially public) psychiatry has not occurred.

Factors Modifying the Impact of the Right to Refuse Treatment

Psychiatrists, as we have seen in several instances, are not circumspect in their response to legal developments that affect their field. Their reaction to the right to refuse treatment was no exception; and indeed, the validity of some of their concerns was confirmed by experience. Two of their predictions, however, proved to be inaccurate: the incidence of treatment refusal was much less, in most settings, than psychiatrists had feared; and long-term refusers—those who were supposed to be "rotting with their rights on"—are evidently quite uncommon. The unexpected mildness of these two effects has substantially mitigated the anticipated negative impact of the right to refuse treatment. Why they were not disastrously severe (as most psychiatrists had prophesied) demands explanation.

The roots of psychiatrists' overestimation of the likely incidence of refusal of treatment lay deep in the popular skepticism toward psychiatry discussed in Chapter 1. It is difficult not to be influenced by what one hears or reads in the media, even when one perhaps ought to know better. By the late 1970s, media coverage of psychiatry for nearly two decades had been replete with attacks on the quality of psychiatric care and on the inadequacies of psychiatrists themselves. One clear implication of these attacks was that, without the power of coercion (including the ability to coerce treatment), psychiatry would wither and die as patients rejected care.[122]

However stoutly psychiatrists resisted the critiques of the labeling theorists and other "anti-psychiatrists," they inevitably were affected by them. Many psychiatrists wondered about the legitimacy of the powers they wielded,[123] and some tried to reject them altogether.[124] Most psychiatrists, of course, remained firm in the belief that mental illness deserved treatment, and that the disordering effects of such illness often meant that the patient had to receive treatment involuntarily. But they felt embattled and came to believe that many—even most—patients and a large segment of the general public would reject their views. Perhaps, if psychiatrists lost their coercive powers, they might find few patients with serious mental illnesses who were willing to accept their ministrations.

Psychiatrists' misreading of the probable extent of treatment refusal emanated, in part, from this mind-set. Many psychiatrists assumed that medication refusal would be rampant and contagious, especially among involuntary patients who had already refused voluntary hospitalization. They believed that, if one patient on a unit refused medication, the others would follow suit as soon as they realized that they could "get away with it." Ironically, this assumption was premised on acceptance of several of the core arguments of psychiatry's most severe critics: that medications do disproportionately little good for most patients, considering their side-effects; that most patients, recognizing this poor benefit/risk ratio, would reject medications if permitted to do so; and conversely, that only the threat of coercion keeps patients taking their medications.[125] Given this model, it was logical to decry the right to refuse treatment as the beginning of the end of in-patient psychiatry.

Yet even in jurisdictions where the most expansive right to refuse treatment is recognized—in Massachusetts, for example—only a small percentage of patients (under 10 percent on average) refuse medications for significant periods of time. Involuntary patients are no more likely to refuse treatment than voluntary patients.[126] Even most patients who express strong doubts about whether they have an illness or whether they need treatment acquiesce to taking medications.[127]

What do these data say about the assumptions underlying the contagion model of treatment refusal? It appears that psychiatrists were misled by the loud protestations of a small number of current and former patients. Most patients, even when they are unwilling to endorse the idea that they may be ill or in need of treatment, appear to recognize at some fundamental level their need for care and the utility of the medications prescribed for their treatment. Surveys of patient groups support this idea. Among mentally ill persons in California who responded to a patient-initiated questionnaire, 51 percent said that they found medications "very helpful" or "somewhat helpful." Almost two-thirds described taking medication as one of their "coping reactions to stress."[128]

These attitudes appear to extend, at least in part, to involuntary treatment. In an Ohio study, 63 percent of patients said that they should *not* be able to refuse medication when they were "not in control" or "dangerous."[129] Only 20 percent said they should be able to refuse under all circumstances. At their time of discharge from a New York hospital, seventeen of twenty-four patients who had been treated with medications against their will reported that they believed the medication had been necessary and important for their successful treatment.[130] The resistance of most patients to taking medication appears to be a myth.

There is, of course, another possible explanation for the relatively low rate of treatment refusal—one less reassuring to psychiatry. Perhaps, since most refusing patients whose cases are taken to formal review are ultimately treated, other patients learn that attempts to refuse medication are futile. Given the rates of overturned refusals, especially in states with judicial review, this explanation is somewhat plausible. But it ignores important data from the prospective studies. Most patients who refuse medication do not reach the stage of being compelled to reaccept it by reviewing authorities; they drop their refusal "voluntarily." (Some patients, of course, may feel pressured to accept medication by the prospect of prolonged hospitalization as a consequence of their refusal.) And a substantial number (almost one-quarter in Hoge et al.'s Massachusetts study) are "successful" refusers: their refusal goes unchallenged.[131] It seems unlikely, therefore, that the prospect of coercion per se is critical (although it may sometimes occur) to mentally ill persons' acceptance of treatment with medication. Instead, it appears that psychiatrists were simply too quick to assimilate the prejudices of their critics.

Why so few patients remain hospitalized and go permanently untreated—or in the pungent phrase of the era, "rot with their rights on"—is more difficult to answer. One might expect, as many psychiatrists clearly did, that some proportion of refusing patients would be found competent to decide about treatment and yet would not be ready for discharge from the hospital. That proportion might be particularly high if their refusal was ratified by judges who were sympathetic to patients' rights and skeptical of the effects of antipsychotic medications. If the medications were essential to these patients' treatment, they could be expected to deteriorate—or at least not to improve—and to languish indefinitely on hospital wards. Each element of the chain of logic makes sense, but such patients are evidently so scarce that it is difficult to identify even one. Why?

In part, psychiatrists seem to have misjudged the extent to which treatment refusal would become a legal, rather than a clinical problem. The implicit conceptual model on which they based their assumptions stipulated that refusal would occur when patients were implacably hostile to psychiatry, when they were unable to recognize their mental disorders, or when they harbored bizarre or paranoid delusions about the intentions of treating physicians. If opposition to treatment were based on these grounds, patients could not be "talked out of" their refusals. Consequently, if refusals were to be resolved, large-scale external intervention would be necessary, with all the costs that would imply.

Data from studies that inquired into the reasons for patients' refusal of treatment challenge these conclusions. To be sure, large percentages of refusal evidently were based on denial or delusions.[132] But a substantial percentage of patients who refused treatment appeared to rest their decisions on factors that may not have been irrational at all. In the Hoge and colleagues study from Massachusetts, 35 percent of patients cited side effects of the medications as the basis of their refusal.[133] A California report put this figure at 24 percent; a study from New York, at 40 percent; and one from Ohio, at 34 percent.[134] When records of the review process in Ohio were examined, 14 percent of patients claimed at their hearings that they were refusing because of side-effects.[135] Furthermore, some patients who say that the medication is not helping them (another frequently offered reason for refusal) are probably right. Rather than manifesting denial of their illness, they may simply be reporting accurately the limitations of therapeutic effectiveness on conditions that are notoriously difficult to treat.

Just because patients cite side-effects or the ineffectiveness of medications as the reasons for their rejection of treatment, of course, does not mean that denial or delusional factors are not involved. Patients may learn that refusals are more likely to be respected if they complain of side-effects, or they may mistakenly or delusionally believe that physical sensations attributable to some other cause are due to the medication. Evidence presented by Van Putten and colleagues, however, suggests both that side-effects are more common than many clinicians may believe and that they correlate strongly with patient resistance to medication.[136] About one-quarter of patients in their study had a dysphoric response to a single dose of antipsychotic medication, and two-thirds of the dysphoric group stopped their medications within two weeks.[137]

If a large percentage of patients' refusals originate in real problems they are having with antipsychotic medications, rather than in hostility to psychiatry or in phenomena such as denial or illness-based delusions, it should be possible to end many refusals by negotiating with patients about the dose and type of medication. Such patients should be susceptible to reassurance that certain effects are not related to the medications at all, or that they can be reduced by the addition of another drug that counteracts some of the effects of the first medication. In fact, this is exactly what the data suggest. Recall that, in Hoge et al.'s prospective study, 54 percent of patients reaccepted medication voluntarily after discussions with their psychiatrist.[138] An early study of treatment refusal, conducted soon after the initial order in *Rogers,* found that twenty-three of twenty-eight refusers restarted their medication within 24 hours.[139] Although the data are less direct, similar findings can be identified from other studies. One-third of all petitions for judicial review in New York State are withdrawn before the hearing occurs, suggesting that the negotiation process continues even as both sides await their day in court.[140] Ohio data show that a substantial number of refusers agree to accept medication at each of the early stages of the state's multilevel review process.[141]

Another outcome of negotiation also appears possible. When patients' refusals are based on reasonable perceptions of a poor benefit/risk ratio (which may be the case for chronic patients with intractable symptoms), they may be able to persuade their psychiatrists to respect their desires to decline medication. Or patients may argue for a trial period off the prescribed medications to see whether they can manage without them, which is often a reasonable treatment strategy. Hoge et al.'s data show that nearly half of the 23 percent of refusals that ended without patients' being treated fell into these or similar categories.[142] Moreover, psychiatrists may decide to abide by patients' requests for now, hoping to win them over in time and not wanting to alienate them entirely from the treatment process.

Thus, to the extent that psychiatrists saw treatment refusal as an issue that, once raised, could only be resolved by the courts, they misinterpreted the phenomenon. Refusal based on delusions or outright denial of the disorder is not uncommon, of course, and it can indeed be intractable. But most instances of refusal of medication, whatever the basis for the initial decision by the patient, are resolved fairly rapidly by clinical negotiation and never reach formal review by the courts or any other body. Consequently, although it is not rare, refusal is usually self-limited and its clinical consequences are usually abbreviated. Failure to recognize these realities explains much of the psychiatric profession's overestimation of the negative impact of a right to refuse treatment.

Another part of the reason for the failure to detect patients "rotting" in hospital wards, however, may have less positive implications. During the 1980s and early 1990s, as pressures from state officials (in the public sector) and third-party payers (in the private sector) led to sharp decreases in average length of stay,[143] psychiatrists probably became more comfortable about discharging patients who were still quite symptomatic. Thus, some individuals who might otherwise have languished untreated in the hospital now roam the streets untreated and just as ill. It is difficult to estimate the degree to which this is occurring, but such a process is consistent with the "racheting-up" of standards for gaining admission to and remaining in a psychiatric facility or unit, as described in Chapter 2.

Outcomes of the small percentage of cases that reach the review process indicate that psychiatrists also miscalculated the results that would follow from the process of reviewing refusals, particularly when that process was placed in judicial hands. Most psychiatric commentators assumed that judges would generally (or at least frequently) uphold patients' refusals, supporting their civil liberties against the coercive power of the state. In fact, however, that has rarely been the case. A review by the Massachusetts Department of Mental Health of 18 months' experience with judicial review of patients' refusals, as required by the decision in *Rogers,* showed that 98.6 percent of 1,514 cases resulted in approval of the petition for involuntary treatment.[144] Other Massachusetts studies have yielded comparable figures.[145] In New York, rates of judicial override of refusals have been reported at 80 percent (for a forensic facility),[146] 87 percent,[147] 91 percent,[148] 92 percent,[149] 95 percent,[150] and 100 percent.[151] California figures range from 76 percent[152] to 88 percent[153] to 100 percent.[154] A Minnesota study reported that 100 percent of cases submitted to a court resulted in an order for involuntary treatment;[155] results from a Wisconsin forensic hospital were identical;[156] and a Washington State study found judicial treatment orders were issued 90 percent of the time.[157]

Interestingly, the results are somewhat different in instances of review by clinical or administrative processes that avoid the courts. These are more likely to *uphold* patients' refusals. Although several studies show 94 to 100 percent rates of override of patients' objections after review by the medical director of a hospital or an independent clinician,[158] some of the lowest rates of override also derive from these systems. Medical director review resulted in rates of approval of treatment of only 71 percent[159] and 80 percent[160] in an Ohio forensic hospital,[161] and of 65 percent in a New York civil facility.[162] A subsequent clinical/administrative review process adopted in Ohio, in which a panel reviewed refusals utilizing a rights-driven model, with several levels of appeal possible, yielded override rates of 51 percent and 81 percent in two civil facilities.[163] A larger Ohio study of six months' experience at eight hospitals found override rates of 77 percent.[164] Two studies of a similar review process in Minnesota found 67 percent of refusers treated involuntarily in one study,[165] and 87 percent in another.[166]

In any event, it is clear that only a small minority of refusals are upheld by the reviewing body; and given the continuing trend toward judicial review, the percentage is likely to become even smaller in the future. The feared scenario of untreated patients deteriorating, becoming violent, and filling the back wards has not happened, because almost all cases pursued to court (which appear to be the cases in which psychiatrists feel most strongly that treatment with medication is needed) or—to a lesser degree—to clinical/administrative review systems result in orders for treatment.

Why is this the case? Clearly, a good deal of triage takes place before the hearings occur. Most refusers agree to reaccept medication. Some petitions are dropped or never initiated because the psychiatrist is persuaded that a trial period without medication is reasonable, the patient will be found competent, or the refusal will be upheld on some other grounds. Thus, it seems likely that only the strongest cases for overriding refusal—involving patients whose refusal is linked to the effects of their illnesses, and who can therefore be considered incompetent to make treatment decisions—reach the hearing stage.

It is probably true, as well, that the patients most feared by psychiatrists are relatively rare: patients who need medications but refuse them on reasonable grounds, and then deteriorate significantly but not to such an extent that they become incompetent and can be treated involuntarily. Persistent refusers, when competent, either tend to be able to negotiate some compromise with their caregivers or are sufficiently intact to be able to survive outside the hospital, encouraging administrators to discharge them. Permission for involuntary treatment appears to be easy to obtain.

Yet in some respects the figures for override of patients' refusals by the courts are too one-sided. It is plausible that studies from so many jurisdictions should show that *no* refusals, or at most only a tiny percentage, are upheld? In the Massachusetts Department of Mental Health study, for example, were 98.6 percent of the 1,514 patients reviewed really incompetent, and would that many of them have consented to medication if they had been competent to do so (the latter conclusion embodying the "substituted judgment" criterion required under Massachusetts law)?[167]

Unfortunately, observational studies of the kind that helped us understand the civil commitment process have not been conducted with hearings on treatment refusal. Thus, we are left to speculate in a more or less informed fashion. In this regard, it seems warranted to conclude that some of the same factors that impel judges at civil commitment hearings to hospitalize patients who are brought before them—even when the criteria for commitment are, strictly speaking, not met—are at work here. The commonsense model of decision making for the mentally ill may be employed for refusal of treatment as well.[168] Regardless of the legal standard, it may be difficult for judges to forbid treatment of people who are obviously mentally ill and distressed and who, according to their physicians, would benefit from such treatment.

Are the paradoxical figures showing that panels staffed by clinicians and administrators are more likely than the courts to uphold patients' refusals compatible with this explanation? In light of their clinical training, why aren't the members of these panels even more moved than are judges to impose treatment whenever they see the need for it? Although the suggestion here is reasonable, two explanations may account for the apparent anomaly. First, the experienced clinicians and administrators who staff the review panels may simply have a firmer basis for disagreeing with the judgment of psychiatrists who request authority to treat over patients' objections. Unlike judges, they can find independent grounds for refusing permission to treat—for example, a conclusion that medication is unlikely to benefit the patient.[169]

Second, clinicians seem to be more willing to take cases to the clinical panels than they are to go to court. This may relate to the extra time and paperwork required for court hearings, or perhaps to the greater discomfort of being subjected to cross-examination and other formalities of the legal process. Whatever the explanation, data from several facilities in New York before and after the shift from clinical/administrative review panels to the system of judicial review show drops of 60 percent or more in the number of cases brought for review.[170] This may mean that more "borderline" cases, in which the decision about whether to treat over patients' objections is a close call, come before clinical review panels, resulting in a larger proportion of cases in which permission to treat is refused.[171]

More detailed studies of the decision-making process would be welcome; but whatever the explanation, the tendency of judges to agree with petitioning psychiatrists and to authorize treatment is clearly overwhelming. This is one more factor that has mitigated the impact of a right to refuse treatment, but perhaps at the cost of denying some competent patients the right to make their own decisions about treatment.

The Future of the Right to Refuse Treatment

The right to refuse treatment with medication continues to be one of the most contentious issues in mental health law. Each side uses the available empirical data to promote its case. Psychiatrists, who are still overwhelmingly hostile to the practice, point to the very real costs associated with allowing committed patients to refuse treatment. In addition, they speculate about as yet unmeasured costs, including the possibility that patients for whom treatment with medication is delayed may subsequently suffer more severe and intractable mental disorders.[172] Patients' rights advocates point out that the most extreme predictions of the doomsayers never occurred, and they argue that the system can tolerate the cost of respecting patients' decisionmaking rights.

As with so many of the policy debates in the field of mental health, empirical data may inform the discussion, but they do not resolve it. Ultimately, what one thinks about the right to refuse treatment turns on an interaction between the available data and one's beliefs about the purposes of civil commitment of the mentally ill. The key question that must be answered is: Does it make sense to hospitalize persons against their will and then allow them to refuse treatment for the conditions that precipitated their confinement?

Adherents of a quarantine model of civil commitment respond with a resounding, "Yes." They view the state as having a limited right to intervene in people's lives, and they accept governmental intrusions only when the safety of other persons is at stake or when the subjects of the interventions themselves may be endangered. State action is legitimate in these circumstances, they argue, only insofar as it is needed to ameliorate the immediate threat. Once safety is assured, the government must back off. Thus, since hospitalization is frequently sufficient to protect patients and others from the consequences of their illnesses, the state's interest extends only to effecting such persons' confinement.[173]

What makes this reasoning problematic is that the state has generally chosen not to exercise its power to protect persons from themselves or other people prospectively. Where harm to other people is concerned, the state limits its interventions to situations in which criminal acts already have occurred. Part of the justification for punishing such acts may be a desire to protect the community from further danger. But a prediction that a person will act in a harmful fashion—even a prediction that seems very well founded—constitutes an insufficient basis for state intervention.[174] This is why recidivistic violent felons are released from prison at the end of their sentences even if they give every indication (and indeed express the intention) of committing violent crimes in the future.

Similarly, the state generally allows persons whose behavior may endanger their own lives to take significant risks without interference. Mountain climbers, bungee jumpers, hang gliders, and auto racers bear testament to our tolerance for hazardous pastimes. People who smoke, drink alcohol to excess, and fail to wear seatbelts benefit, as it were, from a similar degree of tolerance. The passion aroused by exceptions to this rule—witness the debates over motorcycle helmet laws, seat belt laws, and criminal penalties for possession of marijuana and other illegal drugs—confirms the validity of the general principle. Furthermore, the exceptions are usually justified on the basis of the impact of the prohibited practices on third parties (for example, the economic costs of treating motorcyclists with head injuries), rather than on the victims themselves.

Mentally ill people, however, are treated differently. In every state in this country, and in most nations around the world, they may be confined preventively merely on the basis of a prediction of their exhibiting behavior harmful to others or to themselves. The quarantine theories of civil commitment fail to explain this anomaly. Why can we quarantine the mentally ill, but not other people?

The obvious place to begin a search for the answer is in some characteristic peculiar to mental illness. But plausible possibilities must be separated from implausible ones. It cannot be, for example, that the state can preventively confine mentally ill persons because they are more likely to be dangerous than are people who are not mentally ill. To begin with, the data supporting this proposition are equivocal.[175] Moreover, we do not confine the mentally ill as a class; instead, we require individualized determinations of the likelihood of dangerous behavior, based (in many jurisdictions) on evidence of acts in the recent past. What stops us from doing the same with persons who are not mentally ill but who are seen as threats to public safety?

Nor can it persuasively be argued, as some have tried to do, that the unpredictability of the mentally ill makes them more fitting subjects for prospective interventions, once some probability of dangerous behavior has been shown. If their behavior is indeed less predictable (a claim that, as far as I know, has never been demonstrated), it should be exceptionally difficult to identify mentally ill persons who require confinement. Why not instead focus the state's attention and resources on neutralizing the purportedly more predictable, mentally healthy threats to public order and safety? Beyond that, it is difficult to see why unpredictability is a suitable criterion on which to base a distinction of this degree of importance. Few victims would care (except perhaps for purposes of a lawsuit for negligence against the wrongdoer's guarantor) whether the person who injured them was acting predictably or unpredictably.

Does the impaired decisionmaking competence that often attends mental illness provide an explanation for the differential treatment of the mentally ill? Perhaps it did in an earlier time, when mental illness and incompetence were believed to be coterminous. State laws now generally recognize, however, that most mentally ill people are not legally incompetent. Yet, few states include incompetence as one of the criteria that must be met before commitment can be effected. Some commentators argue in favor of limiting commitment, for reasons of fairness, to incompetent persons. But there is no evidence, in most jurisdictions, that the current system looks to incompetence as a justification for committing the mentally ill.

Much more reasonable, it seems to me, is the conclusion that we target mentally ill persons for intervention because their problematic behavior is thought likely to be ameliorated in a manner beneficial both to them and to society at large. Insofar as their violence or attempts at self-harm derive from their illnesses, treatment serves the dual function of bringing their distressing symptoms under control and diminishing the risks they pose to others and to themselves. Although the desire to protect society is insufficient justification in our constitutional system for depriving persons of liberty when they have not been convicted of committing a crime, the additional paternalistic rationale tips the balance. The therapeutic restraints on freedom that encumber mentally ill people do not just work to the advantage of the mentally healthy majority; they help the mentally ill, as well.[176]

This analysis suggests that an inherently paternalistic element exists even in so-called "police power"–based commitment statutes. Quarantine is not enough to justify confinement indefinitely, even when harm to others alone motivates commitment. Treatment must also be provided. To fail to treat committed persons, when that treatment is essential for them to regain their liberty, undercuts the rationale that legitimates civil commitment. It permits, at least in theory, the indefinite detention of persons who have not committed crimes, denying their right to liberty while offering them no corresponding gain.

What of the argument that it is unjust to treat competent persons against their will? If we are serious about according competent persons the right to run their own lives, the proper question before us is: Why are we committing competent people in the first place? Is it because they are dangerous to other people? If so, and if they have competently declined treatment, let them bear the criminal sanctions that any other citizen would face for acts of violence. Is it because they are dangerous to themselves? If so, and if they are truly competent, let them determine the risks they choose to run, just as we let competent medical patients decline even potentially life-saving treatment.

Excluding competent persons from involuntary commitment, as Alan Stone suggested almost two decades ago,[177] would eliminate the disjunction between the power to commit and the power to treat in a manner that accommodated the concerns of civil libertarians and others about trenching on the rights of competent people. Moreover, it would extend those persons' right of refusal to proposed hospitalization—a significant interference with their liberty—not merely to proposed administering of medication.

There may be reasons why our social system chooses not to go this route. Adding incompetence as a criterion for involuntary commitment would shrink the number of persons eligible for hospitalization as compared with current dangerousness-based criteria.[178] The ability to confine dangerous but competent persons in hospitals is undoubtedly useful in some cases, for political and other reasons, even if the legitimacy of such actions is suspect. Our society may not be willing to give up this option.

If this is the preferred choice, as it has been in most states to date, it implies that even competent people may be hospitalized for their good and for the general welfare. It reflects a societal decision to limit the powers of competent persons to choose how to lead their lives. Given that involuntary hospitalization of the mentally ill can only be justified paternalistically, what is the logic behind allowing persons who cannot choose whether to avoid hospitalization to choose whether to decline treatment? Having made an initial decision to intervene (at least partially) for the benefit of competent mentally ill persons, we should bite the bullet and take the next step as well, permitting nonconsensual treatment when that is necessary for the restoration of their freedom. Otherwise, we undermine the legitimacy of the entire process.[179]

To stop the argument here, however, is to ignore the import of the empirical studies of treatment refusal. Allowing patients to object to treatment, forcing reappraisal of their situation by the treating physician or by outside reviewers, often results in a decision to alter treatment, and sometimes in a decision to suspend it altogether. This suggests that the process of review has some utility—a conclusion that, on reflection, should not be surprising. Standards in psychiatric hospitals (particularly state hospitals) have often been poor, and this was a motivating force in at least some of the early treatment refusal cases.[180] But permitting patients (unless they are found to be incompetent) to refuse treatment that is necessary for the restoration of their freedom is an odd mechanism indeed for addressing the quality of care. If our central concern is about the adequacy of treatment, why should a patient have to refuse medication before independent review of this issue takes place? Are more passive patients to be punished with neglect because of their compliance?

It would be far better to insist that the treatment of every patient be reviewed for appropriateness, as is routinely done in teaching hospitals, where attending psychiatrists, subspecialty consultants, and outside clinicians accomplish that goal. To do so would require additional resources, to be sure, but there seem to have been few problems in covering the costs of expensive, time-consuming judicial review procedures. One would like to think that it would be equally possible to generate the funds needed to pay for interventions that are directly aimed at improving the quality of care.

At its core, the right to refuse treatment is a logical conundrum. In the guise of granting patients decisionmaking rights, it fosters a stunted form of paternalism that cannot fulfill the goals that alone justify commitment. It may be that the tendency of judges to go along with psychiatrists' recommendations for treatment reflects their discomfort with this situation and their effort to set it straight.[181] But as I argued in the context of civil commitment in Chapter 2, to rely on such behavior to compensate for counterproductive legal rules is less desirable than to change the rules themselves.

The costs of the right to refuse treatment—admittedly somewhat less than critics had feared—are not worth bearing, given that more attractive alternatives exist for achieving the rather modest benefits. Protecting the rights of competent persons can be accomplished more effectively by excluding competent mentally ill people from the reach of commitment statutes. Short of that, it makes no sense to create a system that allows us to hospitalize people against their will and then decline to treat them with medication, when such treatment is essential to their regaining their liberty.

References

1. H. Hurd, ed., *The Institutional Care of the Insane in the United States and Canada,* vol. 2 (New York: Arno Press, 1973) [reprint of 1916 ed. (Baltimore, Johns Hopkins Press)], pp. 645–53.
2. G. N. Grob, *Mental Illness and American Society: 1875–1940* (Princeton, N.J.: Princeton University Press, 1983), pp. 224–28.
3. L. V. Briggs, *History of the Psychopathic Hospital, Boston, Massachusetts* (New York: Arno Press, 1973) [reprint of 1922 ed. (Boston: Wright & Potter)].
4. P. S. Appelbaum, "Can Mental Patients Say No to Drugs?" *New York Times Magazine,* March 21, 1982, pp. 46ff.
5. *Rogers v. Okin,* 478 F. Supp. 1342 (D. Mass. 1979). Other allegations in the suit dealt with the use of seclusion and restraint at the facility, allegedly in violation of state law.
6. A. Deutsch, *The Mentally Ill in America,* 2d ed. (New York: Columbia University Press, 1949).
7. E. S. Valentine, *Great and Desperate Cures: The Rise and Decline of Psychosurgery and Other Radical Treatments for Mental Illness* (New York: Basic Books, 1986).

8. For discussions of the history of informed consent, see P. S. Appelbaum, C. W. Lidz, and A. Meisel, *Informed Consent: Legal Theory and Clinical Practice* (New York: Oxford University Press, 1987); R. R. Faden and T. L. Beauchamp, *A History and Theory of Informed Consent* (New York: Oxford University Press, 1986); and M. S. Pernick, "The Patient's Role in Medical Decisionmaking: A Social History of Informed Consent in Medical Therapy," in *President's Commission for the Study of Ethical Problems in Medicine and Biomedical and Behavioral Research: Making Health Care Decisions,* vol. 3 (Washington, D.C.: U.S. Government Printing Office, 1982), pp. 1–35.

9. *Slater v. Baker and Stapleton,* 95 Eng. Rep. 860 (K.B. 1767), p. 862.

10. *Schloendorff v. Society of New York Hospital,* 105 N.E. 92 (N.Y. 1914), p. 93.

11. Appelbaum, Lidz, and Meisel, *supra* note 8.

12. E. S. Glass, "Restructuring Informed Consent: Legal Therapy for the Doctor-Patient Relationship," *Yale Law Journal* 79: 1533–76 (1970); R. E. Simpson, "Informed Consent: From Disclosure to Patient Participation in Medical Decisionmaking," *Northwestern University Law Review* 76: 172–207 (1981).

13. I. Kant, *Metaphysical Foundation of Morals* (L. W. Beck, Trans.). (Indianapolis, Ind.: Bobbs-Merrill, 1959).

14. J. S. Mill, *On Liberty* (Indianapolis, Ind.: Bobbs-Merrill, 1956).

15. S. J. Brakel and R. S. Rock, *The Mentally Disabled and the Law,* 2d ed. (Chicago: American Bar Foundation, 1971).

16. The first voluntary admission statute was not adopted until Massachusetts passed such a law in 1881, and most admissions to state facilities remained involuntary as late as 1980. S. J. Brakel, "Voluntary Hospitalization," in S. J. Brakel, J. Parry, and B. Weiner, *The Mentally Disabled and the Law,* 3d ed. (Chicago: American Bar Foundation, 1985), pp. 177–201.

17. The theory of who should give substituted consent was not well worked out in nineteenth-century law; but in practice, when family members were available, they usually were relied on for consent to admission and treatment. In their absence, decision making was left, *de facto,* in the hands of physicians. See P. S. Appelbaum and K. N. Kemp, "The Evolution of Commitment Law in the Nineteenth Century: A Reinterpretation," *Law and Human Behavior* 6: 343–54 (1982).

18. M. Kindred, "Guardianship and Limitations upon Capacity," in President's Committee on Mental Retardation, *The Mentally Retarded Citizen and the Law* (New York: Free Press, 1976), pp. 62–87.

19. B. A. Weiner, "Rights of Institutionalized Persons," in S. J. Brakel, J. Parry, and B. Weiner, *The Mentally Disabled and the Law,* 3d ed. (Chicago: American Bar Foundation, 1985), pp. 251–325.

20. B. D. Sales, D. M. Powell, R. Van Duizend, et al., *Disabled Persons and the Law: State Legislative Issues* (New York: Plenum Press, 1982).

21. M. H. Shapiro, "Legislating the Control of Behavior Control: Autonomy and the Coercive Use of Organic Therapies," *Southern California Law Review* 47: 237–356 (1974), pp. 308–09.

22. Massachusetts General Laws, Chap. 123, Secs. 7 and 12.

23. A good summary of these arguments can be found in N. K. Rhoden, "The Right to Refuse Psychotropic Drugs," *Harvard Civil Rights–Civil Liberties Law Review* 15: 363–413 (1980); see also C. J. Dudzik, "The Scope of the Involuntarily Committed Mental Patient's Right to Refuse Treatment with Psychotropic Drugs: An Analysis of the Least Restrictive Alternative Doctrine," *Villanova Law Review* 28: 101–48 (1982–1983).

24. P. R. Friedman, "Legal Regulation of Applied Behavior Analysis in Mental Institutions and Prisons," *Arizona Law Review* 17: 39–104 (1975), p. 74.

25. *Winters v. Miller,* 446 F.2d 65 (2d Cir. 1971).
26. See Shapiro's highly influential discussion of the comparative intrusiveness of treatments, *supra* note 21 at pp. 262ff.
27. *Wyatt v. Stickney,* 344 F. Supp. 373 (M.D. Ala. 1972).
28. *Knecht v. Gilman,* 488 F.2d 1136 (8th Cir. 1973).
29. *Mackey v. Procunier,* 477 F.2d 877 (9th Cir. 1973).
30. *Price v. Sheppard,* 239 N.W.2d 905 (Minn. 1976).
31. The Minnesota court in *Price,* however, based its rationale on an expansive interpretation of the Federal constitutional right of privacy. The *Mackey* court, in its terse opinion, also alluded to this right.
32. *Rogers v. Okin, supra* note 5, at 1367.
33. Id. at 1371.
34. In theory, given the value placed on the right to make one's own decisions, this is the way incompetent decisions of any sort should be overturned. In practice, however, medical treatment decisions for persons thought by their physicians to be incompetent are almost always made by family members, without a judicial determination of the patients' incompetence. See *President's Commission for the Study of Ethical Problems in Medicine and Biomedical and Behavioral Research: Making Health Care Decisions,* vol. 1 (Washington, D.C.: U.S. Government Printing Office, 1982), pp. 182–184. Only when extraordinary treatments are involved (for example, sterilization [P. S. Appelbaum, "The Issue of Sterilization and the Mentally Retarded," *Hospital and Community Psychiatry* 33: 523–24 (1982)]), when no family members are available, or when there is a dispute among family members or between family and physicians do cases involving medical treatment for incompetent patients generally get to court. Depending on the circumstances in such cases, judges may appoint a guardian to make a decision or may authorize treatment themselves. See E. J. Emanuel, "A Review of the Ethical and Legal Aspects of Terminating Medical Care," *American Journal of Medicine* 84: 291–301 (1988); and R. F. Weir and L. Gostin, "Decisions to Abate Life-sustaining Treatment for Nonautonomous Patients: Ethical Standards and Legal Liability for Physicians After *Cruzan." Journal of the American Medical Association* 264: 1846–53 (1990).
35. *Rogers v. Okin,* 634 F.2d 650 (1st Cir. 1980).
36. *Mills v. Rogers,* 457 U.S. 291 (1982).
37. *In the Matter of Richard Roe III,* 421 N.E.2d 40 (Mass. 1981).
38. *Rogers v. Commissioner, Department of Mental Health,* 458 N.E.2d 308 (Mass. 1983). The Massachusetts Supreme Judicial Court's decision was not the end of the tortuous procedural history for *Rogers.* The federal First Circuit Court of Appeals reconsidered the case in light of the state court's findings, and held that the newly declared state law rights (though they exceeded those derived from the federal Constitution) created federally enforceable due process rights under the Fourteenth Amendment. See *Rogers v. Okin,* 738 F.2d 1 (1st Cir. 1984). The case was remanded to the federal district court in which it began for the issuance of a decree to that effect.

Thus, it is the Massachusetts Supreme Judicial Court's decision that ultimately defined the rights of the plaintiffs in *Rogers.* Judge Tauro's original decision and the initial ruling of the First Circuit Court of Appeals were mooted by the subsequent proceedings.
39. For a critique of this standard, see T. G. Gutheil and P. S. Appelbaum, "Substituted Judgment and the Physician's Ethical Dilemma: With Special Reference to the Problem of the Psychiatric Patient," *Journal of Clinical Psychiatry* 41: 303–5 (1980).

40. P. Schaeffer, "Court Rules that Mental Patients Have Right to Refuse Treatment," *Clinical Psychiatry News,* January 1980, p. 1ff.
41. Brief *amicus curiae* of the American Psychiatric Association, *Rogers v. Okin, supra* note 35. Of course, some overstatement is customary in documents of this sort.
42. It is uncommon for judges themselves to achieve much notoriety as a result of the opinions they author. Commentators, even when they strongly disagree with the rationale of an opinion, usually focus on perceived faults in the legal reasoning, without paying a great deal of attention to the author. In the case of *Rogers,* however, considerable venom was directed toward Judge Tauro himself, who was mentioned by name in many psychiatric responses to the case. See, e.g., T. G. Gutheil and P. S. Appelbaum, "The Patient Always Pays: Reflections on the Boston State Case and the Right to Rot," *Man and Medicine* 5: 3–11 (1980); and the comments of Alan Stone ("This judge has totally ignored reality."), *supra* note 40. This is an indication, I think, of just how personally aggrieved psychiatrists were at Judge Tauro's opinion.
43. *Rogers v. Okin, supra* note 5, at 1360.
44. Id. at 1367.
45. Id. at 1360.
46. See, e.g., P. S. Appelbaum and T. G. Gutheil, "The Boston State Hospital Case: 'Involuntary Mind Control,' the Constitution and the 'Right to Rot,' " *American Journal of Psychiatry* 137: 720–23 (1980); S. J. Brakel and J. M. Davis, "Taking Harms Seriously: Involuntary Mental Patients and the Right to Refuse Treatment," *Indiana Law Review* 25: 429–73 (1991); and M. A. Solomon and J. M. Davis, "The Refusal of Antipsychotic Medication: A Clinical View," *Developments in Mental Health Law* 3(1–2): 1ff (January–June 1983).
47. Appelbaum and Gutheil, *supra* note 46.
48. E. F. Walker and J. Rossiter, "Schizophrenic Patients' Self-perceptions: Legal and Clinical Implications," *Journal of Psychiatry and Law* 17: 55–73 (1989); S. E. Taylor, *Positive Illusions: Creative Self-Deception and the Healthy Mind* (New York: Basic Books, 1989), Chapter 6.
49. B. S. Herrington, "U.S. Court Upholds Drug Refusal Right," *Psychiatric News* 14(23): 1ff (December 7, 1979); Brief *amicus curiae,* American Psychiatric Association, *supra* note 41.
50. Brief *amicus curiae,* American Psychiatric Association, *supra* note 41, p. 34.
51. "To Treat or Not to Treat: Who Should Decide? Roche Report," *Frontiers of Psychiatry* 11(3): 1ff (March 1, 1981); S. H. Nelson, "Should There Be a Right to Refuse Treatment?" in A. E. Doudera and J. P. Swazey, eds., *Refusing Treatment in Mental Health Institutions—Values in Conflict* (Ann Arbor, Mich.: AUPHA Press, 1982), pp. 88–94.
52. S. Schultz, "The Boston State Hospital Case: A Conflict of Civil Liberties and True Liberalism," *American Journal of Psychiatry* 139: 183–88 (1982).
53. A. A. Stone, *Law, Psychiatry and Morality* (Washington, D.C.: American Psychiatric Press, 1985), pp. 147–48.
54. Nelson, *supra* note 51, p. 91.
55. T. G. Gutheil, "In Search of True Freedom: Drug Refusal, Involuntary Medication, and 'Rotting with Your Rights On,' " *American Journal of Psychiatry* 137: 327–28 (1980), p. 327.
56. Nelson, *supra* note 51.
57. S. Rachlin, "One Right Too Many," *Bulletin of the American Academy of Psychiatry and the Law* 3: 99–102 (1975).
58. M. J. Mills, J. A. Yesavage, and T. G. Gutheil, "Continuing Case Law Develop-

ment in the Right to Refuse Treatment," *American Journal of Psychiatry* 140: 715–19 (1983); Rachlin, *supra* note 57.

59. Brief *amicus curiae* of the American College of Neuropsychopharmacology, *Rogers v. Okin, supra* note 35.

60. Robert Sovner, M.D., quoted in Appelbaum, *supra* note 4.

61. S. L. Halleck, "Legal and Ethical Aspects of Behavior Control," *American Journal of Psychiatry* 131: 381–85 (1974).

62. A. A. Stone, "The Right to Refuse Treatment: Why Psychiatrists Should and Can Make It Work," *Archives of General Psychiatry* 38: 358–62 (1981), p. 361.

63. M. D. White and C. A. White, "Involuntarily Committed Patients' Constitutional Right to Refuse Treatment: A Challenge to Psychology," *American Psychologist* 36: 953–62 (1981).

64. I. N. Perr, "Refusing Treatment—Who Shall Decide?" *Bulletin of the American Academy of Psychiatry and the Law* 10: 233–47 (1982), p. 235.

65. P. S. Appelbaum, "The Right to Refuse Treatment with Antipsychotic Medications: Retrospect and Prospect," *American Journal of Psychiatry* 145: 413–19 (1988).

66. *Riese v. St. Mary's Hosp. & Medical Center,* 243 Cal. Rptr. 241 (Ct. App. 1987); *People v. Medina,* 705 P.2d 961 (Colo. 1985); *Goedecke v. State Dep't of Institutions,* 603 P.2d 123 (Colo. 1979); *Jarvis v. Levine,* 418 N.W.2d 139 (Minn. 1988); *Rivers v. Katz,* 495 N.E.2d 337 (N.Y. 1986); *In re the Mental Health of K.K.B.,* 609 P.2d 747 (Okla. 1980); *Henderson v. Yocum,* No. M17948A (S.D. Cir. Ct., Feb. 19, 1987); *State ex rel. Jones v. Gerhardstein,* 416 N.W.2d 883 (Wis. 1987).

67. The exception is the Oklahoma court in *In re the Mental Health of K.K.B., supra* note 66.

68. This is consistent with traditional restrictions on the powers of guardians in cases involving extraordinary decisions. See P. S. Appelbaum, "Limitations on Guardianship of the Mentally Disabled," *Hospital and Community Psychiatry* 33: 183–84 (1982);.

69. See, e.g., *Rivers v. Katz, supra* note 66.

70. *Davis v. Hubbard,* 506 F. Supp. 915 (W.D. Ohio 1980); *U.S. v. Leatherman,* 580 F. Supp. 977 (D.D.C. 1983); *Jamison v. Farabee,* No. C 780445 WHO (N.D. Cal. Apr. 26, 1983), reported in *Mental Disability Law Reporter* 7: 436ff. (1983); *Opinion of the Justices,* 465 A.2d 484 (N.H. 1983). In practice, *Jamison* was superceded by the decision of a California Court of Appeals in *Riese v. St. Mary's, supra* note 66.

71. One state, Utah, as the result of a court decision (*Colyar v. Third Judicial District Court,* 469 F. Supp. 424 [D. Utah 1979]), and a second state, Kansas, on a statutory basis, have adopted an entirely different approach. Commitment is predicated on a finding of incompetence to make treatment decisions, in addition to whatever other dangerousness criteria may be met. Following an adjudication of incompetence at the commitment hearing, treatment is permitted to proceed at physicians' discretion. An attempt to implement this approach in Florida was struck down by the courts on state constitutional grounds; the commitment courts were held not to have the authority to make competence determinations. See *Bentley v. State ex rel. Rogers,* 398 So. 2d 992 (Fla. Dist. Ct. App. 1981).

72. Of course, this approach assumes that an objectively definable concept of benefit to patients exists outside the patients' own determination of their interests. For a discussion of the circumstances under which this may not be true, see P. S. Appelbaum and W. F. Schwartz, "Minimizing the Social Cost of Choosing Treatment for the Involuntarily Hospitalized Mentally Ill Patient: A New Approach to Defining the Patient's Role," *Connecticut Law Review* 24: 433–85 (1992).

73. *Stensvad v. Reivitz*, 601 F. Supp. 128 (W.D. Wis. 1985) at 131.
74. *Johnson v. Silvers*, 742 F.2d 823 (4th Cir. 1984); *Dautremont v. Broadlawns Hospital*, 827 F.2d 291 (8th Cir. 1987); *Anderson v. State of Arizona*, 663 P.2d 570 (Ct. App. 1982); *Stensvad v. Reivitz*, *supra* note 73.
75. *Rennie v. Klein*, 462 F. Supp. 1131 (D.N.J. 1978), *aff'd in part*, 653 F.2d 836 (3rd Cir. 1981), *vacated and remanded*, 102 S. Ct. 3506 (1982), *on remand*, 700 F.2d 266 (3rd Cir. 1983); *R.A.J. v. Miller*, 590 F. Supp. 1319 (N.D. Tex. 1984); *Project Release v. Prevost*, 551 F. Supp. 1298 (E.D.N.Y. 1982), *aff'd*, 722 F.2d 960 (2nd Cir. 1983).
76. *Rennie v. Klein*, *supra* note 75.
77. *Project Release v. Prevost*, *supra* note 75.
78. *R.A.J. v. Miller*, *supra* note 75.
79. *Rennie v. Klein*, *supra* note 75.
80. *Youngberg v. Romeo*, 457 U.S. 308 (1982).
81. *Washington v. Harper*, 110 S. Ct. 1028 (1990).
82. *Johnson v. Silvers*, *supra* note 74; *Dautremont v. Broadlawns Hospital*, *supra* note 74; *Stensvad v. Reivitz*, *supra* note 74; *R.A.J. v. Miller*, *supra* note 75; *Project Release v. Prevost*, *supra* note 75; *U.S. v. Charters*, 863 F.2d 302 (4th Cir. 1988).
83. A. Meisel, "The Rights of the Mentally Ill Under State Constitutions," *Law and Contemporary Problems* 45: 7–40 (1982); M. L. Perlin, *Mental Disability Law: Civil and Criminal*, vol. 2 (Charlottesville, Va.: Michie, 1989), pp. 349–50 and Chapter 10, especially pp. 942–44.
84. Many state constitutions have provisions whose wording is identical or very similar to those found in the federal constitution. Thus, state courts can interpret individual rights more expansively than the federal courts may have chosen to do, based on the same language. State courts, of course, cannot limit rights recognized by federal courts under the U.S. Constitution or federal statutes.
85. See the post-1982 cases cited *supra* note 66.
86. *Rivers v. Katz*, *supra* note 66; *State ex rel. Jones v. Gerhardstein*, *supra* note 66.
87. *Harper v. State*, 759 P.2d 358 (Wash. 1988).
88. M. Irwin, A. Lovitz, S. R. Marder, J. Mintz, W. J. Winslade, T. Van Putten, and M. J. Mills, "Psychotic Patients' Understanding of Informed Consent," *American Journal of Psychiatry* 142: 1351–54 (1985); S. R. Marder, E. Swann, W. J. Winslade, T. Van Putten, C-P. Chien, and J. N. Wilkins, "A Study of Medication Refusal by Involuntary Psychiatric Patients," *Hospital and Community Psychiatry* 35: 724–26 (1984).
89. D. A. Soskis, "Schizophrenic and Medical Inpatients as Informed Drug Consumers," *Archives of General Psychiatry* 35: 645–47 (1978).
90. R. L. Binder and D. E. McNiel, "Involuntary Patients' Right to Refuse Medication: Impact of the *Riese* Decision on a California Inpatient Unit," *Bulletin of the American Academy of Psychiatry and the Law* 19: 351–58 (1991) [7 percent of patients on locked unit in university hospital]; J. D. Bloom, L. R. Faulkner, V. M. Holm, R. A. Rowlinson, "An Empirical View of Patients Exercising Their Right to Refuse Treatment," *International Journal of Law and Psychiatry* 7: 315–28 (1984) [4 percent of admissions to an Oregon state hospital over one year]; L. A. Callahan and W. V. Rubin, "Informed Consent and the Administration of Medication in Ohio's Public Psychiatric Hospitals: A Delicate Balance," Ohio DMH, November 1989 [two civil hospitals, 9 and 12 percent of patients]; J. R. Ciccone, J. F. Tokoli, C. D. Clements, and T. E. Gift, "Right to Refuse Treatment: Impact of *Rivers v. Katz*," *Bulletin of the American Academy of Psychiatry and the Law* 18: 203–15 (1990) [under 5 percent of patients in two New York hospitals over

several time periods]; J. R. Ciccone and J. F. Tokoli, "Treatment Refusal and Judicial Activism: A Re-examination," presented at the annual meeting of the American Psychiatric Association, New York City, May 16, 1990 [follow-up to earlier study, showing figures essentially stable at below 2 percent]; F. Cournos, K. McKinnon and B. Stanley, "Outcome of Involuntary Medication in a State Hospital System," *American Journal of Psychiatry* 148: 489–94 (1991) [0.37 percent of patients in state hospitals in New York City in 1985]; B. S. Gurian, E. H. Baker, S. Jacobson, B. Lagerbom, and P. Watts, "Informed Consent for Neuroleptics with Elderly Patients in Two Settings," *Journal of the American Geriatric Society* 38: 37–44 (1990) [17 percent of elderly patients in a general hospital psychiatric unit]; R. Keisling, "Characteristics and Outcome of Patients Who Refuse Medication," *Hospital and Community Psychiatry* 34: 847–48 (1983) [2.4 percent of patients over five months at D.C. hospital]; D. B. Langmeyer, personal communication, July 6, 1988 [2 percent of patients in North Carolina state hospitals in 1986]; S. Levin, J. S. Brekke, and P. Thomas, "A Controlled Comparison of Involuntarily Hospitalized Medication Refusers and Acceptors," *Bulletin of the American Academy of Psychiatry and the Law* 19: 161–71 (1991) [15.6 percent of patients on university hospital unit in California]; J. M. Zito, T. J. Craig, and J. Wanderling, "New York Under the *Rivers* Decision: An Epidemiologic Study of Drug Treatment Refusal," *American Journal of Psychiatry* 148: 904–9 (1991) [1 percent of admissions in New York State over one year, 1986–1987]; J. M. Zito, S. Haimowitz, J. Wanderling, and R. M. Mehita, "One Year Under *Rivers:* Drug Refusal in a New York State Psychiatric Facility," *International Journal of Law and Psychiatry* 12: 295–306 (1990) [1.3 percent of involuntary patients; 0.6 percent of total]; J. M. Zito, D. D. Hendel, J. E. Mitchell, and W. W. Routt, "Drug Treatment Refusal, Diagnosis, and Length of Hospitalization in Involuntary Psychiatric Patients," *Behavioral Sciences and the Law* 4: 327–37 (1986) [18 percent of involuntary patients in Minnesota state hospital]; J. M. Zito, S. L. Lentz, W. W. Routt, and G. W. Olson, "The Treatment Review Panel: A Solution to Treatment Refusal?" *Bulletin of the American Academy of Psychiatry and the Law* 12: 349–58 (1984) [15 percent of patients in Minnesota state hospital over 20 months].

91. Ciccone, Tokoli, Clements, and Gift, *supra* note 90.
92. Zito, Haimowitz, Wanderling and Mehita, *supra* note 90; Zito, Craig, and Wanderling, *supra* note 90.
93. P. S. Appelbaum and T. G. Gutheil, "Drug Refusal: A Study of Psychiatric Inpatients," *American Journal of Psychiatry* 137: 340–45 (1980).
94. Gurian et al., *supra* note 90. The minimum duration of refusal that was sufficient for inclusion in this study was not specified.
95. S. K. Hoge, P. S. Appelbaum, T. Lawlor, J. C. Beck, R. Litman, A. Greer, T. G. Gutheil, and E. Kaplan, "A Prospective, Multi-center Study of Patients' Refusal of Antipsychotic Medication," *Archives of General Psychiatry* 47: 949–56 (1990).
96. With regard to the last of these factors, Levin and coworkers, who reported that nearly 16 percent of admissions to their general hospital psychiatric unit in California were referred to a court in an attempt to override refusals, suggested that the high incidence of review sought in their study reflected the pressures they faced from third-party payers (Levin et al. *supra* note 90): insurers were reluctant to pay for hospitalization unless either patients were receiving active treatment or, at a minimum, all options for administering treatment (that is, court review of refusal) were being pursued. Further, the insurance companies were impatient with prolonged discussions with patients aimed at resolving refusal by mutual agreement.

Thus, treating psychiatrists were impelled into the courts, whereas they might not have been in public hospitals (such as those studied by Hoge and colleagues), where patients tend to be uninsured.

97. L. Callahan, "Changing Mental Health Law: Butting Heads with a Billygoat," *Behavioral Sciences and the Law* 4: 305–14 (1986); J. T. Young, J. D. Bloom, L. R. Faulkner, J. L. Rogers, and P. K. Pati, "Treatment Refusal Among Forensic Inpatients," *Bulletin of the American Academy of Psychiatry and the Law* 15: 5–13 (1987).

98. M. G. Farnsworth, "The Impact of Judicial Review of Patients' Refusal to Accept Antipsychotic Medications at the Minnesota Security Hospital," *Bulletin of the American Academy of Psychiatry and the Law* 19: 33–42 (1991); P. Rodenhauser, C. E. Schwenker, and H. J. Khamis, "Factors Related to Drug Treatment Refusal in a Forensic Hospital," *Hospital and Community Psychiatry* 38: 631–37 (1987); P. Rodenhauser, "Treatment Refusal in a Forensic Hospital: Ill-use of the Lasting Right," *Bulletin of the American Academy of Psychiatry and the Law* 12: 59–63 (1984). The two Rodenhauser studies, yielding incidence rates of 35 and 36 percent, were performed in the same facility at more or less the same time as the Callahan study (*supra* note 97), which reported an 11 percent incidence rate. The basis for this discrepancy is difficult to determine from an examination of the reports themselves.

99. R. D. Miller, M. R. Bernstein, G. J. Van Rybroek, and G. L. Maier, "The Impact of the Right to Refuse Treatment in a Forensic Patient Population: Six-month Review," *Bulletin of the American Academy of Psychiatry and the Law* 17: 107–19 (1989).

100. Twenty-nine of the ninety-one refusers (32 percent) subsequently accepted medication voluntarily.

101. L. A. Callahan, "The Impact of a Medication Administration Policy on a State Mental Health System," Ohio DMH, 1987; J. M. Zito, W. W. Routt, J. E. Mitchell, and J. L. Roerig, "Clinical Characteristics of Hospitalized Psychotic Patients Who Refuse Antipsychotic Drug Therapy," *American Journal of Psychiatry* 142: 822–26 (1985).

102. Bloom, Faulkner, and Holm, *supra* note 90; P. J. Davidson, "Medication Refusal and Physical Restraint," presented at the annual meeting of the American Psychiatric Association, San Francisco, May 1989; Dominican Santa Cruz Hospital, "Implementation of *Riese v. St. Mary's* Decision at Dominican Santa Cruz Hospital Mental Health Unit," unpublished manuscript, April 17, 1990; Miller et al., *supra* note 99; Hoge et al., *supra* note 95; P. S. Hyde and D. Roth, "Informed consent in the administration of psychotropic medications in Ohio's Public Psychiatric Hospitals," presented at the annual meeting of the National Association of State Mental Health Program Directors, 1990 [although rates of seclusion and restraint increased in this study, refusers had no greater involvement in reported incidents than did nonrefusers]; Levin et al., *supra* note 90; Rodenhauser et al., *supra* note 98; Young et al., *supra* note 97.

103. Rodenhauser et al., *supra* note 98.

104. Hoge et al., *supra* note 95.

105. Levin et al., *supra* note 90.

106. Dominican Santa Cruz Hospital, *supra* note 102. The report compares a twelve-month period prior to the introduction of a right to refuse treatment, during which five assaults occurred, with a nine-month period after the right was established, during which twenty assaults were committed.

107. Callahan and Rubin, *supra* note 90.

108. Levin et al., *supra* note 90.
109. Hoge et al., *supra* note 95.
110. Dominican Santa Cruz Hospital, *supra* note 102.
111. Hoge et al., *supra* note 95.
112. P. Rodenhauser, "Lasting Rights and Last Rites: A Case Report," *Bulletin of the American Academy of Psychiatry and the Law* 14: 281–86 (1986).
113. Massachusetts Department of Mental Health, untitled report, draft dated July 7, 1988 (final report never issued).
114. J. Veliz and W. S. James, "Medicine Court: *Rogers* in Practice," *American Journal of Psychiatry* 144: 62–67 (1987).
115. Farnsworth, *supra* note 98.
116. Massachusetts DMH, *supra* note 113.
117. See, e.g., Ciccone, Tokoli, Clements, and Gift, *supra* note 90. There have, however, been several reports of extensive delays associated with administrative review, too. See F. Cournos, K. McKinnon, and C. Adams, "A Comparison of Clinical and Judicial Procedures for Reviewing Requests for Involuntary Medication in New York," *Hospital and Community Psychiatry* 39: 851–55 (1988); and I. N. Hassenfeld and B. Grumet, "A Study of the Right to Refuse Treatment," *Bulletin of the American Academy of Psychiatry and the Law* 12: 65–74 (1984).
118. Zito, Craig, and Wanderling, *supra* note 90.
119. Farnsworth, *supra* note 98.
120. Massachusetts DMH, *supra* note 113; Hoge et al., *supra* note 95.
121. F. H. Deland and N. M. Borenstein, "Medicine Court: II. *Rivers* in Practice," *American Journal of Psychiatry* 147: 38–43 (1990); Ciccone, Tokoli, Clements, and Gift, *supra* note 90; Zito, Haimowitz, Wanderling, and Mehita, *supra* note 90.
122. See, e.g., J. Chamberlin, *On Our Own: Patient Controlled Alternatives to the Mental Health System* (New York: Hawthorn, 1978).
123. J. Robitscher, *The Powers of Psychiatry* (Boston: Houghton Mifflin, 1980).
124. M. Lakovics, J. Jiminez, J. Echer et al., "Institutional Psychiatry" [Letter], *Psychiatric News* 7(2): 2 (January 19, 1972).
125. R. Plotkin, "Limiting the Therapeutic Orgy: Mental Patients' Right to Refuse Treatment," *Northwestern University Law Review* 72: 461–525 (1977).
126. Hoge et al., *supra* note 95.
127. J. McEvoy, L. J. Apperson, P. S. Appelbaum, P. Ortlip, J. Brecosky, K. Hammill, J. L. Geller, L. H. Roth, "Insight in Schizophrenia: Its Relationship to Acute Psychopathology," *Journal of Nervous and Mental Disease* 177: 43–47 (1989).
128. J. Campbell and R. Schraiber, *The Well-Being Project: Mental Health Clients Speak for Themselves* (Sacramento, Calif.: California Department of Mental Health, 1989).
129. Callahan and Rubin, *supra* note 90.
130. H. I. Schwartz, W. Vingiano, and C. B. Perez, "Autonomy and the Right to Refuse Treatment: Patients' Attitudes After Involuntary Medication," *Hospital and Community Psychiatry* 39: 1049–54 (1988). The decision to administer the questionnaire in this study at the time of (but prior to) patients' discharge from the facility raises the question of whether patients were concerned about giving the "right" answer, so as not to endanger their release. Replication of this important study with a larger sample, interviewed at some point after release from the facility, would be a valuable contribution to our knowledge of patients' reactions to involuntary treatment.

131. Hoge et al., *supra* note 95.
132. DeLand and Borenstein, *supra* note 121; S. L. Godard, J. D. Bloom, M. H. Williams, and L. R. Faulkner, "The Right to Refuse Treatment in Oregon: A Two-year Statewide Experience," *Behavioral Sciences and the Law* 4: 293–304 (1986); Miller et al., *supra* note 99; Rodenhauser et al., *supra* note 98; J. D. Wilson and M. D. Enoch, "Estimation of Drug Rejection by Schizophrenic Inpatients, with Analysis of Clinical Factors," *British Journal of Psychiatry* 113: 209–11 (1967); Zito, Haimowitz, Wanderling, and Mehita, *supra* note 90.
133. Hoge et al., *supra* note 95. Interestingly, the treating psychiatrist (unaware of patients' responses to this question) identified side-effects as a causative factor in only 7 percent of cases.
134. Levin et al., *supra* note 90; Hassenfeld and Grumet, *supra* note 117; Callahan, *supra* note 97.
135. Callahan and Rubin, *supra* note 90.
136. T. Van Putten, P. R. A. May and S. R. Marder, "Response to Antipsychotic Medication: The Doctor's and the Consumer's View," *American Journal of Psychiatry* 141: 16–19 (1984).
137. See also T. Van Putten, "Why Do Schizophrenic Patients Refuse to Take Their Drugs? *Archives of General Psychiatry* 31: 67–72 (1974); and T. Van Putten, P. R. A. May, S. R. Marder, et al, "Subjective Response to Antipsychotic Drugs," *Archives of General Psychiatry* 38: 187–90 (1981).
138. Hoge et al., *supra* note 95.
139. Appelbaum and Gutheil, *supra* note 93.
140. Zito, Craig, and Wanderling, *supra* note 90. There may, of course, be other reasons for petitions to be withdrawn than patients' reacceptance of medication. For example, patients may be discharged or transferred, or the psychiatrist may conclude that a court is unlikely to grant the request for involuntary treatment or may even conclude that medication is not really necessary at this time.
141. Callahan and Rubin, *supra* note 90.
142. Hoge et al., *supra* note 95.
143. Median length of stay for all psychiatric admissions in 1986 (the most recent data available) was 15 days. For patients with schizophrenia, the overall figure was 19 days, but only 13 days in general hospital units. Most observers believe length of stay has continued to decline since 1986. M. J. Rosenthal, L. J. Milazzo-Sayre, and R. W. Manderscheid, "Characteristics of Persons Using Specialty Inpatient, Outpatient and Partial Care Programs in 1986," in R. W. Manderscheid and M. A. Sonnerschein, eds., *Mental Health, United States 1990* (Rockville, Md.: NIMH, 1990), pp. 139–72.
144. Massachusetts DMH, *supra* note 113. *Rogers* also required hearings for patients who were accepting medication but were thought to be incompetent to do so. If their incompetence is confirmed, the judge must make a finding regarding what their competent desires would be and must authorize or fail to authorize medication on that basis. Of 702 cases of this sort heard, every one resulted in approval of treatment.
145. Gurian et al., *supra* note 90; Hoge et al., *supra* note 95; S. K. Hoge, T. G. Gutheil, and E. Kaplan, "The Right to Refuse Treatment Under *Rogers v. Commissioner:* Preliminary Empirical Findings and Comparisons," *Bulletin of the American Academy of Psychiatry and the Law* 15: 163–69 (1987); Veliz and James, *supra* note 114.
146. P. Sauvayre, "The Relationship Between the Court and the Doctor on the Issue of an Inpatient's Refusal of Psychotropic Medication," *Journal of Forensic Sci-*

ences 36: 219–25 (1991) [32 of 40 petitions were approved at Kirby Forensic Center].

147. Zito, Haimowitz, Wanderling, and Mehita, *supra* note 90 [13 of 15 petitions were approved].

148. Ciccone and Tokoli, *supra* note 90 [30 of 33 cases from a private hospital and a state-operated facility over two years were approved for treatment; these figures update the report in Ciccone, Tokoli, Clements, and Gift, *supra* note 90].

149. Zito, Craig, and Wanderling, *supra* note 90 [statewide experience for one year, 331 of 358 petitions for treatment were approved].

150. Cournos et al., *supra* note 117 [18 of 21 applications were approved, which would yield an 86 percent rate, but 2 of the 3 not approved were dismissed for procedural reasons; a fairer calculation would be based on a total of 19 cases, of which 18 were approved].

151. DeLand and Borenstein, *supra* note 121 [15 of 15 cases from the Central New York Forensic Center were approved for treatment].

152. Dominican Santa Cruz Hospital, *supra* note 102 [42 of 55 petitions were approved from a private hospital].

153. Binder and McNiel, *supra* note 90 [28 of 32 were approved from a locked unit in a university hospital].

154. Levin et al., *supra* note 90 [31 of 31 cases were approved from a university hospital].

155. Farnsworth, *supra* note 97 [25 of 25 were approved].

156. Miller et al., *supra* note 99 [39 of 39 petitions were approved].

157. Davidson, *supra* note 102 [167 of 186 cases submitted from a state hospital were approved].

158. Bloom et al., *supra* note 90 [80 of 84 refusers (95 percent) were ordered treated]; Ciccone and Tokoli, *supra* note 90 [90 of 95 (94 percent) of refusals were overturned in two Rochester, New York, area hospitals]; Cournos et al., *supra* note 90 [51 of 52 cases were approved for treatment (98 percent) in New York City under administrative review]; Godard et al., *supra* note 135 [stateside results from Oregon, which has a system of independent psychiatrist review, found that 412 of 432 refusals (95 percent) were overturned]; Keisling, *supra* note 90 [9 of 9 refusals were overridden at a federal hospital in Washington, D.C.]; Young et al., *supra* note 102 [100% override of 33 refusers at an Oregon forensic hospital]. All of these studies come from systems with treatment-driven models; only need for treatment (and not competence) were considered by the reviewers, unless they chose to consider competence on an individual basis.

159. P. Rodenhauser and A. Heller, "Management of Forensic Psychiatry Patients Who Refuse Medication—Two Scenarios," *Journal of Forensic Sciences* 29: 237–44 (1984) [131 of 185 hearings resulted in treatment being approved].

160. Callahan, *supra* note 97 [68 patients were allowed to refuse medications, and 264 were forced to take them; for purposes of this calculation, the 147 patients who entered the review process but ultimately signed consent forms are excluded].

161. The system studied in these reports, based on the court order in *Davis v. Hubbard*, 506 F. Supp. 915 (D. Ohio 1980), allowed override of refusals in case of emergencies (that is, when there was "at least probable cause to believe that the patient is presently violent or self-destructive, and in such condition presents a present danger to himself, other patients or the institution's staff"). Competence did not have to be considered in those circumstances. Otherwise, competent patients had a right to refuse treatment. For incompetent patients in nonemergency situations, a judicial hearing was required to override refusal.

162. Hassenfeld and Grumet, *supra* note 117 [5 of 8 cases in which refusers did not

voluntarily reaccept were approved for treatment]. A treatment-driven system of review was in place.

163. Callahan, *supra* note 97. Calculating rates of override is not always straightforward. In one hospital in this study, out of 84 persons entering the review process, 28 were treated involuntarily and 27 had their refusal upheld. The remaining patients signed consent forms, had their petitions withdrawn, or did not have the outcome recorded. I consider this a 51 percent rate of override, based on 28 of the 55 patients who went through the review process without being withdrawn at any point, and for whom data are available. For reasons that are not clear to me, the author concludes that the rate of override was 74 percent. Similarly, at the second hospital, of 45 cases that entered the review process, 25 were treated involuntarily, 6 had their refusals upheld, and 14 had other dispositions or are accounted for in missing data. I calculate the rate of override in this facility at 81 percent (25 of 31 who actually went through the process), although the author describes it as an 89 percent rate. But by either calculation, the bottom line is the same: a much lower rate of override than in most studies of judicial review. In almost all cases in which refusal was permitted to continue, the decision was based on a finding that the patient had the capacity to make the decision for himself or herself.

164. Hyde and Roth, *supra* note 102. Again, the calculation of override rates from the data presented is not a simple matter. Out of 163 patients who entered the review process, 130 are accounted for. Presumably the rest represent missing data. Of the 130 patients for whom records exist, 30 accepted medication voluntarily at some point in the process and can be excluded from further analysis, since resolution of their cases occurred outside the review system. Of the remaining 100 patients, 77 were treated over their objections.

165. Zito, Lentz, Routt, and Olson, *supra* note 90 [127 of 193 nonemergency cases were approved for treatment]. Retroactive approval of emergency treatment occurred in 95 percent of all cases.

166. Farnsworth, *supra* note 98 [20 of 23 nonemergency cases were approved]. The rate was approximately the same for emergency cases.

    Ironically, although clinical/administrative review procedures appear to be more likely to support patients' refusals, the trend in state courts has been to reject these approaches in favor of judicial review, ostensibly in the name of greater protection of patient' rights. Thus, of the states in which studies of clinical/administrative review have been performed, New York and Minnesota now have a court-mandated judicial review process, and the Ohio system is under challenge in the courts. (See *Rivers v. Katz, supra* note 66; *Jarvis v. Levine, supra* note 66; and Class Action Complaint, *Cleveland v. Ohio Department of Mental Health,* No. 89CV-05-3658, Ct. Common Pleas, Franklin Cty; 1989) When the shift from clinical/administrative to judicial review occurred in Minnesota, rates of overturning patients' objections rose substantially. (See Farnsworth, *supra* note 98. The rate of overturning refusals under a clinical/administrative system was 87 percent (20/23); once judicial review was imposed, the rate rose to 100 percent (9/9). These figures are for nonemergency cases; rates for emergency cases are almost identical.) With the increasing dominance of judicial review models, even fewer refusals are likely to be upheld after review.

167. Massachusetts DMH, *supra* note 113.

168. C. A. B. Warren, *The Court of Last Resort: Mental Illness and the Law* (Chicago: University of Chicago Press, 1982). See the discussion of Warren's work in Chapter 2.

169. Appelbaum and Schwartz, *supra* note 72.

170. Ciccone, Tokoli, Clements, and Gift, *supra* note 90. Updated figures, suggesting that the drop was even greater and was sustained over time, were presented by Ciccone and Tokoli, *supra* note 90.

171. Appelbaum and Schwartz, *supra* note 72.

172. R. J. Wyatt, "Neuroleptics and the Natural Course of Schizophrenia," *Schizophrenia Bulletin* 17: 325–51 (1991).

173. For some patients, of course, hospitalization itself and the impact of the hospital milieu, or the effects of nonsomatic interventions such as psychotherapy or activities therapies, may be sufficient to enable them to return to life outside the hospital. There is no justification for involuntary medication in such cases.

174. This general rule is illustrated by the well-known case of Dallas Williams, a multiple violent offender who was discharged from custody despite a firm prediction that he would "repeat his patterns of criminal behavior, and might commit homicide." In this case, the prediction turned out to be accurate. See excerpts from the involved legal proceedings in his case in J. Katz, J. Goldstein, and A. M. Dershowitz, *Psychoanalysis, Psychiatry, and Law* (New York: Free Press, 1967), pp. 526–35.

175. J. Monahan, *The Clinical Prediction of Violent Behavior* (Rockville, Md.: NIMH, 1981).

176. Of course, historically the paternalistic rationale for civil commitment in this country lies even closer to the surface. "Need for treatment" was the major justification for involuntary commitment from the inception of the commitment system in the early 1800s until the current generation of statutes were adopted in the late 1960s through the 1970s. Indeed, several states in recent years have added overtly paternalistic components to their dangerousness-oriented commitment statutes. (See the discussion in Chapter 2.)

177. Stone, A. A. *Mental Health and Law: A System in Transition* (Rockville, Md.: NIMH, 1975).

178. S. K. Hoge, P. S. Appelbaum, and A. Greer, "An Empirical Comparison of the Stone and Dangerousness Criteria for Civil Commitment," *American Journal of Psychiatry* 146: 170–75 (1989); S. K. Hoge, G. Sachs, P. S. Appelbaum, A. Greer, and C. Gordon, "Limitations on Psychiatrists' Discretionary Civil Commitment Authority by the Stone and Dangerousness Criteria," *Archives of General Psychiatry* 45: 764–69 (1988).

179. This conclusion is entirely consistent with the ruling of the U.S. Supreme Court in *Washington v. Harper* (*supra* note 84), in which involuntary treatment of a prisoner who met Washington State's commitment standards was permitted without inquiry into his decision-making competence. The decisions of lower courts that have endorsed treatment-driven models of adjudicating treatment refusal—which implicitly permit the involuntary treatment of competent, mentally ill persons—indicate further support for this principle. (See the cases cited *supra* note 74 and 75.)

180. P. S. Appelbaum and T. G. Gutheil, "The Right to Refuse Treatment: The Real Issue Is Quality of Care," *Bulletin of the American Academy of Psychiatry and the Law* 9: 199–202 (1981); see also the comments by Judge Stanley Brotman on his concerns regarding quality of psychiatric care in state facilities in the *Rennie v. Klein* litigation. S. S. Brotman, "Behind the Bench on *Rennie v. Klein*," in A. E. Doudera and J. P. Swazey, eds., *Refusing Treatment in Mental Health Institutions—Values in Conflict* (Ann Arbor, Mich.: AUPHA Press, 1982), pp. 31–41.

181. Appelbaum, *supra* note 65.

5

The Insanity Defense: Moral Blameworthiness and Criminal Punishment

On March 30, 1981, a troubled 25-year-old man with a .22-caliber pistol lurked in the crowd outside the Washington Hilton, where President Ronald Reagan was addressing a luncheon gathering of 3,500 AFL-CIO delegates. As the President emerged from the hotel lobby, the crowd surged toward him. Carefully positioned in the front rank, the young man pulled the pistol from his jacket and began firing. His first shot hit presidential press secretary James Brady over his left eye, entering the frontal lobe of his brain. The next bullet struck a Washington police officer; the third barely missed a presidential aide. A Secret Service agent who was attempting to shield the President took the fourth round in his abdomen, as the President was shoved by another agent into the Presidential limousine. The fifth shot smashed into the car's bulletproof window, behind which a startled Ronald Reagan was huddled. Only one round remained in the gun. As the young man squeezed the trigger for the last time, the bullet ricocheted off the rear fender of the limousine, entered the vehicle through the still-open door, and struck the President on the left side of his chest. The assailant, his gun now empty, was wrestled to the ground by Secret Service agents. Within hours, one of his apparent goals was achieved: the name John Hinckley, Jr., was emblazoned in the consciousness of millions of people in the United States and around the world.[1]

The nation was stunned by the assault on President Reagan and waited nervously for word of his medical condition. Surgeons at George Washington University Hospital, to which the President had been rushed, operated immediately to stanch the bleeding and remove the bullet from his lung. A visibly confused White House staff attempted to reassure the public, but it was days before the President himself was able to issue a statement, and several weeks before he clearly reassumed command of the country. In retrospect, his condition appears to have been much more tenuous than was suggested by the cautiously upbeat press conferences at George Washington University Hospital. Young Mr. Hinckley almost succeeded in killing the President of the United States.

If the President's ordeal and the nation's anguish were over in a matter of weeks, Hinckley's own private purgatory was just beginning. His father, a wealthy Colorado oilman, hired a prominent Washington defense attorney, Vincent Fuller, to prepare his son's case. Fuller's problem was evident to every person with access to a television. The videotape of the attempted assassination had been broadcast hundreds—perhaps thousands—of times. Dozens of bystanders had witnessed the act itself. Hinckley's actions and—it seemed—his guilt were unquestionable. His prospects in court did not look good. Thus, as any reasonable attorney would do in similar circumstances, Hinckley's defense team attempted to strike a bargain with the government: Hinckley would plead guilty to all counts if he were permitted to serve his sentences concurrently, leaving him eligible for parole in 15 years. Not surprisingly, given their seemingly airtight case, the prosecutors refused. They wanted the sentences served consecutively, so that Hinckley, for all practical purposes, would be imprisoned for life.

Defense attorney Fuller and his colleagues were left with few options short of capitulating to the government's demands. The evidence that their client had pulled the trigger and fired the rounds that wounded four people, including the President of the United States, was incontrovertible. But Anglo-American criminal law, in its slow evolution over the centuries, had come to require for conviction more than mere proof that a defendant had committed a prohibited act. The law demanded that the defendant have performed the act while in possession of a particular mental state—a *mens rea* (or "culpable mind"). In the absence of *mens rea,* guilt could not be found nor punishment imposed. This became the cornerstone of Hinckley's defense. Unable to deny that he had committed the acts with which he was charged, his defense team maintained that John Hinckley, Jr., had performed them in a state of mind that did not render him culpable. They entered a plea on Hinckley's behalf of "not guilty by reason of insanity."

The Origins and Development of the Insanity Defense

The moral intuition that a person's mental state might preclude punishment for a crime dates to antiquity. Aristotle argued in his *Nichomachean Ethics* that confusion over the reality of a situation—perhaps a person's delusional belief that he or she was being harmed by another—might provide a moral excuse for persons who acted unlawfully in response to those beliefs.[2] Aristotle's contention, however, had little impact on his contemporaries, who punished perpetrators irrespective of their underlying motives or beliefs.[3] Roman law, however, seems to have inclined toward leniency regarding those who acted under the influence of madness—albeit less on the basis of concerns about moral blameworthiness than on the grounds that such unfortunates already had been punished by fate, and it was not for man to add to their afflictions.[4] Aristotle's conception of the moral significance of one's motivation, though ignored in most criminal law systems of antiquity and the Middle Ages, was embraced by the Church in its canon law.

Scholars differ in their assessment of the impact that these Aristotelian concepts had in the secular world in the intervening centuries,[5] but there is little dispute that they reappeared forcefully in the thirteenth-century writings of the English jurist Bracton, who asserted that a culpable mental state (or *mens rea*) was a necessary component of criminal culpability. "A crime is not committed," he wrote, "unless the will to harm be present." [6] This formulation excluded from moral (and legal) guilt all persons who caused harm unintentionally, including those who may have intended their acts but did not understand their wrongfulness. Children, adults of severely limited intelligence ("idiots" in the parlance of the day), and the seriously mentally ill were the primary members of this last category. Bracton's approach was gradually adopted by the English common law courts. Although initially a finding that the defendant had committed a criminal act but lacked *mens rea* was considered a conviction—so that avoidance of punishment depended on pardon by the Crown—by the beginning of the sixteenth century, juries had acquired the power to acquit such defendants outright.

English courts at first gave their jurors little consistent guidance regarding the test for determining whether *mens rea* was lacking. The best-known and earliest standard was the so-called "wild beast test." To be acquitted under this approach, the defendant had to demonstrate that he did "not know what he was doing, no more than an infant, than a brute or wild beast." Dating to Bracton himself, this formulation was applied as late as 1723, in a case that involved the wounding of one of the courtiers of George II.[7] As it required total behavioral dyscontrol and utter detachment from reality—often referred to as "furious," "frenzied," or "raving" madness—the wild beast test was a rigorous standard unlikely to lead to the exculpation of many defendants.

In the seventeenth and eighteenth centuries, a new test gained ascendance; it required the defendant to prove that he lacked the ability to distinguish between good and evil.[8] This less rigorous standard than the wild beast test increased the likelihood that the placidly insane, along with the mentally retarded, would be acquitted. Whether the wild beast standard or the "good and evil" standard was selected, however, depended solely on the predilections of the trial judge.

It has been difficult to determine how frequently appeal was made to the defendant's lack of *mens rea* by reason of insanity prior to the nineteenth century. Walker's pioneering examination of the records of London's Old Bailey court suggests that the plea grew in popularity in the latter half of the eighteenth century, being offered in over 100 cases during that period—and successfully so in more than half the recorded instances.[9] Why the insanity defense flourished in that era is unclear. Medical testimony was rare, so defendants' mental states were typically described by their family and friends. Whatever the reason for its popularity, by the end of the eighteenth century, when James Hadfield was acquitted by reason of insanity for the attempted assassination of King George III, the authorities recognized that some means of confining the growing number of those so adjudicated was required, lest they be released to try again. Parliament responded to the crisis with the Criminal Lunatics Act of 1800, which allowed indefinite confinement of persons found not guilty by reason of insanity, at the pleasure of the King.[10]

The turning point in Anglo-American law governing criminal nonresponsibility came in 1843 in the wake of yet another attack on a high British government official. Daniel McNaughtan, a young Scotsman, shot and killed Edward Drummond, secretary to the prime minister, under the mistaken impression that his victim was Prime Minister Sir Robert Peel himself. To this day McNaughtan's motives are the subject of vigorous dispute,[11] but it seems clear that he knew that shooting someone was wrong. Thus, he was not eligible for exculpation under the dominant test of the time, which asked whether he knew good from evil. Instead, his attorneys argued that a broader test should be applied. McNaughtan, they claimed, was motivated by a delusional belief that he was being persecuted by Mr. Peel's government. The defense relied on the Aristotelian notion that behavior based on delusional ideas could not serve as the basis for guilt. Chief Justice Tindal, hearing the case, accepted the argument and all but directed the jury to issue an acquittal.

Queen Victoria expressed the horror felt by many of her subjects over the failure to convict McNaughtan. Her concern about the expansion of the standard for exculpation by reason of insanity led her to encourage Peel to take the issue to Parliament. The House of Lords convened a hearing of the common-law judges and put to them a series of questions seeking clarification of the standard and procedures to be applied to insanity defense cases. Chief Justice Tindal, who had presided at McNaughtan's trial, offered the opinion of the group, which thoroughly repudiated the approach he himself had taken to the case. Even if a person were delusional, Tindal reported, "he is nevertheless punishable if he knew that he was acting contrary to the law." Indeed, the touchstone of the inquiry was whether

> at the time of the committing of the act, the party accused was laboring under such a defect of reason, from disease of the mind, as not to know the nature and quality of the act he was doing; or, if he did know it, that he did not know he was doing what was wrong.

In other words, the key was "whether the accused at the time of doing the act knew the difference between right and wrong."[12]

With McNaughtan's case, the impetus that Bracton had given the English law of criminal culpability six centuries before reached its culmination. Defendants lacking evil intent would not be punished for their crimes. Their criminal responsibility would be judged by their ability to distinguish right from wrong—a narrower test than one focused on whether delusional beliefs nurtured the act, but considerably broader then the wild beast test favored by courts in earlier years. To this day, the *McNaughtan* rules (as they came to be called) remain the law in England.

American courts quickly adopted the *McNaughtan* test, but with somewhat less unanimity than their British counterparts exhibited. A popular variant involved adding the so-called "irresistible influence" test to the *McNaughtan* standard, to deal with persons who may have known that they were committing a wrongful act, but felt powerless to stop themselves from doing so.[13] New Hampshire took a unique approach, allowing acquittal "if the [crime] was the offspring or product of mental disease in the defendant."[14] In contrast to attempts made elsewhere to refine the insanity test more precisely, the New Hampshire standard left it open-ended and thus more subject to the influence of jurors' moral sentiments.

Until the mid-twentieth century, the *McNaughtan* test remained dominant in U.S. law, supplemented by an irresistible impulse standard. At that point, however, dissatisfaction began to grow with the century-old approach of the English courts. *McNaughtan* was criticized by both lawyers and psychiatrists as overly narrow in its exclusive focus on knowledge of right and wrong, and its failure to take into account impairments in reasoning, affect, and perception, which modern psychiatry had shown to be core characteristics of mental disorder.[15] The federal appeals court in Washington, D.C., under the influence of Judge David Bazelon, who was then enamored with the potential contributions of psychoanalytic psychiatry to the criminal law, sought to replace *McNaughtan* with a broader standard designed to facilitate a full understanding of the varied effects of mental disorder on criminal behavior. In *Durham v. U.S.* (1954), the court reached back to the approach adopted by New Hampshire more than 80 years before, holding that "an accused is not criminally responsible if his unlawful act was the product of a mental disease or defect."[16]

Motivated by similar concern about the scope of *McNaughtan,* yet un-willing to leave juries entirely without guidance, the American Law Insti-tute (ALI) at about the same time offered a modification of *McNaughtan* as part of its *Model Penal Code.* The ALI test combined the *McNaughtan* and irresistible impulse standards, but relaxed *McNaughtan's* narrow focus on cognition:

> A person is not responsible for criminal conduct if at the time of such conduct as a result of mental disease or defect he lacks substantial capacity to appre-ciate the criminality [wrongfulness] of his conduct, or to conform his conduct to the requirements of the law.[17]

One difference between the ALI standard and traditional tests is that, under the ALI standard, defendants must only manifest a lack of "substan-tial capacity" with regard to their relevant functions, rather than the com-plete absence of capacity implied in earlier formulations.[18] Moreover, the phrase "appreciate the criminality of his conduct" was construed to permit inquiry into a broader range of mental functions, including perceptual dis-tortion, errors in reasoning, and affective impairments, than were compre-hended under the older focus on "knowing" right from wrong. In particu-lar, delusional persons—such as the depressed mother who kills her baby, believing that it is the only way to save the child from a life of sin and subsequent perdition—were at risk for exclusion under a strict *McNaughtan* standard, but were likely to be included under the ALI test.

One further aspect of the insanity defense deserves attention. In about half the states and in the federal courts (where Hinckley was later tried), the burden of proving that the defendant met the requirements for criminal responsibility was placed on the prosecution, which had to demonstrate the defendant's substantial capacity beyond a reasonable doubt. This was sim-ilar to the prosecution's burden with regard to other aspects of its case. The remaining states placed the burden on the defendant to prove that substan-tial capacity had been lacking, although in these states the standard of proof to be met was only a preponderance of the evidence. This seemingly tech-nical rule had an enormous impact on the trial of John Hinckley, Jr.

The Hinckley Trial

In early May 1982, thirteen months after the attempted assassination of President Reagan, the Hinckley trial began.[19] The task for Vincent Fuller and the rest of the defense team was to present to the court a claim that John Hinckley, Jr., met the ALI standard for criminal nonresponsibility at the time of the attack. Once the defense raised the issue, Roger Adelman, the federal prosecutor, and his colleagues bore the burden of proving be-yond a reasonable doubt that Hinckley had been legally sane.

Clearly, John Hinckley, Jr., was more than a little odd. The son of a wealthy Colorado oilman and his wife, Hinckley had been a shy child—a "momma's boy" with few friends. His father, distracted by the demands of his business career, was often absent during John Jr.'s formative years and never seems to have bonded with his son. During his high school years, when many adolescents come out of their childhood shells, the younger Hinckley became even more withdrawn, retreating to his room to listen to records and entirely avoiding contact with the opposite sex. After his graduation from high school, things only got worse: Hinckley drifted in and out of college, to Hollywood for an unrealistic shot at fame as a songwriter, and back and forth to and from his parents' Colorado home. Each attempt at independence was a failure. Hinckley remained dependent on the largesse of his increasingly frustrated father.

In 1976, at the age of 21, Hinckley first saw the movie *Taxi Driver*, a film about a child prostitute and the cabbie who becomes obsessed with rescuing her, an obsession that leads to homicide. Like the character in the film, Hinckley became enraptured by the prostitute, an attachment he transferred to the actress who had portrayed her, Jodie Foster. In 1980, Hinckley, who claimed he saw the movie fifteen times, concocted a story about enrolling in a writers' workshop at Yale, where Foster was a student, to persuade his parents to finance a trip there. He tracked Foster to her dormitory, left messages for her, and spoke with her several times on the phone. Not surprisingly, she was not interested in a relationship with this peculiar young man.

But Jodie Foster was never far from the mind of John Hinckley, Jr. He began to form the idea of attracting her attention by committing a violent act, an act as dramatic as the one devised by Travis Bickle, the unstable protagonist in *Taxi Driver*. Hinckley bought several handguns and began tracking President Jimmy Carter, then in the midst of his reelection campaign. Whatever the reason, the assault he was planning never occurred. Once more, Hinckley returned to Colorado. This time, his parents decided that their prodigal son needed professional help. Hinckley saw a local psychiatrist, John Hopper, for the next few months. The therapy, though, proved superficial, with Hinckley never revealing his violent fantasies. Dr. Hopper took a behavioral approach, setting deadlines for his reluctant patient to get a job and to leave his parents' house. When Hinckley failed to make progress with a job search and wandered off to New York, his exasperated father decided that he could stand it no longer. Meeting his son at the Denver airport, he gave him $200 and told him he was on his own. Slightly more than three weeks later, John Hinckley, Jr., shot the President outside the Washington Hilton.

No one could question the proposition that Hinckley was disturbed. But was he so disordered on the afternoon of March 30, 1981, that he lacked substantial capacity to appreciate the wrongfulness of his actions or to conform his behavior to the law? On this question, the expert witnesses for the prosecution and for the defense disagreed. Park Dietz, a forensic psychiatrist and the lead witness for the prosecution's group of experts, characterized Hinckley as having a personality disorder but as being fully aware of the nature of his actions and exquisitely in control of them. Dietz testified that, although Hinckley's belief that assassinating the President would gain him the affections of Jodie Foster was unrealistic, it was the product of narcissism and naivete—not psychosis. There was even reason to believe that Hinckley, in response to implicit suggestions by defense psychiatrists, had fabricated reports of symptoms that might result in his being characterized as more severely mentally ill than he really was.

The three psychiatrists and one psychologist who testified for the defense saw things differently. Hinckley, in their view, had been psychotic— out of touch with reality—at the time of the crime. His beliefs about the likely impact of his actions on the Yale undergraduate with whom he was obsessed were frankly delusional, based on magical thinking that resisted reasoned challenge. Defense experts pointed to Hinckley's long downhill slide, his disjointed poetry, and even to alleged atrophy of the cortex of his brain to support their conclusions that Hinckley was more than just a badly mixed-up 25-year-old. He suffered, the defense experts asserted, from an insidious form of schizophrenia; and his illness was intimately linked to his decision to kill the President. Hinckley's last act before leaving for the Washington Hilton had been to pen a letter to Jodie Foster, in which he begged her "to please look into your heart and at least give me a chance, with this historical deed, to gain your respect and love." Driven by the delusion that his act would lead to union with his previously unimpressed love object, Hinckley was powerless to appreciate the wrongfulness of his crime or to stop himself from committing this "historical deed."

Observers monitoring the trial in the daily newspaper and television accounts were uncertain which side the jury found more persuasive, but most thought that the prosecution was getting the better of the argument. In the end, though, the prosecution's burden of proof was simply too great for it to satisfy. A perplexed and, at times, angry jury felt constrained by the trial judge's charge that, unless the prosecution had proved Hinckley sane beyond a reasonable doubt, it could not find him guilty. After four days of deliberation, the jury unanimously decided that John Hinckley, Jr., was not guilty by reason of insanity.[20]

Reaction to the Hinckley Verdict

Shocked by the Hinckley verdict, the country plunged into an intense reexamination of the insanity defense. When the nation as a whole sat in the jury box, the consensus was that John Hinckley, Jr., deserved to be punished for his acts. Any system that allowed him to escape punishment, regardless of the rationale, was fundamentally flawed. It was too easy to be exculpated on the basis of insanity.

Commentators trumpeted this message from the op-ed pages of the nation's newspapers. "The most morally indefensible crimes are becoming the most legally defensible," complained conservative columnist George F. Will.[21] At some distance from Will in the political spectrum, the *New York Times'* Russell Baker dispensed with his usual satire to condemn the trial unequivocally "as an exercise in legal absurdity [that] would be hard to improve on."[22] Political leaders reacted similarly. The comments of Republican Senator Strom Thurmond, chairman of the Senate Judiciary Committee, were typical:

> It is deeply troubling to me when the criminal justice system exonerates a defendant who obviously planned and knew exactly what he was doing. This case has demonstrated . . . that there is something fundamentally wrong with the expanded modern insanity defense.[23]

Democratic Speaker of the House Thomas "Tip" O'Neill, Jr. pronounced himself "shocked."[24] Speaking for the administration, Attorney General William French Smith urged that "[t]here must be an end to the doctrine that allows so many persons to commit crimes of violence, to use confusing procedures to their own advantage, and then to have the door opened for them to return to the society they victimized."[25]

There seemed to be plenty of blame to go around for the unpopular outcome of the case. Psychiatrists came in for their share of reproach. Political columnist Tom Wicker pronounced psychiatry the biggest loser in the case, surely an opinion shared by many within and outside the profession.[26] Many people had concluded after this "dismaying spectacle," Wicker wrote, that "these doctors are little better able to agree than any two laymen might be on who's sane or insane." Beyond that, the obvious implication was "that the opinion of some psychiatrists, at least, may be for sale."[27] George F. Will described the expert testimony in the Hinckley trial as "a cacophony of loopiness," and cautioned that "today's rent-a-psychiatry is charlatanism laced with cynicism."[28]

Other critics aimed their remarks at the legal rules of proof under which the trial was conducted. President Reagan, the chief target of the attack, held his peace for nearly two weeks after the verdict, but then he lambasted the law for putting "on the backs of the prosecution the need to prove that someone was sane." In his usual folksy style, he observed, "If you start thinking about even a lot of your friends, you have to say, 'Gee, if I had to prove they were sane, I would have a hard job.' "[29] The *New York Times,* without venturing an opinion on the mental status of the President's friends, endorsed the idea of shifting the burden of proof of nonresponsibility to the defendant.[30]

Many people, however, thought the problem lay with the insanity defense itself. Abolition was widely discussed and found advocates among politicians who sensed the public's outrage.[31] Tinkering with the standard was also proposed, with reforms ranging from a return to *McNaughtan* (which some observers thought would have resulted in Hinckley's conviction[32]) to removal of the so-called "volitional" arm of the ALI test, a modern version of the old irresistible impulse test.[33] Few peopled seemed satisfied with the *status quo*.

Naturally, there were exceptions. Psychiatrist Alan Stone, rarely reluctant to offer a minority point of view, dismissed the argument over the formulation of the insanity test as unworthy of the attention it was receiving. The insanity defense, he argued, is "a pimple on the nose of justice, but the patient is dying of congestive heart failure."[34] Federal court of appeals Judge Irving Kaufman similarly urged care, lest "momentary outrage in response to a particular verdict . . . lead to incautious response."[35] And some commentators bucked the tide of passion sweeping the editorial pages of the nation to argue that the Hinckley verdict was not inappropriate and that the jurors correctly "saw that Hinckley had the right to be put in the care of psychiatrists, not jailers."[36] For the moment, though, the voices urging restraint were lonely ones. The vast majority of political and intellectual leaders, as well as the public at large, were convinced that the insanity defense was fundamentally flawed in its current form. They demanded reform.

Changing the Insanity Defense

There was no shortage of proposals aimed at satisfying the public's mood for change. Professional organizations, including the American Medical Association (AMA), the American Psychiatric Association (APA), and the American Bar Association (ABA) rapidly assembled task forces to review the insanity defense and to recommend new approaches. Mental health advocacy groups, such as the National Mental Health Association and the Mental Health Law Project, did the same. State legislatures and the U.S. Congress rushed to conduct hearings at which witnesses excoriated the current situation and presented a wide range of options for new legislation.

Significantly, the seed of discontent germinated by the Hinckley verdict fell on ground already tilled by several years of efforts at insanity defense reform. These pre-Hinckley reforms, by and large, were precipitated by the broader changes that overtook mental health law in the 1970s. As greater attention was paid to the rights of the mentally ill, the condition of insanity acquittees came under closer scrutiny, too. This process gained momentum from the efforts of legal advocacy groups, whose focus on the rights of mental patients has been described in previous chapters. Legal rights applied initially to civilly committed patients were soon extended to persons hospitalized after being found NGRI (not guilty by reason of insanity).[37]

In many states, the indefinite detention to which NGRI acquittees historically had been subject was ended. The burden was placed on the state to demonstrate at periodic recommitment hearings that these persons, who after all had not been convicted of a crime, met the usual criteria—mental illness and dangerousness—that would allow continued detention under civil commitment statutes.[38] Contentions that persons who had been found NGRI should be subject to especially rigorous standards of readiness for release because of the greater risk they presented to society were shrugged off by patients' advocates, who argued that the inability of psychiatrists to predict future dangerousness made detention of any class of persons undesirable in all but the rarest cases.[39]

This libertarian evolution of the law governing disposition of insanity acquittees fueled a fierce public backlash. In some states, the public's reaction came in response to unfortunate local episodes in which NGRI acquittees who had been released from confinement committed notorious acts of violence.[40] Elsewhere, the public's apprehension about the prospect of such events provoked statutory efforts to limit the reach of the insanity defense. Eleven states altered their insanity defense procedures in the three years prior to Hinckley's attempt on President Reagan's life, and eight additional states made changes in the interval between the attack and the trial. In almost every case, the changes were designed to make it more difficult for defendants to win an NGRI acquittal or to be released from an institution after a finding that they were not criminally responsible.[41] Many of these changes offered models for those seeking reform after the Hinckley verdict.

The wave of reform in the years following the Hinckley trial took several forms: abolition of the insanity defense, narrowing of the legal standards for insanity, a shift of the burden of proof to the defendant, restrictions on expert testimony, changes in the posttrial disposition of insanity acquittees, and institution of an entirely new verdict of "guilty but mentally ill." I consider each of these changes in turn.

Abolition of the Insanity Defense

A good example of how pre-Hinckley reforms laid the groundwork for subsequent efforts is provided by probably the most dramatic reform suggested in the wake of Hinckley's acquittal—abolition of the insanity defense. Both

Idaho and Montana had abolished the special defense of not guilty by rea-son of insanity in the years leading up to the Hinckley trial.[42] In contrast, to the usual motivation for changes in the law of insanity, Montana's action was not impelled by the outcome of a particular case. Rather, abolition reflected a general discontent with the nature of expert testimony in insanity defense cases.[43] Idaho's move, on the other hand, came in response to the attempted murder of a nurse by a defendant who previously had been ac-quitted by reason of insanity of the rapes of two women.[44]

How was it possible for these states to abolish the insanity plea, when the rule that, to be culpable, a defendant must have acted with *mens rea* is so deeply embedded in American law? The answer lies in the evolution of the concept of *mens rea* in the nineteenth and twentieth centuries. When the insanity defense applied only to defendants who met the "wild beast" test, there could be little question that an insanity acquittee lacked *mens rea*. As the tests expanded in scope, however, legal scholars began to talk about narrow and broader senses of *mens rea*. In the narrow meaning of the term, *mens rea* was present if the perpetrator intentionally performed the prohibited act.[45] Thus, whereas people who committed criminal acts while sleepwalking or during an epileptic seizure lacked *mens rea* even in the narrow sense, a delusional person who assaulted a bystander because he thought the person was bombarding his mind with radio waves did have this narrow type of *mens rea*. The person who acted on his delusions, un-like the sleepwalker or epileptic, fully intended to commit the assault that resulted in the criminal charges.[46]

From this perspective, the insanity defense provided an additional ex-cuse—a special defense, in legal terms—for a criminal act, above and be-yond the absence of *mens rea*. If so, the insanity defense could be abolished without damaging traditional notions of the essential nature of criminal law. Opponents of abolition, of course, argued that the normally relevant aspects of a defendant's mental state, whether called *mens rea* or denoted by an-other term, encompassed more than mere intention, including precisely the aspects embraced by the dominant tests for criminal nonresponsibility: ap-preciation of the nature of one's actions, and the ability to control them.[47] Courts in Idaho and Montana, however, did not adopt this broader view. As long as the state still had to meet the burden of proving that the defen-dant acted with *mens rea* in the narrow sense—and the defense still had the right to challenge that contention—the courts found no constitutional obsta-cles to abolition of the special defense of insanity.[48]

The intellectual foundations for the abolitionist argument were drawn from the writings of Norval Morris, a University of Chicago law profes-sor.[49] Morris contended that the special defense of insanity, taken on its own terms, was morally bankrupt because, in practice, it was hopelessly underinclusive. The defense was premised on the idea that persons who lacked the power to make a meaningful choice could not be considered morally blameworthy. Yet various conditions other than mental illness that limited the power to choose, such as social deprivation, were excluded from consideration by the law. And even within the permitted exception, many persons who might qualify for exculpation as insane never had a chance to raise the insanity plea, because they lacked the resources to pay competent lawyers and expensive experts. Thus, according to Morris, the argument in favor of the insanity defense proved too much. The only morally consistent course was to reject a special defense of insanity altogether. If a defendant's mental illness merited consideration at any time in the criminal justice process, it was most reasonably considered at the sentencing stage, when dispositional alternatives that allowed treatment to occur could be selected.

The call for abolishing the insanity defense quickly attracted converts. Within a month after the Hinckley verdict, Republican Senator Orrin Hatch of Utah introduced federal legislation, consciously modeled on the Montana and Idaho statutes, that effectively would have abolished the special insanity defense, leaving mentally ill defendants only the option of falling back on the narrow *mens rea* approach. Attorney General William French Smith immediately announced the Reagan administration's support for the Hatch bill.[50] Heavily influenced by Morris's views, the American Medical Association became the only professional group to endorse abolition.[51] While the AMA's leaders were probably motivated in large part by embarrassment over the "battle of the experts" that so often characterized insanity defense trials, they also argued that "an insanity defense justified solely or primarily on moral grounds is an anachronism in the modern scheme of criminal administration." In the end, though, the abolitionists failed to win the day. Congress did not pass the Hatch bill, and only one state—Utah—joined the ranks of those who rejected the special defense of insanity in favor of a *mens rea* approach.[52] The unpopularity of abolition, however, did not translate into an endorsement of the *status quo*. Instead, other reform proposals, more moderate in their effect on the system, came to the foreground.

Narrowing the Legal Standard

The reason that the insanity defense left much to be desired, many critics argued, was because the standards on which it was based were simply too broad. Professor Richard Bonnie, a University of Virginia law professor, was the most articulate exponent of this point of view.[53] Bonnie argued that the "volitional prong" of the ALI test—a reworked version of the irresistible impulse doctrine—was problematic because "there is no scientific basis for measuring a person's capacity for self-control or for calibrating the impairment of that capacity." Experts were thus led into ungrounded speculation, which undermined the foundation of the insanity defense as a whole.

Working behind the scenes with the American Psychiatric Association and the American Bar Association, Bonnie persuaded both groups to endorse his proposal. In a much quoted phrase, the APA contended that "[t]he line between an irresistible impulse and an impulse not resisted is probably no sharper than that between twilight and dusk."[54] The ABA maintained:

> The principal problem with continuing utilization of the volitional or "control" test is that the test is combined with vague or broad interpretations of the term "mental disease." And it is the mixing of these two ephemeral notions that results inevitably in unstructured expert speculation regarding the psychological causes of criminal behavior.[55]

With the support of major professional groups, the idea of dropping the volitional prong attracted growing enthusiasm in Congress. As the many alternative proposals for insanity defense reform made their way through committee, they were dropped one by one in favor of a modified version of the Bonnie test. Ultimately, the Comprehensive Crime Control Act of 1984, the first statute to establish an explicit standard for the insanity defense in the federal courts, adopted the following language:

> It is an affirmative defense to a prosecution under any Federal statute that, at the time of the commission of the acts constituting the offense, the defendant, as a result of a severe mental disease or defect, was unable to appreciate the nature and quality or the wrongfulness of his acts. Mental disease or defect does not otherwise constitute a defense. (Sec. 402)

Ten states followed Congress's lead in altering their insanity defense standards in the years after the Hinckley trial. Three states adopted a modified ALI standard similar to the federal rule, while the remainder reverted to a *McNaughtan* test or some emendation thereof.[56] In either case, the volitional standard, which focused on defendants' ability to control their behavior, was rejected.[57]

Shifting the Burden of Proof

One of the most widely endorsed legal reforms related to the insanity defense consisted of shifting the burden of proof from the prosecution to the defendant in the 50 percent of U.S. jurisdictions in which the government had previously carried the burden. This single factor had been cited by members of the Hinckley jury as the single most decisive factor in the outcome in the case. Professional groups were divided on the point. The APA declined to take a position on the issue, seeing it as a matter of legal procedure that was outside the organization's expertise to judge.[58] The ABA, on the other hand, tried to draw a finer line, endorsing shifting the burden of proof to the defendant only in jurisdictions that retained both cognitive and volitional standards for insanity. With regard to states that had eliminated the volitional prong, the bar group felt that defendants had been sufficiently hobbled, and it urged that the burden of proof remain with the prosecution.[59]

But the commonsense view expressed by President Reagan when he wondered how anyone could be proved "sane beyond a reasonable doubt" won the day in Congress. The new federal statute placed the burden of proof on the defendant to establish, by clear and convincing evidence, that he or she met the criteria for legal insanity. Seventeen states also modified their burden of proof, with thirteen of them shifting the burden onto the defendant. By 1990, thirty-seven of the fifty-one American jurisdictions had made defendants responsible for proving their impairments.[60]

Restricting Expert Testimony

Another procedural rule that played a role in the Hinckley trial (and subsequently became a focus for reform) permitted expert witnesses to comment directly on whether or not the defendant met the legal test for insanity. This question of whether experts should be allowed to offer testimony on the "ultimate issue" in a case had long been the subject of controversy in the psychiatric and legal communities.[61] Proponents of admitting ultimate issue testimony argued that it allowed witnesses to be maximally helpful to the trier of fact, and that, in any event, efforts to restrict it would only lead attorneys and experts to conspire to convey the experts' ultimate opinions in other ways. The most recent revision of the Federal Rules of Evidence prior to the Hinckley trial had embraced this argument and declined to restrict expert testimony.[62] Jurors in the Washington courtroom in which Hinckley was tried were thus treated to the spectacle of experts for the defense and experts for the prosecution differing with each other directly on whether the defendant met the ALI standard.

Following the Hinckley verdict, the American Psychiatric Association led the attack on the rule permitting ultimate issue testimony.[63] Questions of legal insanity, the APA maintained, reflecting the usual arguments against ultimate issue testimony, did not involve matters about which psychiatrists had special expertise. Rather, these determinations relied on moral judgments regarding the blameworthiness of the defendant and the appropriateness of punishment. To allow psychiatric experts to offer opinions on the ultimate issue encouraged "impermissible leaps in logic" that inevitably confused the jury. Psychiatrists should be limited to testifying about the "defendant's mental state and motivation"—matters about which they as psychiatrists had demonstrated expertise. A beneficial side-effect of such a rule would be a reduction in the degree of public disagreement manifested by experts for the opposing sides, because "in many criminal insanity trials both prosecution and defense psychiatrists . . . agree about the nature and even the extent of mental disorder exhibited by the defendant at the time of the act."[64]

By and large, the APA proposal received favorable comment from the press.[65] Some commentators thought they detected an underlying current of self-interest on the part of the psychiatric profession in extricating itself from the most contentious aspect of insanity trials,[66] but others took it as a reassuring sign of professional humility about the proper scope of psychiatric knowledge.[67] The ABA already had before it a similar proposal that had been drawn up by its task force working to develop a set of Criminal Justice Mental Health Standards, which it ultimately endorsed.[68]

When Congress passed its insanity defense reform bill, the new statute expressly altered the Federal Rules of Evidence on this point:

> No expert witness testifying with respect to the mental state or condition of a defendant in a criminal case may state an opinion or inference as to whether the defendant did or did not have the mental state or condition constituting an element of the crime charged or of a defense thereto. Such ultimate issues are matters for trier of fact alone. (Rule 704)

Altering Posttrial Disposition

The most frequent change in the law governing the insanity defense after the Hinckley trial had nothing to do with what happened in court. Public concern had been mounting through the 1970s over the rapidity with which insanity acquittees, who once faced long (if not permanent) confinement, were being returned to the streets.[69] Some states already had begun experimenting with means of maintaining greater control over persons found not guilty by reason of insanity. Oregon, for example, created a Psychiatric Security Review Board (PSRB) to which insanity acquittees were committed for a period that could extend up to the maximum length of time they might have been confined had they been found guilty.[70] (Despite its name, the PSRB had only one psychiatrist among its five members.) The PSRB, functioning something like a parole board, was empowered to decide when acquittees could be released from confinement and under what conditions, and when rehospitalization was necessary. In its statement on the insanity defense, the APA urged other states to consider the Oregon model.[71]

Although only four states besides Oregon had modified their posttrial procedures during the three years before Hinckley's attempted assassination of the President, thirty-one states took such steps during or after his trial.[72] A number of these states implemented conditional release programs that bore more or less similarity to the Oregon plan.[73] Others instituted fixed periods of mandatory commitment after an NGRI finding, even in the absence of demonstrable dangerousness and mental illness—the criteria required for commitment of civil patients. Some states varied the rigor of their posttrial procedures, depending on whether the defendant's act had involved violence; required that subsequent commitment and release proceedings be conducted in the trial court, where the acquittee was less likely to "slip through the cracks"; and shifted to the acquittee the burden of proving that he or she was no longer dangerous or mentally ill. These efforts were given a boost by the U.S. Supreme Court's decision in *Jones v. U.S.*, in which the justices upheld the constitutionality of automatic commitment of insanity acquittees, confinement (on the basis of dangerousness) for longer than the maximum sentence that could have been imposed had the defendant been found guilty in a regular criminal trial, and placement on the acquittee of the burden of proving nondangerousness.[74]

Instituting the Guilty but Mentally Ill Verdict

One final, curious effort at reform should be noted. In 1974, the Michigan Supreme Court ordered the release of all insanity acquittees who could not meet civil commitment criteria.[75]

Of the 270 acquittees then being detained, 214 were soon released.[76] Within a year, the inevitable crimes of violence occurred, leading to a call for changes in the insanity defense that would enable the state to continue to confine criminals who, although mentally ill, had committed violent acts. In response to this demand, the Michigan legislature crafted a new verdict for criminal trials: guilty but mentally ill (GBMI).[77] Defendants who pled not guilty by reason of insanity could instead be found GBMI, if the jury concluded that they had been mentally ill at the time of the offense but did not meet the standard for legal insanity. A GBMI finding resulted in the defendant being sentenced as if he or she had been found guilty. If required, treatment of the mental disorder could be provided, but in a penal setting.

Taken at face value, the GBMI verdict seemed to add little to existing options. Although its name suggested an intermediate verdict between findings of guilty and of NGRI, in practice the effect of a GBMI verdict is identical to that of a guilty verdict. What then was the point of the new legislation? Lawmakers apparently believed that jurors would be led by the concept—but not the reality—of a compromise finding to select a GBMI verdict for at least some proportion of defendants who would otherwise have been found NGRI.[78] Reacting to this, academics denounced GBMI as "disingenuous"[79] and a "moral slight of hand"[80]—an option that "hoodwinks the jury in the decisional process and . . . hoodwinks the public."[81] "For all the difference it makes," one critic commented "the verdict 'guilty but mentally ill' could just as well be 'guilty but cirrhosis' or 'guilty but flat feet.' "[82]

Nonetheless, even before the furor over the Hinckley trial occurred, the GBMI verdict held some appeal to politicians who felt a need to "do something," no matter how disingenuous, about the insanity defense. A Task Force on Violent Crime set up by the U.S. Attorney General had endorsed the idea of a federal GBMI statute in its final report in 1981.[83] The expressed aim of the recommendation was to provide another option for juries who might otherwise return a generous verdict out of sympathy for a mentally ill defendant who failed to meet the standard for an insanity defense. Shortly after the assault by John Hinckley, Jr., on the President, the states of Illinois, Indiana, and New Mexico followed Michigan in enacting the verdict. In the aftermath of the Hinckley trial, despite condemnation of the GBMI option by groups as diverse in their views of insanity defense issues as the APA, the ABA, the AMA, and the National Mental Health Association, eight other states passed GBMI legislation.[84]

Other Approaches

Not every proposal in the aftermath of the Hinckley verdict called for tightening the insanity defense. The National Mental Health Association convened a panel chaired by former Democratic Senator Birch Bayh, which recommended retaining the ALI standard and the essence of the current procedures.[85] In contrast, the Mental Health Law Project (MHLP), an advocacy group that had been at the forefront of the movement for patients' rights in the 1970s, suggested that an insanity standard even broader than the ALI test should be adopted.[86] Harkening back to a suggestion made by Judge David Bazelon after he had become disenchanted with the "product of mental illness" test embodied in his *Durham* opinion, the MHLP proposed that the criteria for establishing legal insanity essentially be left to the collective conscience of the jury. They urged a standard that read:

> A defendant is not responsible if at the time of his unlawful conduct his mental or emotional processes or behavior controls were impaired to such an extent that he cannot justly be held responsible for his act. (p.7.)

There was little question, though, about the direction in which the dominant mood of the times lay. Public sentiment strongly favored limiting the reach of the insanity defense. Of the forty-one efforts at reform attempted in twenty-eight states between April 1981 and December 1990, almost all were aimed at doing precisely that.[87]

Consequences of Insanity Defense Reform

Most of the reforms enacted on the heels of the Hinckley verdict were designed to reduce the number of defendants who in future were adjudged

NGRI. To what extent was this expectation realized? Compared with the other reforms of mental health law we have considered so far, the impact of changes in the insanity defense have less commonly been empirically investigated. Indeed, much of the available data come from a single, remarkable effort undertaken by sociologist Henry Steadman and his colleagues.[88] This section relies heavily on their findings.

Steadman and his group began by identifying five states that had enacted major changes in their insanity defense laws between 1978 and 1984 (California, Georgia, Montana, New York, and Ohio). Three additional states that had not made such changes were selected for comparison (New Jersey, Washington, and Wisconsin). Because insanity pleas are filed and adjudicated at the county level, and because few states compile detailed information on such cases centrally, data were culled almost entirely from written records of trial courts. Counties were selected for study in such a way as to account for roughly two-thirds of the NGRI acquittals in each state. In most counties, dockets or case files were pulled by hand to determine whether an insanity plea was pursued at any point in the proceedings. More than 1 million indictments were examined to identify 8,979 insanity pleas. Data were collected for at least three years before and after each major reform. Characteristics of the defendants, the processing of the cases, and their outcomes were recorded by the research team.

Consequences of Abolition

The value of this intensive examination of the NGRI process is demonstrated by Steadman et al.'s findings regarding the most dramatic—and seemingly definitive—reform of the insanity defense, Montana's landmark abolition of the special defense of insanity in 1979. (Although a plea of insanity technically could still be filed in Montana after 1979, the verdict was only applicable to defendants who lacked *mens rea,* which effectively abolished the independent defense of insanity.)[89] As one would expect, the rate of successful mental health defenses dropped sharply. In the three years prior to reform, the number of NGRI verdicts had ranged from three to fourteen per six-month period. During the six-and-a-half years after reform, only five *mens rea* acquittals occurred, and three of them took place in the first year after abolition, when substantial confusion may have prevailed regarding the state of the law.[90]

Up to this point, Steadman et al.'s case findings are fairly predictable consequences of abolition of the special defense of insanity: a near disappearance of exculpation of mentally ill defendants. The researchers were puzzled, though, about another finding. To their surprise, nearly four years after the special defense was abolished, the number of mental state pleas filed annually in Montana had not declined. Searching for some incentive that might explain this anomaly, they discovered that many defendants who filed a *mens rea* defense were found incompetent to stand trial in a preliminary hearing and were sent to the state hospital. A large proportion of these defendants (79 percent) subsequently had their charges dismissed or deferred, so that they never came to trial. Thus, defendants still found mental state pleas desirable, because these were likely to lead to dismissal of the charges, once treatment of the mental disorder had occurred.

A comparison of this ad hoc system with the processing of defendants prior to abolition is instructive. Before abolition, 72 percent of those found incompetent to stand trial ultimately were determined to be NGRI. This is almost identical to the figure representing those who were never brought to trial after abolition. Moreover, both historically and demographically, the group of defendants who had been found NGRI prior to reform looked very similar to the group of patients who were now being called incompetent to stand trial and, after hospitalization, were having their charges dismissed.[91]

Although it appeared at first blush that abolition had achieved its desired goal—limiting the number of mentally ill defendants not subject to disposition under normal criminal proceedings—a closer look suggested the contrary. Defendants who previously had been found NGRI and, after trial, had been hospitalized for treatment were now, in roughly similar numbers, being found incompetent to stand trial and were being hospitalized for treatment before trial occurred. Once their treatment was successfully completed, they were released without imposition of criminal sanctions. Further confounding the expectations of the advocates of abolition, the length of stay for defendants who had mental health-related outcomes actually decreased after elimination of the insanity defense[92]; that is, on average, those found NGRI prior to reform were held longer in hospitals than were those found incompetent to stand trial after reform.[93] Steadman and his group summarized their findings on this point in the following way:

> After the reform, most mental disease or defect cases . . . were being found IST [incompetent to stand trial], their charges dismissed or deferred, and they ended up being hospitalized in the same settings where NGRI cases had been sent. Faced with the loss of one avenue, the legal and mental health systems simply found another way to accomplish the same end. If a person's mental status was seen as sufficient to warrant reduced criminal responsibility, they were found IST and committed to the same hospital and the same wards where they would have been confined if they had been found NGRI. (p. 136)

Although the Steadman et al. study is by far the most systematic examination of the consequences of abolition, it does not stand alone in suggesting a paradoxical outcome. Two years after Utah statutorily abolished the special defense of insanity, the clinical director of forensic psychiatry at Utah State Hospital, Peter Heinbecker, reviewed the state's experience.[94]

During the roughly ten years when the ALI standard was operative in Utah (1973–1983), only seven defendants were found NGRI. In the two years following abolition of the special defense, however, another seven defendants were exculpated under the *mens rea* law. In other words, abolition of the more generous standard of exculpation was followed by a fivefold increase in the annual rate of successful mental state defenses. Heinbecker, after reviewing the records of each of these cases, concluded that in virtually no case did the defendant fail to manifest *mens rea;* that is, these findings of criminal nonresponsibility did not appear to be justifiable under the *mens rea* statute. All of the post-reform nonresponsibility findings were the result of pleas negotiated between prosecutors and defense attorneys ''as a mutually acceptable way of disposing of the lawsuit.'' Thus, in two out of the three states that abolished the special defense of insanity—at least for the years immediately following reform—abolition proved ineffective at ensuring that defendants were tried and punished as common criminals for their wrongful acts.[95]

Consequences of Changes in Legal Standards and the Burden of Proof

Given the difficulty researchers had in verifying the anticipated effects of abolishing the special defense of insanity, it might be expected that studies of less drastic reforms, such as modifying the insanity test, would have similar paradoxical outcomes. To a large extent, this indeed has been the case. Studies conducted prior to the latest round of insanity defense reforms had yielded conflicting evidence regarding the impact of changes in statutory language governing the standard for insanity. When jurisdictions in the 1950s and 1960s expanded the scope of their insanity standards, replacing the *McNaughtan* standard with the ALI test or (in the District of Columbia) with the *Durham* standard, increases in the number of NGRI acquittals were generally observed.[96] Pasewark and colleagues, however, found no differences in the rates at which insanity pleas were filed and NGRI verdicts were obtained as Wyoming moved, between 1973 and 1979, from a *McNaughtan* standard to an ALI standard with a bifurcated trial to an ALI standard with a single trial.[97] Psychologist Ira Packer, looking at Michigan's 1975 adoption of the ALI standard in place of a combined *McNaughtan* and irresistible impulse rule, similarly found no change in the number of acquittals per year or in the percentage of arrests per year that led to NGRI findings.[98] These studies, however, all dealt with situations in which insanity standards were broadened, generally during periods of popular and judicial support for dealing more leniently with mentally ill offenders. Even if a clear pattern could be discerned in these instances, it might not apply to the immediate pre- and post-Hinckley context, in which standards were tightened and hostility toward the insanity defense was growing.

To test the effects of narrowing the insanity standard following the attack by John Hinckley, Jr., on President Reagan, Steadman and his collaborators examined the impact of statutory change in California. That state dropped the ALI standard in July 1982, adopting in its place a form of the *McNaughtan* standard and thereby essentially eliminating the volitional prong of the insanity test.[99] Both insanity pleas and acquittals declined throughout much of the study period, as anticipated, but the decrease had already begun prior to adoption of the new insanity standard, and the rate of decline appeared unaffected by the new law. Rather than constituting a reaction to the altered insanity standard, the fall-off in insanity pleas seems to be due to a change in 1979 in the terms of commitment for persons found NGRI. The California legislature, in response to a state supreme court decision, authorized NGRIs to be held for up to the longest term of imprisonment they could have received, if found guilty, excluding credits for good behavior. Moreover, hospitals increasingly began to hold NGRI acquittees for that maximum term. Since convicts serving their sentences in the state prison system typically received time off for good behavior, defendants who pled NGRI thereby opened up the possibility of being confined longer than they probably would have been if found guilty. It is little wonder that, with these disincentives in place, the rate of NGRI pleas began to fall. On the other hand, among defendants who did plead NGRI in the post-reform period, despite the more stringent standards, the success rate did not change significantly, nor did the characteristics of the persons who employed the insanity defense. Moreover, the length of time that defendants who were found NGRI were detained did not change at all. Thus, the most widely heralded reform of the post-Hinckley era—dropping the volitional prong of the ALI test (of which California's standard was one version)—appeared to have no independent impact on the success with which the insanity defense could be employed.

Another common legislative reaction to the Hinckley verdict involved shifting the burden of proof of insanity to the defendant, extricating the state from the uncomfortable position of having to prove that the person was sane. Steadman's group again has provided the only follow-up data. They looked at the effects of shifting the burden of proof to the defendant, focusing on Georgia, (which reformed its procedures in 1978) and New York (which followed suit in 1984). In both states, shifting the burden of proof led to a decrease in the rate at which insanity pleas were filed and in the overall number of NGRI verdicts—the expected result of the reform.[100] Thus, in contrast to the effects of tinkering with the insanity standard (as California did) or abolishing the special defense of insanity altogether (as in Montana and Utah), placing the burden of proof on the defendant appears to have a demonstrable impact in reducing the rate of insanity pleas and NGRI findings, and in tending to limit the plea to a more severely mentally ill group of defendants, for whom it might well be more appropriate.

Consequences of Changes in Posttrial Disposition

Posttrial procedures also came in for their share of attention in the wave of insanity defense reforms that occurred during the late 1970s and early 1980s. Few states pursued abolition of the insanity defense, making it inevitable that some defendants would be found NGRI. The prospect that insanity acquittees, especially murderers and sex offenders, would be released (after brief and ineffectual treatment) to the community, only to repeat their crimes, struck a primordial chord of fear in many members of the public. Indeed, some proponents of the insanity defense argued that it was less the NGRI verdict itself than the possibility of recidivism that was responsible for the intensity of popular opposition to the insanity defense. Both advocates and opponents of the insanity defense, therefore, had strong motivations to design systems of posttrial detention and supervision that minimized the risk of repeated offenses. This meant, in most cases, reversing the trend established during the 1960s and 1970s of adopting similar procedures for the release of insanity acquittees as for patients who were civilly committed. In particular, proposed reforms emphasized ensuring that, once insanity acquittees were released from the hospital, the state did not relinquish its coercive power over them altogether. The most crucial posttrial reforms in the handling of insanity acquittees were designed to guarantee that the state could monitor their status, require continuing treatment, and easily reconfine them when necessary, after they had been released to the community.[101]

Given that the dispositional changes were intended to reduce the rate of new crimes committed by NGRI acquittees, we need some sense of the baseline rate of criminal recidivism in this group if we are to judge the success of such efforts. Unfortunately, but perhaps not surprisingly, the extant data leave a great deal to be desired. Most studies base their recidivism rates on arrest data, and the relation of these to actual criminal behavior is always uncertain. Beyond this, studies are difficult to compare because of varying lengths of follow-up, different definitions of recidivism, and uncertainty about the degree of supervision to which acquittees were actually subject. Nonetheless, we can conclude with some assurance that naturalistic rates of recidivism are quite substantial. Pre-reform New York data on 148 persons who were found NGRI during the period from 1971 to 1976 and who were released by August 1981 showed that 32 percent had arrests of some kind after release to the community—23 percent of the sample being arrested for a felony.[102] Arrest rates in an Oklahoma study were almost identical, while a Canadian study of 200 NGRIs who were followed for an average of six-and-a-half years found recidivism (defined as arrest and revocation of release for arrestable behaviors) at 41 percent and rates of violence at 20 percent.[103]

In the late 1970s, Oregon undertook what has become the most widely discussed reform of posttrial procedures for NGRIs. Its Psychiatric Security Review Board (PSRB) is the most intensively studied posttrial reform model, with numerous reports published by psychiatrist Joseph Bloom and his colleagues.[104] Given the high rate of recidivism demonstrated in other studies, the close follow-up and the ability to rehospitalize acquittees rapidly that characterize the Oregon system appear to have had a substantial positive effect. A review of the first five years of PSRB operations showed that only 13 percent of its subjects had been charged with new crimes while on conditional release and that another 5 percent had been charged during an escape, while on pass, or while in the hospital[105]; after nine years, the overall arrest rate for the group had dropped to 15 percent.[106] Another way to examine PSRB effectiveness is to compare arrest rates prior to, during, and after PSRB involvement. A sample of 137 schizophrenic subjects who had been on conditional release for at least one year had a rate of 0.41 criminal contacts (apparently equivalent to arrests) per person per year, compared with 0.69 contacts per person per year prior to their index offenses.[107] Only 3 of these subjects were charged with serious crimes. In another sample, arrest rates increased from 0.2 per person per year to 0.54 per person per year after PSRB jurisdiction over the study's subjects was terminated.[108] The full nine-year sample showed a drop in arrest rates from 0.5 per person per year prior to the index offense to 0.3 per person per year after discharge from PSRB oversight, with a significant shift toward less serious offenses.[109]

Other programs of close community supervision have had varying recidivism rates, ranging from 2 percent among a highly specialized sample in Illinois[110] to 22 percent in New York[111] to 32 percent in California[112] to 56 percent in Maryland[113] to 67 percent in Hawaii.[114] Comparisons are problematic because selection procedures and criteria among the programs differed greatly, as did the intensity of follow-up, the ease with which subjects could be confined if they violated terms of release, and the periods over which subjects were followed to ascertain the rate of recidivism. There is one common element, however: successful programs appear to be aggressive in revoking the release of subjects who violate its terms.

Wiederanders, for example, in evaluating California's CONREP program for insanity acquittees, found one-year arrest rates of 5.8 percent— significantly less than the 27.3 percent rate for acquittees who were released unconditionally.[115] There was no difference in rate of reconfinement when rehospitalization was taken into account, although the unconditionally released group probably spent more time in confinement. Lower rates of recidivism in California are largely bought at the price of periods of civil detention. Similarly, in Oregon, 67 percent of subjects who were hospitalized after trial in the first nine years of that state's PSRB spent the entire study period in the hospital, and 68 percent of all time spent under PSRB jurisdiction was hospital time. Among acquittees placed on conditional release, 56 percent experienced revocation or voluntary rehospitalization.[116]

If generalization is possible, it suggests that intensive community supervision is more effective at detecting decompensation and initiating rehospitalization than it is at maintaining acquittees safely in the community. Nonetheless, during the period an acquittee can be kept in the community, costs to the state are reduced and the acquittee enjoys greater liberty, which may aid in adjustment after supervision is ended. Cross-jurisdictional research is badly needed to assess the comparative effectiveness of different approaches and to identify the program elements most directly responsible for a positive outcome.

Consequences of the GBMI Verdict

That oddity of twentieth-century insanity defense law—the guilty but mentally ill verdict—is the final reform to consider. Its goal was to provide an alternative to the NGRI verdict that would divert some mentally ill defendants to prison. The earliest data, naturally, come from Michigan, the state that gave birth to GBMI in 1975. A review of the six years following implementation of the verdict showed no significant change in the rate of defendants pleading NGRI or in the number of those attaining NGRI verdicts.[117] It is tempting, on the basis of these data, to conclude that adopting the GBMI verdict had no impact on rates of NGRI findings in Michigan, especially since defendants who were found GBMI seemed to resemble defendants found guilty more than they did NGRIs.

Critics, however, have pointed out problems with that conclusion.[118] Michigan made multiple changes in its insanity defense law at the same time that it instituted the GBMI verdict—including centralizing insanity evaluations, changing the insanity standard, and providing a new definition of mental illness. Indeed, given that rates of NGRI pleas almost tripled from 1975 to 1981, the absence of change in the rate of NGRI verdicts could be taken as an indication that GBMI had a substantial effect as an alternative disposition. Studies in other states ran into similar problems.[119]

Once again, therefore, we turn to the Steadman et al. study for the best estimate of the outcome of adopting a GBMI verdict. Steadman's group examined Georgia, which enacted a GBMI approach in 1982. The study, using data for the period from three years before to three years after the change, found no difference in the rate of NGRI pleas. Successful pleas decreased, but this reflected a trend that began before the GBMI verdict and did not accelerate during the study period. Although overall effects were hard to demonstrate, there did seem to be some impact in cases of more serious crimes. Before reform, 20 percent of insanity pleas in murder cases were successful; afterward, the success rate dropped to 7 percent, while 25 percent were found GBMI. Conversely, before reform 75 percent of murder defendants were found guilty, while after reform that rate fell to 50 percent. The GBMI verdict, therefore, seems to have drawn from both pools.

The process by which defendants were found GBMI, all studies agree, differed from what proponents of the verdict had anticipated. The GBMI verdict was aimed at juries. The idea was to provide an alternative verdict that jurors could select when they believed that a defendant was mentally ill but were reluctant to exculpate him or her entirely. The Georgia data, however, showed that 75 percent of GBMI verdicts came through plea negotiations, 19 percent after bench trials, and only 6 percent as a result of jury trials. In Michigan, 60 percent of GBMIs came from uncontested pleas, and 20 percent from jury trials[120]; in Pennsylvania, 82.5 percent came from pleas[121]; and in South Carolina, no one was found GBMI by a jury.[122]

Why should defendants plead GBMI when the statutory consequences are no different from those flowing from a finding of guilty, and when some GBMIs might receive effectively longer sentences than persons simply found guilty?[123] Various answers have been suggested, including ignorance on the part of lawyers and defendants of the implications of the verdict, and defense attorneys who falsely persuaded their clients that a GBMI finding represented a partial victory. In the Georgia murder cases that Steadman et al. examined, the motivation is less obscure. Although defendants pleading GBMI got longer sentences than those found guilty after unsuccessfully pleading insanity, none received the death penalty. Georgia prosecutors apparently accepted GBMI pleas when they were persuaded that mental illness at least partially mitigated the offenders' culpability, and judges responded accordingly.[124]

To summarize the data on the consequences of insanity defense reform, it seems fair to say that many of the reformers' expectations were not realized. Abolition of the insanity defense has not affected the number of mentally ill defendants who avoid punishment for their acts. Tinkering with the standard for insanity—the subject of endless debates and countless articles in legal and mental health literature—similarly has had little impact. The guilty but mentally ill verdict may have had some impact in high-profile cases, but not for the reasons its proponents expected. Moreover, the data are limited and—in more ways than one—the jury is still out. Tightening posttrial supervision of NGRI acquittees may reduce the number of offenses they subsequently commit, but largely at the cost of keeping them confined for long periods of time. The only change for which the data indicate a clear effect consists of shifting the burden of proof to the defendant. That seemingly minor procedural detail appears substantially to decrease the number of persons acquitted by reason of insanity. Given all the fuss over insanity defense reform, these are slim pickings indeed.

Why the Limited Impact of Insanity Defense Reforms?

Why did changes in the law governing the insanity defense have so little impact on the number of persons who are excused from punishment by virtue of their mental state? An important part of the explanation may lie in a fundamental misconception underlying many insanity defense reform efforts. In the wake of the Hinckley trial, the belief was widespread that large numbers of defendants "beat the rap" by pleading insanity, finding psychiatrists whose mistaken or suborned testimony supported their fraudulent claims, and persuading jurors bewildered by psychiatric jargon and overcome by misplaced sympathy that they were "mad" and not "bad." The resulting diversion of defendants from prisons to mental hospitals—from which they were thought to be released with undue haste—was perceived to be playing a significant role in the supposed breakdown of law and order. If rules that disproportionately favored defendants could be changed, conventional wisdom maintained, the inevitable results would be a sharp drop in the number of persons found NGRI and a concomitant increase in those who received their due punishment.[125]

This argument pivoted on the premise that the insanity defense played a major role in the criminal justice process, freeing myriad defendants from punishment each year. But this core premise was seriously flawed. Only a minuscule percentage of defendants ever entertain insanity defenses, and fewer still are successful with them. Steadman et al.'s data, the most comprehensive on the subject, show that rates of insanity pleas in the eight jurisdictions they studied ranged from 0.30 percent of felony indictments in New Jersey, to 5.74 percent in Montana.[126] Moreover the success of an NGRI plea could not be taken for granted, since rates varied from a low of 7.31 percent of such pleas in Montana to a high of 87.36 percent in Washington State. Overall, 0.93 percent of 967,209 felony indictments in the states studied resulted in NGRI pleas, of which 26 percent were successful. In general, the higher the rate of NGRI pleas to all pleas the lower the success rate. These data are in keeping with the rates found in other studies.[127] Lande, for example, reported that, of 104,434 criminal cases heard in federal trial courts from 1987 to 1989, only 24 defendants were found NGRI, a rate of 0.02 percent. One explanation for the failure of many reforms to reduce NGRI findings, therefore, is that such a small proportion of defendants are found NGRI in the first place. There is simply not much room for change.

Of course, even if only a small fraction of defendants are found NGRI, their numbers could be reduced further if means of preventing "unjustified" insanity verdicts from being reached could be found. But the assumption that a large percentage of NGRI acquittees succeeded in fooling the system by feigning mental disorder to avoid punishment appears unwarranted. Although direct tests of the legitimacy of individual insanity verdicts are wanting, indirect evidence suggests that the stereotype of a malingering defendant, with an astute lawyer and a "bought and paid for" psychiatrist, fooling gullible jurors is off the mark. The vast majority of successful insanity defenses occur without trial, as a result of negotiated pleas between prosecutors and defense attorneys. Bloom's group in Oregon, for example, found that 86 percent of NGRIs committed to that state's PSRB had negotiated their verdicts with prosecutors, while another 10 percent had bench trials (trials before a judge, with no jury involved), and only 4 percent had been found not responsible by a jury.[129] The Steadman et al. data reveal similar figures in the states they studied.[130] If anyone is being fooled here, it is not naive jurors, but tough prosecutors and trial court judges—persons not generally given to letting culpable defendants off the hook.

Further evidence for the integrity of the current system comes from studies attempting to establish the most influential factors in the outcome of insanity defense cases. Researchers are unanimous in concluding that the major correlate of a finding of insanity is the opinion of the forensic examiner or team of examiners who evaluated the defendant. In independent studies in Colorado, in New York, and in Illinois and Ohio, the rate of concurrence between examiners' opinions and judicial findings was 88 percent[131]; a study in Hawaii found a rate of 93 percent.[132] Of course, if the examiners themselves were being fooled by defendants, there would be little comfort in these figures. Thus, it is reassuring that the major predictor of a clinical opinion supporting an insanity defense was the presence of a psychotic disorder.[133] Aggregate data of this sort cannot eliminate the possibility that some abuses are occurring. Examiners may be fooled, prosecutors may be complacent, judges may be inept, and juries may be gullible. The data, however, are consistent with a system that is generally doing what it is supposed to be doing: identifying a small proportion of defendants undeserving of punishment because their behavior was affected by serious mental impairment. Reforms aimed merely at improving the current system would seem to have little scope within which to achieve their goals.

Most reforms, though, were not targeted simply at helping judges and jurors make better decisions. Changes such as narrowing the standard for nonculpability and introducing a GBMI verdict were designed to alter and restrict the population eligible for an NGRI finding. Moreover, even less radical means of tinkering with the insanity defense process—such as restricting ultimate-issue testimony by experts—might be expected to have some impact on the process, especially with regard to the cases, however few, now inappropriately resolved. Why have such effects been so difficult to demonstrate?

Useful in answering this question is a body of data generated outside the courtroom, in the experimental models of psychologists studying decision making by persons asked to simulate the role of jurors in insanity defense trials. Although the data are helpful and impressively consistent, some cautions about interpreting them are in order. Most studies of decision making in relation to the insanity defense have involved college students as subjects—hardly a sample representative of the general population. The stimuli they have used include edited trial transcripts, brief written vignettes, and videotapes meant to simulate key elements of a trial. In most cases, subjects' decisions were reached individually, without the joint deliberation that is a defining characteristic of the jury system. Finally, subjects in the studies are well aware that the verdicts they render involve hypothetical cases with no real-world impact. Given these methodological problems, therefore, this group of studies should be taken as offering suggestive rather than conclusive evidence of the functioning of jurors and other decision makers in the insanity defense process.

The effect of the various insanity tests in mock jurors' decisions has been a prime focus of these studies. For example, psychologist Norman Finkel provided subjects (usually college students) with vignettes of insanity defense cases.[134] Participants were asked to reach decisions regarding the appropriate verdict—not guilty, guilty, or NGRI—and the tests they were asked to apply were varied systematically. Among the insanity tests Finkel compared were the "wild beast" test; *McNaughtan; McNaughtan* combined with an irresistible impulse rule; the ALI standard; the new federal insanity test; and a more complex decisionmaking framework called the "disability of mind" approach. Although participants routinely distinguished among the cases they reviewed, judging some to be more worthy of NGRI verdicts than others, their willingness to find a defendant not guilty by reason of insanity was not at all affected by the standard they were instructed to use. Even more startling, subjects given the same cases without any instructions as to which test to apply did not differ in their verdicts from the other groups.[135] Ogloff, comparing subjects instructed to apply *McNaughtan* with those told to utilize the ALI standard after watching a trial videotape, similarly found no difference between the groups in the rate of NGRI findings.[136] Indeed, when asked to list the factors that were important to their decisions, his subjects ranked many considerations ahead of the legal standard.

How might the data be interpreted? With due caution, given the caveats previously noted, it appears that persons asked to make judgments of criminal responsibility begin with some innate sense of which offenders deserve punishment and which do not. Finkel found that his subjects were able to develop fairly elaborate rationales for their decisions, calling on different factors depending on the nature of the case, but with little correspondence to any particular legal test.[137] Ogloff concluded that his subjects may simply have been using their visceral instincts, judging whether the defendants they were "trying" justly could be held responsible for their acts. If these findings are generalizable to real-life juries—and to prosecutors and judges, who make most decisions regarding NGRI verdicts—they may explain the peculiar difficulty investigators such as Steadman have had in finding demonstrable effects of alterations in insanity standards. Beyond this, such an explanation seems consistent with the surprising survival of procedures that are used to avoid punishing certain mentally ill defendants in jurisdictions that have entirely abolished the affirmative defense of insanity.[138]

Another set of experimental studies looked at the consequences of procedural changes at insanity defense trials. The federal Insanity Defense Reform Act of 1984, for example, altered the Federal Rules of Evidence to prevent expert witnesses from commenting directly on whether defendants met the relevant standard for legal insanity. Behind this move lay concern about the interjection of experts' personal biases into their conclusions, a concern magnified by the dominant role expert opinions seem to play in insanity defense cases. Testing the premise that exclusion of testimony addressing the ultimate issue of insanity would reduce the number of NGRI findings, Fulero and Finkel gave a hypothetical written case description to 271 subjects.[139] They found no significant difference in the incidence of NGRI decisions based on whether the expert presented testimony about the defendant's mental disorder only in clinical terms, related the clinical condition to the legal standard, or directly addressed the ultimate issue of insanity.

A group of Canadian psychologists took a more sophisticated look at this question, exposing 460 subjects to transcripts that varied along several dimensions, including whether the expert testimony characterized the defendant as having been psychotic, whether an ultimate opinion was offered on the insanity question, and the degree of confidence (60 percent, 80 percent, or 100 percent) expressed by the expert.[140] Although the expert's conclusions regarding whether the defendant was psychotic had a significant effect on subjects' verdicts, the presence or absence of an opinion framed in terms of the legal test for insanity had no effect at all. Interestingly, expert opinions regarding psychosis only exerted an effect on subjects when the experts claimed 80 percent certainty. Professions of 60 percent or 100 percent certainty failed to sway the mock jurors—one perhaps seeming too close to chance and the other too cocksure. The authors concluded that the impact of expert testimony, especially regarding the ultimate issue of insanity, may well be overrated.

It is worth underscoring the caution with which conclusions from mock juror studies must be approached. For example, Ogloff found no effect on subjects' decisions in two separate studies from manipulating the burden and standard of proof.[141] Indeed, when questioned after having made their decisions, only two-thirds of his subjects could remember which party had the burden of proof, and only one-half recalled the standard of proof (for example, beyond a reasonable doubt) they had been asked to employ. Yet, Steadman et al. found in actual cases that reallocating the burden of proof to the defendant was the most potent intervention a state could make to reduce the rate of insanity findings.[142]

Another example of apparent differences in decision making between mock jurors and their real-life counterparts comes from several studies that have examined the impact of introducing a verdict of guilty but mentally ill. Several sets of investigators have found profound effects on rates of NGRI verdicts of instructing mock jurors that they could find a defendant GBMI. Rates of GBMI verdicts in the studies ranged from 34 percent[143] to 68 percent[144] to a staggering 73 percent[145] and 75 percent.[146] In contrast, studies of states that have adopted a GBMI verdict have demonstrated that, if introducing a GBMI option has an effect at all, it is an exceedingly subtle one.

Nonetheless, other kinds of data support what appear to be the central messages of the mock juror studies: that statutory criteria play a limited role in decision making about the insanity defense, and that altering statutory language may not be a very effective way of achieving change. Researchers have developed evidence that other factors exert a major influence on whether a defendant is found NGRI. Boehnert, for example, compared 30 successful NGRIs with an equal number of defendants who pled NGRI but were found guilty.[147] She concluded that perpetrators of more heinous crimes tended to be found guilty, even though subjects in the two groups had roughly equivalent degrees of mental disorder.[148] Indeed, commentators have often observed that notorious defendants—Sirhan Sirhan, "Son of Sam," and Jeffrey Dahmer come readily to mind—no matter how crazy, are almost always found guilty.[149] Perhaps the major reason for the controversy following the Hinckley verdict was its perceived violation of this rule. Conversely, for crimes below a certain threshold of heinousness, the perception that defendants either do not warrant punishment or deserve to be treated for their disorders may lead to findings of insanity, regardless of the legal parameters in effect.[150]

Unfortunately, more investigation of how the insanity defense operates occurs in psychology laboratories and courtroom archives than in the courtroom itself. But one of the only observational studies of insanity defense cases, conducted by A. C. Singer, a public defender in New Jersey, confirms the impact of nonstatutory factors and extends the list of incentives that may influence NGRI findings.[151] In Singer's study, only five of the forty-six cases she examined involved jury trials; she noted that prosecutors and judges were attracted to NGRI verdicts by the prospect that defendants found NGRI could be held indefinitely, as long as they were thought to be dangerous and had some degree of mental disorder. Moreover, in practice this could be achieved without providing proof beyond a reasonable doubt that they had committed the act charged. The efficiency of accepting a negotiated or uncontested NGRI verdict, rather than undertaking a lengthy trial, also appealed to them. Defense attorneys, on the other hand, took pride in their apparent "success" at avoiding a guilty finding when they negotiated an insanity verdict, regardless of the long-term consequences for the defendant. When an insanity agreement satisfied every party's perceived interests, scant attention was paid to the fine points of statutory law.

The popular assumption that use of the insanity defense is easily modified is based on several incorrect premises. Insanity verdicts are awarded much less frequently than is commonly believed, and no substantial evidence exists to indicate that they are commonly obtained by deceit. Moreover, the verdict appears to be more than an abstract creation of common law and statute. Regardless of what most people tell interviewers in public opinion surveys about their sense that the insanity defense is being abused, when faced with the task of making decisions about mentally ill defendants, they seem to act on an innate sense that punishment should not be imposed in certain cases. Perceptions of which cases should be exempted from punishment are relatively resistant to alteration by rules of law, suggesting that they are embedded in individual moral codes. Many would-be reformers of the insanity defense—especially those who would abolish it altogether—have missed this point. The insanity defense is less an imposition on commonly held notions of morality than an expression of them. As such, although it is susceptible to some degree of modification by the law, the extent to which it can be "reformed" successfully is limited by the reluctance of participants to violate their own moral intuitions.

Future of the Insanity Defense

The impetus for reform following the Hinckley trial was spent by the late 1980s. Past history, however, suggests that a new wave of statutory changes lurks somewhere on the horizon, awaiting the next highly publicized acquittal of a defendant by reason of insanity. Perhaps the crime will be particularly heinous, such as the sexually motivated murder of a young child. Or the victim may be a beloved and respected public figure, since such figures seem disproportionately to stir murderous impulses among persons of dubious mental stability. Almost certainly the testimony of the expert witnesses at trial will be ambiguous and conflicting—some portraying the defendant as hopelessly impaired, others suggesting that the defendant manifested a deliberate and callous disregard for human life. Acquittal will be followed by an outcry: the insanity defense is an abomination that allows the guilty to walk free; something must be done to change it. A new round of reform will begin.

Maybe it is in anticipation of this seemingly inevitable sequence of events that analyses of the insanity defense and proposals for reform continue to flow. The reciprocal relationship between theories of moral responsibility and the insanity defense attracts endless commentary, offering new ways of understanding current approaches,[152] or urging that we reconceptualize our fundamental notions of who should be exculpated from responsibility for their crimes.[153] Certainly, the popular literature on insanity and crime grows apace, fed equally by public fear of and by public curiosity about the link between violence and mental disorder.[154]

How will our society respond to future pressures for reform? The abolitionist imperative seems to have dissipated. Although there will undoubtedly be renewed calls for eliminating an affirmative defense of insanity, the data from Montana and Utah demonstrating the paradoxical effects of such a change are likely to dampen enthusiasm for this approach.[155] But the attraction of further manipulating definitions of legal insanity will remain strong. Are there possibilities beyond modifying the current cognitive and volitional standards? Two other options are likely to enter the debate.

Some scholars remain convinced that finer distinctions need to be drawn among degrees of defendants' culpability. Herbert Fingarette, a professor at the University of California, Berkeley, School of Law, is a leading exponent of this approach. With collaborator Ann Hasse, he proposes that any mental impairment at the time of a crime, including intoxication, be classified as a "disability of mind."[156] Once the jury determined that a defendant had committed the criminal act alleged, it would then have the task of judging whether a disability existed, whether the disability was partial or total, and whether it was voluntarily or negligently induced by the defendant (for example, by consuming alcoholic beverages or by neglecting to take antipsychotic medication). In the last case, the defendant would retain responsibility for his or her subsequent actions. Thus, four verdicts (in addition to "guilty") would be possible: nonculpable disability of mind (equivalent to a finding of insanity), nonculpable partial disability of mind (which would result in a guilty verdict, but might lead to mitigation at sentencing), culpable disability of mind, and culpable partial disability of mind (without mitigating effect). The advantages of this approach, according to proponents, are the elimination of conceptual confusion and a diminution in the impact of expert testimony on juries' decisions.

Finkel, in the name of further clarifying the disability of mind approach, would add two additional verdicts: partially culpable disability of mind and partially culpable partial disability of mind.[157] In a study of students who attempted to apply his schema, Finkel found a marked reduction in the total numbers of cases judged NGRI (which corresponds to nonculpable disability of mind) and judged guilty, with the differences spread out over the remaining categories.[158] He concluded that a broader range of verdict options more accurately reflects the distinctions that jurors make among defendants pleading insanity.

Whatever the conceptual advantages of offering more categories into which defendants can be sorted (and the idea that the disability of mind doctrine offers any advantages at all has been challenged forcefully[159]), the notion sounds like a bad parody of criminal law. Persuasive evidence exists that jurors fail to understand the instructions they are now given, with only three options (guilty, not guilty, and NGRI) under consideration. Providing six alternatives to an NGRI verdict is a recipe for utter confusion. Even in his experimental paradigm, Finkel had to give four pages of written instructions to his subjects to explain the approach. Whether or not his highly motivated psychology students understood the choices, it is unrealistic to expect that ordinary jurors will comprehend them.

An additional, equally significant problem with "disability of mind" or any other schema that multiplies the complexity of decision making in insanity cases is its likely impact on the public at large. Uneducated in legal doctrine, not exposed to trial testimony, and unaware of judges' instructions to juries, ordinary citizens already have enormous difficulty understanding the principles involved in insanity defense cases. Any effort designed to add to this complexity would threaten to undermine the crucial educative function of the criminal law. When the public does not understand proceedings, the temptation to assume that the law is being manipulated to the advantage of particular defendants and against the interests of the common weal becomes irresistible. It is difficult to believe that future reforms will embrace an insanity defense doctrine that is any more complicated than contemporary approaches. Disability of mind seems doomed to be the plaything of scholars.

At the other end of the reform spectrum are proposals to simplify current insanity defense tests. The most powerful of these suggestions is the most straightforward: allow judges or juries to acquit mentally ill defendants when, in the decision makers' judgment, they cannot justly be held responsible for their acts. Judge David Bazelon embraced this approach in the early 1960s, as the D.C. Circuit Court of Appeals was dismantling the "product of mental illness" standard created in Bazelon's opinion in *Durham*.[160] During the controversy following the Hinckley trial, the Mental Health Law Project was a lone voice urging a "justly responsible" approach.[161]

Although it has never been adopted in this country, the idea is unlikely to disappear. It has the virtue of cutting to the core of the rationale for a defense of nonresponsibility by reason of mental illness. We exculpate defendants by reason of insanity precisely because it would be unjust to convict them. Moreover, recent data demonstrating the relative invariance of mock jurors' decisions, regardless of the standard they have been instructed to use, suggest that this is already the test being applied in practice.[162] If so, codifying this approach would have the added benefit of bowing to reality. Instructions to jurors would be simplified immensely, and the public might obtain a clearer view of what the insanity defense is all about.

That the "justly responsible" test has not yet been adopted, however, despite its putative advantages, suggests significant resistance by the legal system. Affording juries unbridled discretion—which is how the justly responsible approach is likely to be seen—has never been popular among legislators and judges. Indeed, the usual impulse of appellate courts has been to require ever greater precision in the framing of the jury's task, and detailed analysis of jury instructions has been a prime focus of appellate decisions. The result has been a proliferation of intricately worded paragraphs and clauses, in the face of increasing evidence that many jurors neither remember nor attend to the instructions they receive. Although juries now, in fact, have considerable discretion in reaching their judgments of insanity, the legal system is likely to remain reluctant to codify that discretion into a rule of law.[163]

We can anticipate, therefore, continued changes in existing cognitive and volitional standards. This might seem like a fool's errand, given the message of empirical research that the nominal standard makes little difference in outcome. But the temptation to alter the wording of the tests will undoubtedly be irresistible (or at least not resisted). Data on the effects of shifting the burden of proof to the defendant may well motivate jurisdictions that have not already done so to make that move. Popularity of the guilty but mentally ill verdict has probably reached its peak and may soon begin to decline. And considerable attention almost certainly will be paid to more intensive follow-up of acquittees after trial, with the Oregon, California, and Maryland systems serving as models for other states.

If we are willing to learn, the post-Hinckley experience has something to teach us about the intrinsic meaning of the insanity defense. Like several of the other aspects of mental health law that we have examined, it is rooted in commonsense perceptions of fairness. Having descended from the Anglo-American legal tradition, our beliefs about the appropriateness of punishment are closely tied to the idea of moral blameworthiness. Those who cannot be blamed, cannot fairly be punished. The insight afforded by the most recent round of reforms in the United States is that perceptions of moral culpability are not easily affected by legal rules. That should allow us to feel more comfortable with the insanity defense as a genuine expression of our most profound moral principles.

References

1. The account of Hinckley's attempt on the life of President Reagan and its aftermath is based on reports found in J. W. Clark, *On Being Mad or Merely Angry: John W. Hinckley, Jr. and Other Dangerous People* (Princeton, N.J.: Princeton University Press, 1990); and L. Caplan, *The Insanity Defense and the Trial of John W. Hinckley, Jr.* (Boston: David R. Godine, 1984).
2. Aristotle, *Nichomachean Ethics, Book Four* (Indianapolis: Bobbs-Merrill, 1962).
3. N. Walker, "The Insanity Defense Before 1800," in R. Moran, ed., *The Insanity Defense. Annals of the American Academy of Political and Social Science* 477: 25–30 (1985).
4. Ibid.
5. Compare ibid. with American Medical Association, "Insanity Defense in Criminal Trials and Limitations of Psychiatric Testimony," *Journal of the American Medical Association* 251: 2967–81 (1984).
6. H. Bracton, *Of the Laws and Customs of England*, cited in Walker, *supra* note 3.
7. *Rex v. Arnold*, 16 How. St. Tr. 684 (1723).
8. Walker, *supra* note 3.
9. Ibid.
10. R. Moran, "The Modern Foundation for the Insanity Defense: The Case of James Hadfield (1800) and Daniel McNaughtan (1843)," in Moran, ed., *The Insanity Defense. Annals of the American Academy of Political and Social Science* 477: 25–30 (1985).
11. See, e.g., R. Moran, *Knowing Right from Wrong: The Insanity Defense of Daniel McNaughtan* (New York: Free Press, 1981). The focus of scholarly argument rests on whether McNaughtan had straightforward political motives for attempting to assassinate Pell—indeed, whether he might have been paid to carry out the act—or whether he was acting on the basis of delusions, as his lawyers later claimed.
12. Ibid.
13. A. S. Goldstein, *The Insanity Defense* (New Haven, Conn.: Yale University Press, 1967).
14. *State v. Jones*, 50 N.H. 369 (1871); see also *State v. Pike*, 49 N.H. 399 (1869).
15. The common critiques of *McNaughtan* are nicely summarized, with an attempted refutation, in Goldstein, *supra* note 13.
16. *Durham v. U.S.*, 214 F.2d 862 (D.C. Cir. 1954). Bazelon later became frustrated with the conclusory testimony of many psychiatric witnesses, who simply testified that the accused's behavior was the "product" of mental disorder, rather than describing the antecedents of the behavior thoroughly so that the finder of fact could draw a considered conclusion. See *Washington v. U.S.*, 390 F.2d 444 (D.C. Cir. 1967). After several attempts at reform, the D.C. Circuit abandoned the *Durham* test in 1972, replacing it with the American Law Institute standard, as discussed in the main text. See *U.S. v. Brawner*, 471 F.2d 969 (D.C. Cir. 1972).

17. American Law Institute, *Model Penal Code,* Sec. 4.01 (1955).
18. Goldstein (*supra* note 13) argues persuasively that, in practice, *McNaughtan* was often *not* interpreted as requiring absolute deficiencies in knowledge of right and wrong.
19. Unless otherwise specified, the description of the Hinckley trial is taken from the sources cited in *supra* note 1.
20. S. Taylor, "Jury Finds Hinckley Not Guilty, Accepting His Defense of Insanity," *New York Times,* June 21, 1982, p. A-1. For an account of the jury's reaction, see S. Taylor, "5 Hinckley Jurors Testify in Senate," *New York Times,* June 25, 1982, p. A-10.
21. G. F. Will, "Hinckley Case Proves Psychiatry and Law Are Incompatible," *Pittsburgh Post Gazette,* June 24, 1982, p. 7.
22. R. Baker, "Hinckley Jury Judged the Psychiatrists," *Pittsburgh Post Gazette,* June 24, 1982, p. 6.
23. Ibid.
24. S. V. Roberts, "High U.S. Officials Express Outrage, Asking for New Law on Insanity Plea," *New York Times,* June 23, 1982, p. B-6.
25. Ibid.
26. T. Wicker, "After the Hinckley Case," *New York Times,* June 25, 1982, p. A-31.
27. Wicker, unlike many critics, also noted that neither of these impressions "was fair to the profession as a whole." Nonetheless, he wondered "whether [psychiatrists] have created the impression that they know more about human behavior than they do." Ibid.
28. Will, *supra* note 21.
29. "Reagan Backs Bids on Insanity Pleas," *New York Times,* July 2, 1982, p. A-12.
30. "Editorial: Killers Can Be Crazy," *New York Times,* June 23, 1982, p. A-26; "Editorial: Instead Prove Insanity," *New York Times,* July 6, 1983, p. 22; "Editorial: Shift the Insanity Burden," *New York Times,* October 17, 1982, p. 16.
31. Roberts, *supra,* note 24.
32. Will, *supra* note 21.
33. American Psychiatric Association, "Statement on the Insanity Defense," Washington, D.C. (December 1982).
34. Stone, A. A. "The Insanity Defense on Trial," *Hospital and Community Psychiatry* 33: 636–40 (1982).
35. I. R. Kaufman, "The Insanity Plea on Trial," *New York Times Magazine,* August 8, 1982, pp. 16–20.
36. C. McCarthy, "Justice and Society Were Well Served by the Hinckley Verdict," *Pittsburgh Post Gazette,* June 24, 1982, p. 7.
37. B. Weiner, "Mental Disability and Criminal Law," in J. Parry, S. J. Brakel, and B. Weiner, *The Mentally Disabled and the Law,* 3d ed. (Chicago: American Bar Foundation, 1985), pp. 693–801.
38. See Judge Bazelon's influential opinion in *Bolton v. Harris,* 395 F.2d 642 (D.C. Cir. 1968); see also *People v. McQuillan,* 221 N.W.2d 569 (Mich. 1974), and *State v. Krol,* 344 A.2d 289 (N.J. 1975).
39. Stone, A. A.: "The Insanity Defense and the Civil Libertarian" [review of L. Caplan, *The Insanity Defense and the Trial of John W. Hinckley, Jr* (Boston: David R. Godine, 1984)] *Harvard Civil Rights–Civil Liberties Law Review* 20: 525–36 (1985).
40. R. C. Petrella, E. P. Benedek, S. C. Bank, and I. K. Packer, "Examining the Application of the Guilty but Mentally Ill Verdict in Michigan," *Hospital and Community Psychiatry* 36: 254–59 (1985).

41. L. Callahan, C. Mayer, and H. J. Steadman, "Insanity Defense Reform in the United States—post-Hinckley," *Mental and Physical Disability Law Reporter* 11: 55–59 (1987).

42. Idaho Code, Sec. 18-207; Montana Code Annotated, Sec. 46-14-201.

43. J. M. Bender, "After Abolition: The Present State of the Insanity Defense in Montana," *Montana Law Review* 45: 133–50 (1984).

44. C. A. Hagan, "The Insanity Defense: A Review of Recent Statutory Changes," *Journal of Legal Medicine* 3: 617–41 (1982). Perhaps illustrating the difficulty of establishing causation for legislative actions, the review by Geis and Meier of the Idaho legislation concludes that no single case motivated reform and fails entirely to mention the episode cited by Hagan. G. Geis and R. F. Meier, "Abolition of the Insanity Plea in Idaho: A Case Study," *Annals of the American Academy of Political and Social Science* 477: 72–83 (1985).

45. For a small number of crimes, mental states other than intention—such as recklessness or gross negligence—constitute the required *mens rea*. And some crimes, such as driving through a stop sign, can be viewed as strict liability offenses for which no particular *mens rea* is required. H. L. A. Hart, *Punishment and Responsibility: Essays in the Philosophy of Law* (Oxford: Oxford University Press, 1968).

46. Law professor Norval Morris has been one of the leading proponents of this point of view. See N. Morris, *Madness and the Criminal Law* (Chicago: University of Chicago Press, 1982).

47. National Mental Health Association, *Myths and Realities: A Report of the National Commission on the Insanity Defense* (Arlington, Va.: NMHA, 1983).

48. *State v. Korell,* 690 P.2d 992 (Mont. 1984); *State v. Searcy,* 798 P.2d 914 (Id. 1990). The U.S. Supreme Court has not been called on to decide whether such abolition violates federally guaranteed rights. But Justice Sandra Day O'Connor, in a recent concurring opinion in a case involving dispositional issues associated with the insanity defense intimated that she, too, believed that abolition transgresses no federal constitutional protections. *Foucha v. Louisiana,* 60 U.S.L.W. 4359, May 18, 1992.

49. Morris, *supra* note 46.

50. "U.S. Moves to Curb Insanity Defense," *New York Times,* July 20, 1982, p. A-18.

51. AMA, *supra* note 5.

52. Utah Code Annotated, Sec. 76-2-305.

53. R. J. Bonnie, "The Moral Basis of the Insanity Defense," *American Bar Association Journal* 69: 194–97 (1983). See also the Bonnie–Morris debate in "Should the Insanity Defense Be Abolished?" *Journal of Law and Health* 1: 117–40 (1986–1987).

54. APA, *supra* note 33.

55. American Bar Association, "Report to the House of Delegates of the Standing Committee on Association Standards for Criminal Justice and Commission on the Mentally Disabled," Washington, D.C., November 17, 1982.

56. Callahan et al., *supra* note 41.

57. There is some irony in the fact that rejection of the volitional prong of the insanity defense followed outrage over the Hinckley verdict. As Alan Stone noted, Hinckley's defense counsel never clearly rested their case on a volitional argument; indeed, they seemed to suggest that Hinckley's appreciation of the consequences of his behavior was impaired. Thus, even had the volitional prong been absent in the law of the District of Columbia, John Hinckley, Jr., probably would have been found not guilty by reason of insanity. A. A. Stone, *Law, Psychiatry and Morality* (Washington, D.C.: American Psychiatric Press, 1985).

58. APA, *supra* note 33.
59. ABA, *supra* note 55
60. H. J. Steadman, M. A. McGreevy, J. P. Morrissey, L. A. Callahan, P. C. Robbins, and C. Cirincione, *Before and After Hinckley: Evaluating Insanity Defense Reform* (New York: Guilford Press, 1993). Only three jurisdictions adopted the more stringent federal standard of proof by clear and convincing evidence. The remainder, with one exception, required defendants to meet a preponderance of the evidence (or "more likely than not") standard.
61. P. S. Appelbaum and T. G. Gutheil, *Clinical Handbook of Psychiatry and the Law,* 2d ed. (Baltimore: Williams & Wilkins, 1991).
62. Federal Rules of Evidence, Sec. 704.
63. APA, *supra* note 33.
64. Ibid. Alan Stone, with his usual perspicacity, noted that this was not true at the Hinckley trial, where psychiatric experts differed on the fundamental nature—psychotic or nonpsychotic—of Hinckley's impairments. See Stone, *supra* 57.
65. See, e.g., "Editorial: Psychiatrists on Insanity" *Washington Post,* January 22, 1983, p. A-16.
66. "Editorial: Not Insane," *Los Angeles Herald-Examiner,* January 27, 1983, p. A-14. The editorial nonetheless endorsed the APA recommendations.
67. E. Goodman, "Psychiatrists Are the Humblest Experts," *Pittsburgh Post-Gazette,* January 25, 1983, p. 4.
68. American Bar Association, *ABA Criminal Justice Mental Health Standards* (Washington, D.C.: ABA, 1989).
69. J. LaFond and M. Durham, *Back to the Asylum* (New York, Oxford University Press, 1992); P. S. Appelbaum, "The Insanity Defense: New Calls for Reform," *Hospital and Community Psychiatry* 33: 13–14 (1982).
70. J. L. Rogers, "1981 Oregon Legislation Relating to the Insanity Defense and the Psychiatric Security Review Board," *Williamette Law Review* 18: 23–48 (1982).
71. APA, *supra* note 33.
72. Steadman et al., *supra* note 60.
73. M. A. McGreevy, H. J. Steadman, J. A. Dvoskin, and N. Dollard, "New York State's System of Managing Insanity Acquittees in the Community," *Hospital and Community Psychiatry* 42: 512–17 (1991); M. K. Spodak, S. B. Silver, and C. U. Wright, "Criminality of Discharged Insanity Acquittees: Fifteen-year Experience in Maryland Reviewed," *Bulletin of the American Academy of Psychiatry and the Law* 12: 373–82 (1984); D. C. Scott, H. V. Zonana, and M. A. Geta, "Monitoring Insanity Acquittees: Connecticut's PSRB," *Hospital and Community Psychiatry* 41: 980–84 (1990); M. R. Wiederanders, "Recidivism of Disordered Offenders Who Were Conditionally vs. Unconditionally Released," *Behavioral Sciences and the Law* 10: 141–48 (1992) [reporting on California's program].
74. *Jones v. U.S.,* 463 U.S. 354 (1983). Automatic posttrial commitment was upheld in the context of the District of Columbia statute, which placed the burden on the defendant to prove insanity.
75. *People v. McQuillen, supra* note 38.
76. R. Slovenko, "Commentaries on Psychiatry and Law: Guilty but Mentally Ill," *Journal of Psychiatry and Law* 10: 541–55 (1982).
77. Michigan Statutes Annotated, Sec. 28. 1059.
78. Slovenko, *supra* note 76.
79. Ibid.
80. Bonnie, *supra* note 53.
81. Slovenko, *supra* note 76.
82. Ibid.

83. *Attorney General's Task Force on Violent Crime: Final Report* (Washington, D.C.: U.S. Department of Justice, August 17, 1981).
84. Steadman et al., *supra* note 60. The additional states were Alaska, Delaware, Georgia, Kentucky, Pennsylvania, South Carolina, South Dakota, and Utah. See the dissenting opinions of the groups cited *supra* notes 5, 33, 47, and 55.
85. National Mental Health Association, *supra* note 47. The report did recommend shifting the burden of proof to the defendant.
86. Testimony of Leonard S. Rubenstein before the Subcommittee on Criminal Justice, Committee on the Judiciary, U.S. House of Representatives (press release, Mental Health Law Project, September 9, 1982).
87. Steadman et al., *supra* note 60.
88. Ibid. I am most grateful to Henry Steadman for making available to me a draft of the book manuscript well in advance of its publication.
89. H. J. Steadman, L. A. Callahan, P. C. Robbins, and J. P. Morrissey, "Maintenance of an Insanity Defense Under Montana's 'Abolition' of the Insanity Defense," *American Journal of Psychiatry* 146: 357–60 (1989).
90. The research team found in interviews that many participants (including lawyers and judges) had been unaware that the state had abolished the special defense of insanity or had ignored the abolition, at least until after the Hinckley verdict in 1982.
91. After reform, defendants who were found incompetent and had pending charges against them dismissed or deferred were more likely to be schizophrenic and less likely to have committed crimes of violence than were pre-reform defendants found NGRI.
92. Steadman et al.'s analysis included small numbers of pre-reform defendants who were found incompetent to stand trial and had charges dismissed or deferred (7); and small numbers of after-reform defendants who were found to have met the *mens rea* nonculpability standard (6) or who were found guilty but sentenced to serve their term in the state hospital (6). Two instances of the latter disposition were included in the pre-reform group. Thus, the analysis is a bit more complex than is suggested in the text. Nonetheless, the vast majority of the pre-reform group were NGRIs (50), and most of the post-reform group were incompetent to stand trial, with charges dismissed or deferred (53). The general conclusions stated in the text are therefore accurate.
93. When researchers broke the data down by type of crime, they found that defendants accused of violent crimes were held about the same length of time before and after reform, whereas those accused of nonviolent crimes were released sooner after reform.
94. P. Heinbecker, "Two Years' Experience Under Utah's *Mens Rea* Insanity Law," *Bulletin of the American Academy of Psychiatry and the Law* 146: 185–91 (1986).
95. A similar outcome was found after Oregon's attempt to prevent defendants whose only psychiatric diagnosis was a personality disorder from pleading NGRI. The number of such defendants who successfully pled insanity did not diminish. S. M. Reichlin, J. D. Bloom, and M. H. Williams, "Post-Hinckley Insanity Reform in Oregon," *Bulletin of the American Academy of Psychiatry and the Law* 18: 405–12 (1990).
96. R. Arens, "The *Durham* Rule in Action: Judicial Psychiatry and Psychiatric Justice," *Law and Society Review* 2: 41–84 (1967); A. Krash, "The *Durham* Rule and Judicial Administration of the Insanity Defense in the District of Columbia," *Yale Law Journal* 70: 905–51 (1961); S. Reynolds, "Battle of the Experts Revisited: 1983 Oregon Legislation on the Insanity Defense," *Willamette Law Review*

20: 303–17 (1984); C. Slobogin, "The Guilty but Mentally Ill Verdict: An Idea Whose Time Should Not Have Come," *George Washington Law Review* 53: 494–526 (1985).

97. R. A. Pasewark, R. L. Randolph, and S. Bieber, "Insanity Plea: Statutory Language and Trial Procedures," *Journal of Psychiatry and Law* 12: 399–422 (1984). In bifurcated trials, the question of whether the defendant intentionally committed the act charged is adjudicated first. If the defendant is found to have done so, a separate proceeding takes place to determine whether the requirements for an insanity defense have been met. Single trials combine these decision points into a unified proceeding at which the trier of fact can find the defendant not guilty, guilty, or NGRI.

98. I. K. Packer, "Insanity Acquittals in Michigan 1969–1983: The Effects of Legislative and Judicial Changes," *Journal of Psychiatry and the Law* 13: 419–34, (1985). Other aspects of the Michigan reforms implemented at the same time included centralized evaluation of defendants who pled NGRI and creation of a guilty but mentally ill verdict.

99. The wording of the new California standard was actually stricter than that of the traditional *McNaughtan* test, in that it seemed to require that the defendant fail both to know the nature and quality of the act *and* to know that it was wrong. Historically, *McNaughtan* was a disjunctive test, allowing the defendant to qualify for exculpation by proving a failure to know either the nature and quality of the act *or* that it was wrong. In 1984, the California Court of Appeals construed the wording of the revised *McNaughtan* test as being equivalent to the traditional standard. See M. A. McGreevy, H. J. Steadman, and L. A. Callahan, "The Negligible Effects of California's 1982 Reform of the Insanity Defense Test," *American Journal of Psychiatry* 148: 744–50 (1991).

100. Rates of successful use of the insanity defense (that is, the ratio of insanity verdicts to insanity pleas), however, did not fall (indeed, in New York they rose), apparently because of a change in the characteristics of the defendants who employed the defense. Fewer defendants who lacked a diagnosis of major (that is, psychotic) mental illness filed an insanity plea, and fewer were successful after the reforms. But the increase in the rate of successful pleas was more than compensated for by the overall decline in the number of pleas filed, leading to a much reduced ratio of insanity verdicts to all verdicts.

101. An interesting, if tangential, finding from the Steadman et al. data on the unexpected consequences of reform in this area deserves comment. Steadman and colleagues looked at New York's reform of its posttrial procedures. The state was among the first to alter its release procedures for insanity acquittees, acting in response to two notorious cases that raised questions about the adequacy of existing procedures for handling mentally ill offenders in the criminal justice system. The New York reforms were multifaceted, including a mandatory thirty-day assessment period for defendants found NGRI, retention of jurisdiction for commitment and recommitment by the trial court, notice to the original prosecutor of petitions for a change in the acquittee's status, and (perhaps most important) empowerment of the trial court to release the acquittee—when this was deemed appropriate—on an "order of conditions." This order, valid for five years and renewable for another five years, specified criteria the acquittee must meet, under supervision by the state's Office of Mental Health, in order to remain at liberty. Revocation of release status could be accomplished by demonstrating to the court that the defendant was again dangerous due to mental disorder.

Steadman and his group gathered data from five of New York's most populous counties over a six-year period. The rate of insanity pleas, which had been increasing before the change in the law, ceased to rise and in fact began a slow (but not statistically significant) decline following passage of the reform measures. When insanity pleas were filed, though, they were more likely to be successful after the new law was implemented; a closer look revealed—contrary to anyone's *a priori* expectations—that the greater rate of success was concentrated among defendants charged with violent offenses. How could one account for this unexpected finding? Steadman et al. suggested that the greater degree of control retained by the criminal justice system over NGRI acquittees made prosecutors and judges more comfortable with the NGRI option. Thus, more mentally ill offenders who might qualify for the verdict were found NGRI, usually as a result of plea bargains. Length of confinement, which was already longer in New York than elsewhere—and longer for insanity acquittees than for those convicted and sent to prison for similar crimes—did not change. Defendants charged with lesser (usually nonviolent) offenses, therefore, had little incentive to pursue an insanity defense. An NGRI verdict might still be attractive to violent offenders, however, and now the system was more willing to grant them that option. The perception of postdisposition control over the acquittee by the court and prosecutors, combined with the stepped-up level of community supervision, reduced the criminal justice system's attitude of uneasiness and suspicion toward the insanity defense. Indeed, the greater control judges and prosecutors were granted was a more important factor in this more favorable view of the defense than any actual increase in the periods of detention imposed following introduction of the reforms.

For a study that demonstrates actual compliance in New York with the requirements of the 1980 reform and shows increased posttrial confinement in secure facilities, see D. C. McClellan, "The New York State Insanity Defense Reform Act of 1980: A Legislative Experiment," *Bulletin of the American Academy of Psychiatry and the Law* 17: 129–51 (1989).

102. R. A. Pasewark, S. Bieber, K. J. Bosten, M. Kiser, and H. J. Steadman, "Criminal Recidivism Among Insanity Acquittees," *International Journal of Law and Psychiatry* 5: 365–74 (1982).
103. R. A Nicholson, S. Norwood, C. Enyart, "Characteristics and Outcomes of Insanity Acquittees in Oklahoma," *Behavioral Sciences and the Law* 9: 487–500 (1991); M. E. Rice, G. T. Harris, C. Lang, and V. Bell, "Recidivism Among Male Insanity Acquittees," *Journal of Psychiatry and Law* 18: 379–403 (1990). These Canadian figures were lower than those for a sample of defendants matched on charge but not found NGRI. Unlike most U.S. studies, the Canadian report included time spent in ordinary civil hospitals as time at risk.
104. The most comprehensive summary of their work appears in J. D. Bloom and M. H. Williams, *Management and Treatment of Insanity Acquittees: A Model for the 1990s* (Washington, D. C.: American Psychiatric Press, 1994). My thanks to Joe Bloom for giving me access to this manuscript prior to publication.
105. J. L. Rogers, J. D. Bloom, and S. M. Manson, "Oregon's New Insanity Defense System: A Review of the First Five Years, 1978 to 1982," *Bulletin of the American Academy of Psychiatry and the Law* 12: 383–402 (1984). The average period during which members of this group were at risk (that is, in the community) is not clear from the report.
106. Bloom and Williams, *supra* note 104. The average period at risk was 12 months.
107. J. D. Bloom, M. H. Williams, and D. A. Bigelow, "The Involvement of Schizophrenic Insanity Acquittees in the Mental Health and Criminal Justice System," unpublished manuscript, 1991.

108. J. D. Bloom, J. L. Rogers, S. M. Manson, and M. H. Williams, "Lifetime Police Contacts of Discharged Psychiatric Security Review Board Clients," *International Journal of Law and Psychiatry* 8: 189–202 (1986).

109. Bloom and Williams, *supra* note 104.

110. J. L. Cavanaugh and O. E. Wasyliw, "Treating the Not Guilty by Reason of Insanity Outpatient: A Two-year Study," *Bulletin of the American Academy of Psychiatry and the Law* 13: 407–15 (1985).

111. McGreevy et al, *supra* note 73.

112. H. R. Lamb, L. E. Weinberger, and B. H. Gross, "Court-mandated Community Outpatient Treatment for Persons Found Not Guilty by Reason of Insanity: A Five-year Follow-up," *American Journal of Psychiatry* 145: 450–56 (1988).

113. Spodak et al., *supra* note 73. A subsequent study found equivalent rates over a five-year follow-up, although patients discharged from the central forensic facility did somewhat better than a more chronically ill group sent to civil hospitals prior to discharge (47 percent rearrest rate vs. 62 percent). See C. Tellefsen, M. I. Cohen, S. B. Silver, and C. Dougherty, "Predicting Success on Conditional Release for Insanity Acquittees: Regionalized versus Nonregionalized Hospital Patients," *Bulletin of the American Academy of Psychiatry and the Law* 20: 87–100 (1992).

114. R. P. Bogenberger, R. A. Pasewark, H. Gudeman, and S. L. Beider, "Follow-up of Insanity Acquittees in Hawaii," *International Journal of Law and Psychiatry* 10: 283–95 (1987).

115. Wiederanders, *supra* note 73.

116. Bloom and Williams, *supra* note 104.

117. G. A. Smith and J. A. Hall, "Evaluating Michigan's Guilty but Mentally Ill Verdict: An Empirical Study," *Journal of Law Reform* 16: 77–106 (1982).

118. Petrella et al., *supra* note 40; B. D. McGraw, D. Farthing-Capowich, and I. Keilitz, "The 'Guilty but Mentally Ill' Plea and Verdict: Current State of the Knowledge," *Villanova Law Review* 30: 117–91 (1985). McGraw et al. also identified statistical problems in the analysis performed by Smith and Hall.

119. A study of the GBMI verdict in Pennsylvania was crippled by incomplete data and the simultaneous shift of the burden of proof to the defendant, which is, (as we have seen) the only change that seems unquestionably to limit the rate of NGRI findings. See R. D. Mackay and J. Kopelman, "The Operation of the "Guilty but Mentally Ill" Verdict in Pennsylvania," *Journal of Psychiatry and Law* 16: 247–68 (1988). The effect of GBMI on NGRI rates could not be determined in a South Carolina study because the rate of NGRIs in that state was negligible (1 to 2 per year) in the first place. See D. W. Morgan, T. M. McCullough, P. L. Jenkins, and W. M. White, "Guilty but Mentally Ill: The South Carolina Experience," *Bulletin of the American Academy of Psychiatry and the Law* 16: 41–48 (1988). The sole multistate study that has been published to date found conflicting data with regard to changes in NGRI rates, probably because of confounding factors that contributed to local variations. See Institute on Mental Disability, *The Guilty but Mentally Ill Verdict: An Empirical Study* (Williamsburg, Va.: National Center for State Courts, 1984).

120. Smith and Hall, *supra* note 117.

121. Mackay and Kopelman, *supra* note 119.

122. Morgan et al., *supra* note 119.

123. Steadman et al., *supra* note 60.

124. That is not to say that persons pleading GBMI cannot be sentenced to death. In fact, at least two state supreme courts have ruled such sentences constitutional in

their jurisdictions. See *Harris v. State*, 499 N.E.2d 723 (Ind. 1986); and *State v. Wilson*, 413 S.E.2d 19 (S.C. 1992). Needless to say, this raises further questions about the meaning of a GBMI verdict.

125. The work of Pasewark and colleagues offers several striking examples of these beliefs. Prior to the Hinckley trial, they surveyed legislators (32 of 92 contacted responded) in Wyoming to get their estimates of the number and success rate of insanity pleas in that state. Subjects were told only that in 1970–1972 the state had recorded 21,012 felony indictments. The mean estimated number of NGRI pleas was 4,458 (range: 0–18,567) and respondents estimated that 1,794 such pleas had been successful (range: 0–13,600). In fact, there were only 102 insanity pleas during the years in question; and of these, just 1 was successful. See R. A. Pasewark and M. L. Pantle, "Insanity Plea: Legislators' View," *American Journal of Psychiatry* 136: 222–23 (1979).

Similarly, a survey of three student and citizen groups just prior to the Hinckley trial asked subjects to estimate the percentage of insanity defense cases among 12,307 indicted felons in the period 1975–1977. Respondents judged that 33–38% of cases involved insanity pleas, and of these 45% were successful. Even when told afterward that, in reality, only 0.8 percent of defendants (*n* = 104) pled insanity and that only 4 percent of these (*n* = 4) were successful, a majority of respondents endorsed the propositions that the insanity defense was overused and that it was abused. See R. W. Jeffrey and R. A. Pasewark, "Altering Opinions About the Insanity Plea," *Journal of Psychiatry and Law* 11: 29–40 (1983).

126. L. A. Callahan, H. J. Steadman, M. A. McGreevy, and P. C. Robbins, "The Volume and Characteristics of Insanity Defense Pleas: An Eight-state Study," *Bulletin of the American Academy of Psychiatry and the Law* 19: 331–38 (1991). Data are averaged across all years of the study (that is, before and after reform). See Table 1, p. 335.

127. M. L. Criss and D. R. Racine, "Impact of Change in Legal Standard for Those Adjudicated Not Guilty by Reason of Insanity 1975–1979," *Bulletin of the American Academy of Psychiatry and the Law* 8: 261–71 (1980); Packer, *supra* note 98; R. A. Pasewark, "Insanity Plea: A Review of the Research Literature," *Journal of Psychiatry and Law* 9: 357–401 (1981); R. A. Pasewark, M. L. Pantle, and H. J. Steadman, "Characteristics and Disposition of Persons Found Not Guilty by Reason of Insanity in New York State, 1971–1976," *American Journal of Psychiatry* 136: 655–60 (1979); P. K. Pati "Insanity Pleas in Oregon" [letter], *American Journal of Psychiatry* 136: 1346–47 (1979); Steadman, H. J. "Insanity Acquittals in New York State, 1965–1978," *American Journal of Psychiatry* 137: 321–26, (1980); C. J. Stokman and Heiber, P. G. "The Insanity Defense Reform Act in New York State, 1980–1983," *International Journal of Law and Psychiatry* 7: 367–84 (1984). See also *infra* note 131.

128. R. G. Lande, "The Military Insanity Defense," *Bulletin of the American Academy of Psychiatry and the Law* 19: 193–201 (1991).

129. J. L. Rogers, J. D. Bloom, S. M. Manson, "Insanity Defenses: Contested or Conceded?" *American Journal of Psychiatry* 141: 885–88 (1984).

130. Steadman et al., *supra* note 123.

131. R. A. Pasewark, R. Jeffrey, and S. Bieber, "Differentiating Successful and Unsuccessful Insanity Plea Defendants in Colorado," *Journal of Psychiatry and Law* 15: 55–71 (1987); H. J. Steadman, L. Keitner, J. Braff, and T. M. Arvanites, "Factors Associated with a Successful Insanity Plea," *American Journal of Psychiatry* 140: 401–5 (1983); R. Rogers, J. L. Cavanaugh, W. Simon, and M. Harris, "Legal Outcome and Clinical Findings: A Study of Insanity Evalua-

tions," *Bulletin of the American Academy of Psychiatry and the Law* 12: 75–83 (1984).

132. K. K. Fukunaga, R. A. Pasewark, M. Hawkins, and H. Gudeman, "Insanity Plea: Interexaminer Agreement and Concordance of Psychiatric Opinion and Court Verdict," *Law and Human Behavior* 5: 325–28 (1981).

133. Steadman et al., *supra* note 131; Pasewark et al., *supra* note 131. It goes without saying that psychosis *per se* does not establish the legitimacy of an insanity defense. A causal link to the defendant's behavior, with the nature and degree of impact specified by the operative standard, is also required. Thus, these data fall well short of conclusive proof of the appropriateness of the current decisionmaking process.

134. N. J. Finkel, "The Insanity Defense Reform Act of 1984: Much Ado About Nothing," *Behavioral Science and the Law* 7: 403–19 (1989); N. J. Finkel, R. Shaw, S. Bercaw, and J. Koch, "Insanity Defenses: From the Jurors' Perspective," *Law and Psychology Review* 9: 77–92 (1985). An integrative summary of his work can be found in N. J. Finkel, "De Facto Departures from Insanity Instructions: Toward the Remaking of Common Law," *Law and Human Behavior* 14: 105–22 (1990).

135. N. J. Finkel and S. F. Handel, "Jurors and Insanity: Do Test Instructions Instruct?" *Forensic Reports* 1: 65–79 (1988).

136. J. R. P. Ogloff, "A Comparison of Insanity Defense Standards on Juror Decision-making," *Law and Human Behavior* 15: 509–31 (1991).

137. N. J. Finkel and S. F. Handel, "How Jurors Construe Insanity," *Law and Human Behavior* 13: 41–59 (1989).

138. A study of insanity defense opinions of four forensic psychiatrists disagreed with these findings. Asked to apply the ALI test, broken down into cognitive and volitional prongs, along with *McNaughtan* and the test proposed by the American Psychiatric Association, the psychiatrists found tests without a volitional prong significantly more restrictive. Although this study is widely cited, the extremely small sample it is based on and its hypothetical nature leaves one uncertain about how much weight should be given its conclusions. See R. W. Wettstein, E. P. Mulvey, and R. Rogers, "A Prospective Comparison of Four Insanity Defense Standards," *American Journal of Psychiatry* 148: 21–27 (1991).

139. S. M. Fulero and N. J. Finkel, "Barring Ultimate Issue Testimony: An 'Insane' Rule?" *Law and Human Behavior* 15: 495–507 (1991).

140. R. Rogers, R. M. Bagby, and M. M. K. Chow, "Psychiatrists and the Parameters of Expert Testimony," *International Journal of Law and Psychiatry* 15: 387–96 (1992). See also their earlier study (which reached similar results), R. Rogers, R. M. Bagby, M. Crouch, and B. Cutler, "Effects of Ultimate Opinions on Juror Perception of Insanity," *International Journal of Law and Psychiatry* 13: 225–32 (1990).

141. Ogloff, *supra* note 136.

142. Steadman, *supra* note 60. In real life, shifting the burden may deter defendants from pleading NGRI, in addition to affecting decision making by judges and juries.

143. N. J. Finkel, "The Insanity Defense: A Comparison of Verdict Schemes," *Law and Human Behavior* 15: 533–55 (1991).

144. R. L. Poulson, "Mock Juror Attribution of Criminal Responsibility: Effects of Race and the Guilty but Mentally Ill (GBMI) Verdict Option," *Journal of Applied Social Psychology* 20: 1596–1611 (1990).

145. C. F. Roberts, E. L. Sargent, and A. S. Chan, "Verdict Selection Processes in Insanity Cases: Juror Construals and the Effects of Guilty but Mentally Ill Instructions," *Law and Human Behavior* 17: 261–75 (1993).

146. J. C. Savitsky and W. D. Lindblom, "The Impact of the Guilty but Mentally Ill Verdict on Juror Decisions: An Empirical Analysis," *Journal of Applied Social Psychology* 16: 686–701 (1986); see also C. F. Roberts and S. L. Golding, "The Social Construction of Criminal Responsibility and Insanity," *Law and Human Behavior* 15: 349–76 (1991); and C. F. Roberts, S. L. Golding, and F. D. Fincham, "Implicit Theories of Criminal Responsibility: Decision Making and the Insanity Defense," *Law and Human Behavior* 11: 207–32 (1987).

147. C. E. Boehnert, "Psychological and Demographic Factors Associated with Individuals Using the Insanity Defense," *Journal of Psychiatry and Law* 13: 9–31 (1985).

148. Supportive findings regarding the inverse relationship between "level of incrimination" and ratings of insanity can be found in a pre-Hinckley study of 312 mock jurors. See R. P. McGlynn and E. A. Dreilinger, "Mock Juror Judgment and the Insanity Plea: Effects of Incrimination and Sanity Information," *Journal of Applied Social Psychology* 11: 166–80 (1981). The "planfulness" of the wrongful act was found to be negatively associated with NGRI verdicts in another mock juror study. See Roberts and Golding, *supra* note 146.

149. Stone, *supra* note 57. The same is true for most assassins or would-be assassins of political figures, including—in the years leading up to the Hinckley trial—Arthur Bremer (who shot George Wallace), and Lynnette Fromme and Sara Jane Moore (who each made attempts on the life of President Ford).

150. Miller et al. reported that abolition of a sex offender commitment statute in Wisconsin led to an increase from 6.5 percent to 21.3 percent in the percentage of sex offenders among NGRIs hospitalized after trial. Many of the cases they reviewed appeared to lack a sufficient objective basis for an NGRI finding. Moreover, none involved the use of force, which they speculated would have led to guilty findings instead of insanity verdicts. See R. D. Miller, J. Staval, and R. K. Miller, "The Insanity Defense for Sex Offenders: Jury Decisions After Repeal of Wisconsin's Sex Crimes Law," *Hospital and Community Psychiatry* 39: 186–89 (1988).

151. A. C. Singer, "Insanity Acquittal in the Seventies: Observations and Empirical Analysis of One Jurisdiction," *Mental Disability Law Reporter* 2: 406–17 (1978).

152. See, e.g., B. B. Sendor, "Crime as Communication: An Interpretive Theory of the Insanity Defense and the Mental Elements of Crime," *Georgetown Law Journal* 74: 1371–1434 (1986); and M. L. Perlin, "Unpacking the Myths: The Symbolism Mythology of Insanity Defense Jurisprudence," *Case Western Reserve Law Review* 40: 599–731 (1989–1990).

153. See, e.g., P. Arenella, "Convicting the Morally Blameless: Reassessing the Relationship Between Legal and Moral Accountability," *UCLA Law Review* 39: 1511–1622 (1992).

154. One of the better examples of the genre is W. Gaylin, *The Killing of Bonnie Garland* (New York: Penguin Books, 1983).

155. Of course, unlike data generated from laboratory experiments, social science data are highly sensitive to the contexts in which they are obtained. Profound changes in public attitudes toward crime, mental illness, or basic notions of justice could produce very different results in the future if attempts were made to replicate the studies cited in this chapter. Extrapolations of current trends to future events is a risky business.

156. H. Fingarette and A. F. Hasse, *Mental Disabilities and Criminal Responsibility* (Berkeley: University of California Press, 1979).

157. N. J. Finkel, *Insanity on Trial* (New York: Plenum Press, 1988).

158. Finkel, *supra* note 143.

159. P. Arenella, Review of Fingarette and Hasse (*supra* note 156), *Columbia Law Review* 80: 420–34 (1980).
160. *U.S. v. Brawner*, *supra* note 16.
161. Rubenstein, *supra* note 86.
162. Ogloff, *supra* note 136; Finkel, "De Facto," *supra* note 134.
163. Consider the comments offered more than forty years ago by the era's leading experts on forensic psychiatry, psychiatrist Manfred S. Guttmacher and law professor Henry Weihofen. Reflecting on New Hampshire's experience with its relatively unstructured "product of mental disease" standard, they noted, "No one has ever demonstrated that the New Hampshire courts have more difficulty than others, or that New Hampshire juries return more dubious verdicts. It is true that the New Hampshire rule turns the problem over to the jury with a minimum of legal rules to guide them, but the lawyers' faith in elaborate instructions as guides which the jury is supposed to take to heart and apply in arriving at a verdict is probably excessive. Most of the verbal niceties of instructions which lawyers quibble over, and over which appellate courts sometimes reverse cases, probably never affect the jury's actual deliberations at all." M. S. Guttmacher and H. Weihofen, *Psychiatry and the Law* (New York: W. W. Norton, 1952), p. 419.

    A partial step in the direction of a "justly responsible" standard was taken by the Rhode Island Supreme Court in *State v. Johnson* (399 A.2d 469, 1979). There, the court adopted an insanity standard endorsed by a minority of the ALI committee: "A person is not responsible for criminal conduct if at the time of such conduct, as a result of mental disease or defect, his capacity either to appreciate the wrongfulness of his conduct or to conform his conduct to the requirements of the law is *so substantially impaired that he cannot justly be held responsible*." [Emphasis added.] Rather than adopting an unstructured test, however, the Rhode Island court retained the outlines of the ALI standard, but modified its threshold requirement by introducing the "justly responsible" formulation.

6

The Consequences of Reform in
Mental Health Law

During periods of cataclysmic change, emotional reactions make objective evaluation all but impossible. Minor perturbations seem to have immense impact, and transitory phenomena are mistaken for permanent alterations. People who speak the loudest or the most provocatively are often mistaken as those most able to shape the course of events. Attempts to predict the future tend to begin with the most dramatic changes to date and to extrapolate upward. Factors that may slow or reverse the tide of reform routinely are ignored.

Such was the case with the turbulent era of reform in mental health law that began in the late 1960s, crested during the following decade, and by the mid-1980s had all but ended. The responses of those caught in the maelstrom—both the advocates of reform and those who opposed it—were characterized by extreme judgments about the impact of the changes, almost always incorrect. Only now, with the equanimity derived from our increasing distance from those tumultuous times, can we begin to assess the true consequences of the receding epoch of reform.

What can we say about the consequences of the reforms in mental health law addressed in the preceding chapters? If generalization is possible across these very disparate areas of law, our conclusion must be that the consequences of reform were much more limited than partisans on either side anticipated. This appears true for changes in commitment law, the imposition of liability on clinicians for patients' violent acts, the introduction of the right to refuse treatment, and the insanity defense reforms that followed in the wake of the Hinckley trial. Perhaps certain areas of mental health law could be identified where this was not the case. I will leave that task to others. Even if they are successful, however, it will not diminish the need to explain the findings before us.

Initially, however, it is important to underscore a critical aspect of the argument offered in the previous chapters. My account should not be perceived as claiming that the reforms in mental health law left no imprint on the mental health system or on the lives of the mentally ill. Since this conclusion badly misrepresents reality, there is value in recapitulating in an abbreviated form why it is false. Let us note, to begin with, the concrete impact of the changes:

- As commitment criteria were tightened, the population of persons eligible for involuntary hospitalization contracted. In areas—and they exist—where dangerousness standards are strictly applied, there has been a marked decrease in the ease with which mentally ill persons can be hospitalized against their will. Moreover, the changes in commitment procedures, particularly the requirements for adversarial hearings, allow patients to challenge their commitments, offering patients, at a minimum, a voice in the process.
- *Tarasoff* and the cases that followed it, along with the statutes passed in reaction to the court decisions, have heightened the sensitivity of clinicians to the risks posed by patients and to the importance of taking protective measures. As a result of court decisions in some duty-to-protect cases—and the reluctance of defense attorneys in a much larger number of cases to risk the vicissitudes of trial—many victims have been compensated for the harms they suffered.
- Patients undergoing treatment in states that have embraced broad versions of the right to refuse treatment can challenge automatic—and perhaps unthinking—use of antipsychotic medications and other agents over their objections. In many cases, they may negotiate alternative regimens more to their liking. Even if ultimately treated against their will, patients can delay this outcome until independent review of their treatment plan occurs.
- Certain insanity defense reforms, often those that attracted least attention, have reduced findings of not guilty by reason of insanity. This result is primarily associated with shifts in the burden of proof from the prosecution to the defendant, and to a lesser extent with the guilty but mentally ill verdict. Moreover, improved postrelease supervision has decreased the rate of new offenses in states that have adopted this approach.

Beyond these effects, which are far from trivial in their own right, lies a pervasive change in attitude that may be the most enduring legacy of the most recent era of reform. The legal rights of mentally ill persons were given scant consideration before the late 1960s. Mental hospitalization, for most of that period, entailed the loss of basic civil liberties, a situation taken for granted by mental health professionals, lawyers, legislators, and the public at large. It is unlikely that this will ever be true again. Once, the dominant assumption was that mentally ill persons could be deprived of their liberties under a wide range of circumstances and with few procedural protections; now the opposite holds true. In the post-reform era, it is axiomatic that services must be provided in a manner that minimizes intrusions on individual rights and maximizes patients' recourse to independent review when infringements occur.

Indeed, the most telling measure of the shift in attitude toward the rights of the mentally ill appeared when legal reforms were suggested that might have benefitted others at some cost to the prerogatives of persons with mental illness. The development of the duty to protect third parties from patients' violence and the pressure to alter the insanity defense are both cases in point. *Tarasoff* and the cases that followed it compromised, to some degree, the confidentiality of persons in psychiatric treatment for the sake of protecting their victims. Insanity defense reform was aimed at limiting the excuses that severely mentally ill persons could offer to avoid punishment for their behavior. Yet even when such measures were enacted, the debate pivoted on precisely the question that was invisible a few decades before: to what extent is it legitimate to abrogate the rights of mentally ill persons for the sake of other goals? The fact that all parties to these controversies now accept the critical nature of this question demonstrates, as no other evidence can, the changes wrought by the decades of reform.

On the other hand, we cannot ignore the lessons of our close examination of the consequences of mental health law reform. Whatever the impacts of the reforms, these were registered on a scale of magnitude far less than most contemporaneous observers had expected. This, too, deserves emphasis:

- In most places, civil commitment reform has not substantially changed either the nature of the committed population or the care with which commitment decisions are made. The most profound effects appear to be of limited duration, with the situation tending to return toward the pre-reform baseline over time.
- The imposition of a duty to protect potential victims from patients' violence, although its effects have been little studied, has not clearly altered the behavior of mental health professionals in cases in which they believe a clear threat exists to a third party. Conversely, the feared demise of psychotherapy as a result of the new rules has not materialized.
- Although patients' right to refuse treatment in general is frequently endorsed, it is rare for courts to uphold the refusal of any given patient. The nearly uniform consequence of a court hearing is treatment against the patient's will. To the extent that the right has had adverse effects on inpatient facilities, these have been far milder than critics originally feared and relate primarily to the delay in resolving patients' refusals.
- The most loudly debated reforms of the insanity defense—including alterations in the legal standard of insanity and outright abolition of a special verdict of not guilty by reason of insanity—have had little effect on rates of punishment for mentally ill people accused of criminal offenses.

Though these outcomes undoubtedly were unanticipated by those who respectively promoted and fought each reform, they might be less surprising to sociologists of law and others who study the effects of legal change. It is commonplace for these scholars to note that the consequences of changes in law are rarely foreseeable at the time of implementation. Few legal initiatives completely fulfill the hopes of their advocates, and even fewer fail to produce some unanticipated reactions, which often tend to undermine the goals of reform. But we ought not to write off the events previously detailed as simply being predetermined by some perverse law of human society stipulating that the effects of any change resemble neither the intentions of its promoters nor the fears of its detractors. To do so would shed little light on the factors that helped limit the impact of the mental health law reforms of the past generation and would offer no guidance as to how such outcomes might be modified in the future. After all, notwithstanding their many unintended consequences, some reforms came closer to fulfilling their expectations than did others.

To reach more meaningful conclusions, we must begin by recognizing that generalization across the mental health law reforms we have considered is complicated by the differences among them. They vary, for example, in the forces that propelled them, the mechanisms (judicial, legislative, or regulatory) of reform, the attitudes of key actors toward the initiatives, the social contexts in which they occurred, and the degree to which they approximated the effects—for good or ill—predicted for them. With this caution in mind, we may still observe some valid generalizations that embrace all of our examples to a greater or lesser extent.

Theoretical and Empirical Underpinnings of Reform

As is evident from the history of the mental health law reforms described in this book, the proposals for change grew in soil fertilized by dubious theoretical or empirical premises about mental illness and the systems created to deal with it. Reformers often were energized by doubts about the existence of mental illness, about the pain caused by its symptoms, and about the efficacy and value of psychiatric treatment.[1] These beliefs led them to question the rationale for civil commitment,[2] the benefits of involuntary treatment,[3] the importance of confidentiality in mental health treatment,[4] and the nature of the link between mental disorder and criminal behavior.[5]

The most extreme views of this sort—often called "anti-psychiatry"— would have led to much more sweeping changes than actually occurred. Civil commitment would have been abolished rather than restructured, voluntary as well as involuntary treatment would have been prohibited, and no allowance whatsoever would have been made for the impact of mental illness on the behavior of persons who commit criminal acts. The fact that these radical alterations, though sometimes advocated, were not adopted indicates that most policy makers recognized that they rested on shaky ground. For the people who wrote the laws and the court opinions, the other motive forces described in Chapter 1—including beliefs about the importance of civil liberties, the negative effects of hospitalization, the benefits of community-based care, and the desire to reduce spiraling mental health costs—often played more significant roles.

Nonetheless, discourse on mental health law reform was shaped in important ways by doubts about the nature of mental disorder and about the value of its current modes of treatment that permeated the cultural milieu of the era. In particular, the balancing of risks and benefits by advocates of new legal initiatives tended to give less weight to interests in promoting treatment and more weight to interests in protecting individual rights. When advocates of greater legal protections for civil committees, for example, pointed to uncertainties about whether mental disorder could be diagnosed meaningfully, or whether treatment was more likely to do harm than good, the argument against strict standards and criminal-style procedures for commitment appeared weak indeed.[6] Similarly, in a milieu in which the basic utility of psychiatric treatment was in question, it was more difficult to argue for preferring protection of confidentiality over protection of potential victims—since, even if the new rules dissuaded people from seeking care, the resulting harm might be of little consequence.[7]

Reforms influenced by these beliefs systematically undervalued the interests of mentally ill people in receiving treatment, and they generally were designed for (or at least had the effect of) impeding access to care. This was true not only when legal initiatives addressed treatment settings *per se,* but even in the criminal law, where many insanity defense reforms were aimed at facilitating punishment rather than at treating persons with mental disorders. This conclusion should not be taken to imply that concerns with civil liberties or the rights of victims are illegitimate considerations in mental health law. Clearly, they are important, and the general acceptance of sweeping procedural changes in civil commitment is evidence of the consensus in favor of respecting individual rights. But as members of a new school of legal thought dubbed ''therapeutic jurisprudence'' regularly point out, the purpose of the mental health system is to treat mentally disordered persons.[8] Legal regulation of that system should be consistent with and should facilitate that goal. When mental health law significantly undercuts patients' interests in treatment, it does not do justice to the mentally ill.

Resistance to Reform

Neglect of treatment interests played an important part in the failure of many of the reforms to achieve the ends desired by their proponents. Though contemporary liberal dogma during the 1960s and 1970s may have called the existence of mental illness into question, most people who came into contact with severely mentally ill persons had little doubt that they were disordered and that something should be done about their condition. This group included judges, lawyers (even lawyers designated to represent mentally ill persons at commitment hearings), jurors (especially in insanity defense trials), mental health professionals, and family members. Many of these participants were also resolved to protect individual rights. They concluded, however, that an excessive regard for such rights should not be allowed to impede unduly the process of providing care and treatment for those for whom—in Carol Warren's pointed phrase—"common sense" dictated that outcome.[9]

A divergence of this sort between the assumptions of those who created the new laws governing mental health treatment and those charged with implementing them would have been of little significance unless the latter possessed sufficient discretion to undermine the reforms in practice. The decentralized nature of the mental health law system, however, ensured that this would be the case. Indeed, the levels at which discretion can be applied to thwart the narrow limits of mental health law are manifold. In civil commitment, for example, family members and mental health professionals have considerable scope in framing their allegations of a patient's committability; attorneys appointed to represent respondents can vary the vigor with which they contest commitment petitions; and judges can elect to apply broader or narrower interpretations of commitment standards. Data reviewed in Chapter 2 suggest that all of these actions occur routinely.

Insanity defense proceedings offer another example. Defense attorneys can decide whether or not to raise an insanity plea, depending on whether the likely consequences are considered desirable for the defendant. Since most insanity defenses are resolved by plea bargaining prior to trial, prosecutors have enormous latitude in negotiating pleas (such as when they are eager to see a mentally ill defendant treated rather than punished), whether or not the defendants meet statutory criteria for insanity. Even when denied this opportunity by the abolition of the insanity defense, prosecutors and judges find means to ensure the same practical outcome, as in Montana, where commitments for incompetence to stand trial took the place of insanity verdicts. For cases that go to trial, the finder of fact (whether judge or jury) has the final word regarding which behaviors deserve exculpation, and the evidence presented in Chapter 5 suggests that this discretion is used freely. Indeed, even acknowledging the limits of current data, insanity verdicts appear to be motivated more by an internalized sense of the appropriateness of punishment than by prevailing legal standards, to which jurors seem relatively impervious.

The effectiveness of mental health law in most contexts depends on the willingness of those who gather information and make decisions—often operating with low visibility—to conform to the dictates of the law. When the law seems wrongheaded, however, unless incentives can be provided for their cooperation or sanctions imposed for their resistance, they will often respond according to their own lights.[10] The more the law appears to deny premises that seem self-evident, the greater becomes the likelihood of such a response. Thus, the divergence between, on the one hand, the common perception of the existence of mental illness and the desirability of treating it (in fact, often, the cruelty of failing to do so), and, on the other, the posture of much mental health law, which sometimes impedes the provision of treatment, has doomed many of the reforms of the last three decades.

Over time, as the impetus for the initial wave of reforms ebbed, this grass-roots reaction has attained greater influence in the legal process. This has been most evident in changes in commitment law in the 1980s and early 1990s, discussed in Chapter 2, which generally have sought to counteract the limitations on the states' commitment powers enacted in the preceding decade. Commitment criteria have been expanded, and some procedural requirements have been relaxed, obviating (to some extent) the need previously felt by those making front-line decisions to disregard the law in day-to-day practice. The addition of options for out-patient commitment is another move in this direction. A similar effort to limit the scope of reforms resulted in legislation aimed at circumscribing therapists' duties toward victims of their patients' violence.

If advocates of reform misjudged the degree to which their views of mental illness were shared by the majority of the population, their opponents—including many mental health professionals—evinced the same failing. Time and again they underestimated their power to resist the new statutes and court decisions, and the extent to which their opinions commanded popular support. Perhaps one ought to be charitable toward their tendency to assume that massive legal changes would translate directly into widespread alterations in the mental health system, with results that affected every aspect of care. Sociologists and political scientists may be sophisticated enough to know how much the law depends for its effectiveness on the cooperation of the citizenry, but there is little reason to expect psychiatrists and clinical psychologists to have been aware of this.

By now, however, one hopes that the lesson is clear: the mental health system so commands the allegiance of ordinary citizens and front-line decision makers with regard to its core treatment functions that a legally precipitated apocalypse is unlikely. Even legal changes that on paper seem capable of causing significant disruption in the delivery of care are usually transmuted in practice into procedures that preserve the system's function. Not that other professions or the public at large will support flouting of patients' rights or intolerably poor levels of care; they will not. Neither, however, will they facilitate legal initiatives that threaten to undermine care for those most in need.

Impact of Other Social Forces

So far, our attention has been focused on factors intrinsic to reform that limited its effects. But external forces played a role in this regard, too. Commitment law again provides the best example. The goal of reducing reliance on involuntary hospitalization was aided in areas where other incentives—primarily fiscal—existed to keep people out of the hospital. When counties were charged for the costs of hospitalizing mentally ill persons in state hospitals, they tended to seek alternatives whenever possible. Indeed, in California, the rates of commitment began to drop when costs for hospitalization were shifted to the counties, well in advance of changes in commitment laws.[11] Similarly, one recently studied Wisconsin county showed no decrease in emergency detentions in the wake of either the *Lessard* decision or subsequent statutory changes, but it registered a marked decline after the state transferred financial responsibility for in-patient care to the county.[12] The availability of community-based alternatives to in-patient hospitalization undoubtedly has a major effect on commitment rates, as well.

Opposing pressures on the commitment system can also be observed. The public's reaction to deinstitutionalization and the ubiquity in large cities of homeless mentally ill persons has stimulated considerable interest in broadening commitment standards.[13] Similarly, acts of violence by mentally ill people—of growing concern in recent years—have led to more liberal interpretations of existing statutes[14] and to pressure for changes that would undo some of the reforms of the 1970s.[15] (We are now beginning to see similar pressures regarding the right to refuse treatment.[16]) In these instances, commitment law on the books and in practice is being shaped by problems resulting from the closing of state mental hospital beds, the failure to provide alternative community services, the disappearance of low-cost housing, and other policies that have contributed to homelessness. It would be impossible to understand the evolution of mental health law without reference to these other factors.

The same can be said for social influences on the duty to protect victims from patients' violence, and on the insanity defense. In the former case, the public's preoccupation with rising rates of violence on the streets probably contributed to the creation and adoption of a duty to protect. Recall the *Tarasoff* court's evocative rationale: "In this risk-infested society, we can hardly tolerate the further exposure to danger that would result from a concealed knowledge of the therapist that his patient was lethal."[17] Insanity defense reform, too, was given added momentum by concerns over violence in the streets and by (often unrealistic) perceptions of the degree to which mentally ill persons contributed to the overall rate of violent crimes.[18]

Again, with time, countervailing social forces appeared. The rapid spread of broad versions of a duty to protect was checked by statutes enacted in part out of concern over the negative impact of malpractice suits. Proposals to narrow the duty were seen in some states as part of a package of "tort reform," limiting the liability burden of physicians and other health-care professionals. In the end, laws were passed that restricted therapists' duties without abolishing them. Insanity defense reforms ran out of steam not because the number of NGRI acquittals dropped dramatically, but because the public's attention was diverted to other causes of mayhem in the streets— particularly the drug epidemic of the latter half of the 1980s.

Mental health law cannot be insulated from the influence of broader social issues, nor is there anything improper about such interactions. All law is molded by the temper of the age. Such forces contribute to the unpredictable long-term consequences of statutory reform, and they always will.

Lessons for the Future of Mental Health Law

Having catapulted into the forefront of legal consciousness in the 1960s and 1970s, mental health law is unlikely ever to return to its prior obscurity. Admittedly, the pace of change has slowed. In most years, however, the U.S. Supreme Court reviews one or two cases related to mental health law, and state courts continue filling in the interstices of the last several decades of legal reform. Courses in mental health law are taught, research is performed, and journals are published. Nonlawyers interested in altering the mental health system, often misinterpreting the real effects of the legal changes they witnessed, still turn to the law to seek their ends. Mental health law will continue to evolve, and undoubtedly there will be periods when the tempo of reform increases.

Can the monumental efforts at reform in the latter decades of the twentieth century teach us anything of value with regard to the future? Perhaps the clearest message of our recent experience is that extreme ideological positions are unlikely to lead to stable reforms. Another generation of activists who doubt the existence of mental illness, minimize the suffering it causes, and downplay the desirability of treating its symptoms will inevitably see their efforts—even if initially successful in the legislatures and courts—undercut on the front lines, where the realities are too clear to be denied.[19] Similarly, advocates of counterreforms who oppose placing any substantive limits on the coercive use of state power and resist offering fair procedures to decide when the rights of mentally ill persons are to be restricted will see their goals frustrated.

There is no single set of interests that alone can or should command the allegiance of those who fashion mental health law, whether on the books or in the field. Neither society's interest in providing treatment to mentally ill persons—particularly in the difficult circumstances in which they deny their need for care—nor its interest in protecting their civil rights stands alone. The purpose of mental health law should be to fashion reasonable compromises between these often-conflicting desiderata. When other, non-treatment interests come into conflict with the rights of mentally ill persons—for example, the protection of the public or the imposition of punishment—the same balance must be struck. Compromise should be considered the goal of efforts to revise mental health laws, not a second-best outcome.

Insofar as compromise depends on consensual agreement on the nature of the situation with which one is dealing, the need for accurate empirical descriptions of key aspects of the mental health system and the effects of legal regulation cannot be overstated. The reforms of the last several decades were initiated in an empirical vacuum, a situation that has only slowly been rectified. Widespread change routinely was pursued with knowledge of neither the current functioning of the system nor the probable consequences of perturbing it. Examples can be culled with little effort from each of the areas examined in this book.

Changes in civil commitment criteria spread across almost every jurisdiction in the United States in less than a decade, although the few available outcome studies failed to agree on the effectiveness of the new laws.[20] A duty to protect patients' potential victims was imposed on mental health professionals on the basis of mere conjecture about the extent to which it might deter patients from seeking needed care.[21] The right to refuse treatment evolved in a milieu in which the proportion of patients who declined treatment, why they did so, and the consequences of their actions were all unknown.[22] At the height of insanity defense reform, only the sketchiest data were available about the rate of NGRI findings (which were wildly overestimated) and the types of defendants who were acquitted[23]; no data existed on the likely consequences of any of the proposed reforms, beyond indications that changes in the standard of insanity would probably have little impact on juries' decisions.[24]

Of course, agreement about the nature of a situation and the probable empirical consequences of legal change, in the face of differing material interests or philosophical tendencies among the parties affected, will not by itself lead to consensus about the path to be selected. But it is axiomatic that the absence of such agreement will vastly complicate the task. Future efforts at reform should begin with establishment of a valid database of information about the nature of the current system. Studies should be designed with input from the various interest groups who have a stake in any reform, so that all parties will agree on the accuracy of the findings, whether or not the results conform to their preconceptions. Since we can identify areas of ongoing interest in which current knowledge is inadequate, a strong rationale exists for developing a program of research—funded by the federal government, the states, and private foundations—to fill these gaps.

Data addressing the nature of the current system are inadequate, however, for intelligently designed reform. Even given agreement on the current situation, consensus on the desirability of change is likely to depend on the perceived consequences of altering the system. Some changes will simply demand too high a price to justify the advantages (if any) they afford. If the costs are too great, one might elect to forgo reform altogether. Alternatively, the selection of one approach among others may depend on careful consideration of its relative effectiveness and potentially adverse effects.

It is no accident that mental health law reform in the last generation is so often described as a "wave" of change that "swept over" the nation. Based on certain preconceptions, often inaccurate, decision makers were quick to follow the lead of other states and jump on the reform bandwagon. At times there appeared to be little independent reflection, and certainly there was little consideration given to other approaches than those adopted by the leader of the pack. The opportunity to study carefully the experience of another jurisdiction before embracing a new legal structure was often squandered. Rational mental health law reform should involve deliberate experimentation by particular jurisdictions, with close examination of the consequences prior to more widespread adoption. Although this is a difficult strategy to carry out in our impulse-ridden political system, examples of such approaches can be found in welfare and health-care reform.[25] Indeed, such a deliberate approach seems to characterize the states' consideration of closer posttrial supervision of insanity acquittees, as more data become available about the impact of various models.[26]

Increased availability of these sorts of data should make possible a different process of changing mental health law. Reform proposals in the future may emanate from a consensus developed among interested parties, including those whose exercise of discretion will strongly influence the ultimate effect of reforms. Compromises could be based on common understandings of the current situation and the likely consequences of the changes. Original goals—individual or group—may be modified as additional experience with proposed mechanisms is accumulated. This process of negotiation is not uncommon in the legislative process, particularly when two or more powerful parties are involved and when legislators are unwilling to chance disturbing the status quo unless assured that all parties acquiesce in the proposed changes.

In mental health law reform, however, many of the parties have little political power and no means to force entry into the bargaining process. Even when they manage to find a place at the table, they may lack the empirical data needed to make their arguments meaningful. A commitment to generating both descriptive and evaluative data, along with a process for seeking agreement and compromise among interest groups, would mark a striking change for mental health law. Although in practice such processes often deviate from the ideal (particularly with regard to the availability of relevant data), they are occurring now—more frequently, I think, as the range of interests that must be accommodated becomes apparent—and they should be encouraged.

The problematic nature of the relationship between law and the social and behavioral sciences has given rise to a series of laments by scholars.[27] Most often they express their regrets at the resistance of the legal system (primarily the courts, but legislatures as well) to taking into account the data they and their colleagues have laboriously gathered, prior to issuing opinions and drafting laws. The reasons for this resistance are multiple and differ from subject to subject, but there is no reason to believe that they are inherent—certainly not with regard to mental health law. As I hope this book has demonstrated, we know a great deal more about how to assess legally relevant aspects of the mental health system and the impact of legal regulation than we have usually taken into account in fashioning policy. It would be a fitting legacy of our information age if the next generation of students of mental health law concluded that, by dint of our efforts, this had changed.

References

1. For a controversial but useful account of the motives of some of the key actors in the mental health law drama of the 1970s, see R. Isaac and V. Armat, *Madness in the Streets* (New York: Free Press, 1990).
2. S. J. Morse, "A Preference for Liberty: The Case Against Involuntary Commitment of the Mentally Disordered," *California Law Review* 70: 54–106 (1982); B. Ennis, *Prisoners of Psychiatry* New York, Harcourt, Brace Jovanovich, 1972.
3. R. Plotkin, "Limiting the Therapeutic Orgy: Mental Patients' Right to Refuse Treatment," *Northwestern University Law Review* 72: 461–525 (1977).
4. J. G. Fleming and B. Maximov, "The Patient or His Victim: The Therapist's Dilemma," *California Law Review* 62: 1025–68 (1974).
5. T. S. Szasz, *Law, Liberty, and Psychiatry* (New York: Collier, 1963).

6. Morse, *supra* note 2.
7. Although the *Tarasoff* court recognized "the public interest in supporting effective treatment of mental illness," one wonders about the effects on the justices' reasoning of possible skepticism about the value of psychiatric treatment. Note, in this regard, the court's statement of the balancing process it went through to arrive at its conclusion that a duty to protect should exist: "If the exercise of reasonable care to protect the threatened victim requires the therapist to warn the endangered party or those who can reasonably be expected to notify him, *we see no sufficient societal interest that would protect and justify concealment.*" [Emphasis added.]
8. D. B. Wexler, *Therapeutic Jurisprudence: The Law as a Therapeutic Agent* (Durham, N.C.: Carolina Academic Press, 1990); D. B. Wexler and B. J. Winick, *Essays in Therapeutic Jurisprudence* (Durham, N.C.: Carolina Academic Press, 1991).
9. C. A. B. Warren, *The Court of Last Resort: Mental Illness and the Law* (Chicago: University of Chicago Press, 1982).
10. G. N. Rosenberg, *The Hollow Hope: Can Courts Bring About Social Change?* (Chicago: University of Chicago Press, 1991).
11. ENKI Research Institute, *A Study of California's New Mental Health Law (1969–1971)* (Los Angeles: ENKI Corporation, 1972).
12. M. J. Leiber, "Civil Commitment in Dane County, Wisconsin: 1969 Through 1984," *Journal of Psychiatry and Law* 20: 207–42 (1992). Interestingly, even this effect was transient, with rates of detention returning to previous levels within four years. The number of patients taken to commitment hearings showed a similar trend, dipping after fiscal reform, and returning to or exceeding previous levels some years later. It is not clear to what extent either of these variables constitutes an appropriate measure. Actual rates of commitment to state facilities would probably provide the best estimate of the impact of the fiscal changes.
13. H. R. Lamb, *The Homeless Mentally Ill: A Task Force Report of the American Psychiatric Association* (Washington, D.C.: APA, 1984).
14. W. Fisher, G. Pierce, and P. S. Appelbaum, "How Flexible Are Our Civil Commitment Laws?" *Hospital and Community Psychiatry* 39: 711–12 (1988).
15. J. Barbanel, "Slaying in Cathedral Spurs Scrutiny of Mental Health Care," *New York Times,* September 26, 1988, p. B-1; C. A. Acker and M. J. Fine, "Families Under Siege: A Mental Health Crisis," *Phildelphia Inquirer,* September 10, 1989, p. 1-A; "Editorial: Psychosis and Civil Rights," *Wall Street Journal,* September 28, 1990; C. W. Dugger, "Threat Only When on Crack, Homeless Man Foils System," *New York Times,* p. A-1. September 3, 1992,
16. M. Gladwell, "Justice on the Edge of Insanity: One Family's History of Mental Illness and Laws That Say It Can Go Untreated," *Washington Post,* May 12, 1993, p. B1ff.
17. *Tarasoff v. Regents of the University of California,* 551 P.2d 334 (Cal. 1976), p. 347.
18. S. V. Roberts, "High U.S. Officials Express Outrage, Asking for New Law on Insanity Plea," *New York Times,* June 23, 1982, p. B-6.
19. I do not mean to suggest that everyone who advocated mental health law reform in the period in question subscribed to or was motivated by these views. However, many of the participants—particularly in the early years—did share these beliefs, and more importantly, the mental health advocacy bar rarely shied away from embracing such assumptions when it seemed advantageous to propound them.
20. Compare ENKI Research Institute, *supra* note 12, with A. L. McGarry, R. K.

Schwitzgebel, P. D. Lipsitt, and D. Lelos, *Civil Commitment and Social Policy: An Evaluation of the Masssachusetts Mental Health Reform Act of 1970* (Rockville, Md.: NIMH, 1981).

21. Fleming and Maximov, *supra* note 4.
22. P. S. Appelbaum and S. K. Hoge, "The Right to Refuse Treatment: What the Research Reveals," *Behavioral Sciences and the Law* 4: 279–92 (1986).
23. H. J. Steadman and J. Braff, "Defendants Not Guilty by Reason of Insanity," in J. Monahan and H. J. Steadman, eds., *Mentally Disordered Offenders: Perspective from Law and Social Science* (New York: Plenum Press, 1983), pp. 109–29.
24. R. J. Simon, *The Jury and the Defense of Insanity* (Boston: Little, Brown, 1967).
25. A description of the classic New Jersey Graduated Work Incentive Experiment can be found in D. P. Moynihan, *The Politics of a Guaranteed Income: The Nixon Administration and the Family Assistance Plan* (New York: Vintage Press, 1973). For an example of experimentation in health care delivery, see W. G. Manning, A. Liebowitz, G. A. Goldberg, W. H. Rogers, and J. P. Newhouse, "A Controlled Trial of the Effect of a Prepaid Group Practice on Use of Services," *New England Journal of Medicine* 310: 1505–10 (1984).
26. J. D. Bloom and M. H. Williams, *Management and Treatment of Insanity Acquittees: A Model for the 1990s* (Washington, D.C.: American Psychiatric Press, 1994); M. A. McGreevy, H. J. Steadman, J. A. Dvoskin, and N. Dollard, "New York State's System of Managing Insanity Acquittees in the Community," *Hospital and Community Psychiatry* 42: 512–17 (1991); M. K. Spodak, S. B. Silver, and C. U. Wright, "Criminality of Discharged Insanity Acquittees: Fifteen-year Experience in Maryland Reviewed," *Bulletin of the American Academy of Psychiatry and the Law* 12: 373–82, (1984); D. C. Scott, H. V. Zonana, and M. A. Getz, "Monitoring Insanity Acquittees: Connecticut's PSRB," *Hospital and Community Psychiatry* 41: 980–84 (1990); M. R. Weideranders, "Recidivism of Disordered Offenders Who Were Conditionally vs. Unconditionally Released," *Behavioral Sciences and the Law* 10: 141–48 (1992).
27. P. S. Appelbaum, "The Empirical Jurisprudence of the United States Supreme Court," *American Journal of Law and Medicine* 13: 335–49 (1987); D. N. Bersoff, "Social Science Data and the Supreme Court," *American Psychologist* 42: 52–58 (1987); M. J. Saks and R. Van Duizend, *The Use of Scientific Evidence in Litigation* (Williamsburg, Va.: National Center for State Courts, 1983); P. W. Sperlich, "Social Science Evidence and the Courts: Reaching Beyond the Adversary Process," *Judicature* 63: 280–89 (1980).

Index

225

court-appointed guardian and, 124
dissolution of presumption of, 121
insanity defense substitute, 182
Informed consent, 118, 129, 130
behavioral modification programs and, 122
commitment as exception to, 130
duty to protect and, 98
medical vs. mental hospital, 117–18, 120
treatment and, 117–18
In-patient population, 50
In re Gault, 28
Insanity defense, 3, 4, 12, 95, 134, 135, 163–
209, 211, 212, 219. *See also* GBMI
verdicts; NGRI acquittees; NGRI
verdicts
abolition of, 172, 173–75, 185, 194, 195,
212, 215
consequences of, 181–83, 192
Aristotelian foundation for, 164–65, 166
burden of proof and, 168, 171–72, 176–77,
193
effects of shifting, 184–85, 211, 184–85,
193
competence to stand trial and, 182, 215
expert testimony and, 177–78
forensic examiners' influence on, 190
frequency of, 166, 180–85, 187, 189–90
future of, 194–98
guilty but mentally ill (GBMI) vs., 179,
187–89
heinousness of crime vs. degree of insanity
and, 193
Hinckley use of, 164, 168–72
hypothetical decisionmaking and, 191–94
indefinite detention and, 173
legal standards for, 168, 175–76, 180, 183–
84
ALI, 168, 172, 175, 177, 180, 183, 184,
191
cognitive, 176
disability of mind, 191, 195–96
in federal court, 176, 191
irresistible impulse, 167, 172, 175, 176,
183
justly responsible, 180, 196–97
lack of effect on jurors, 193, 216
McNaughton, 166–68, 172, 176, 183,
184, 191
mens rea and, 164, 165–66, 174–75,
181, 183
volitional, 176, 177, 184
wild beast standard, 165, 174
moral code about, 194
origins and development of, 164–68
plea bargaining and, 188, 190, 194,
215

posttrial disposition and, 178–79, 185–87,
212
recidivism and, 185
reform of, 172–80
consequences of, 180–89, 211, 212
limited impact of, 189–94
resistance to, 215–16
Insanity Defense Reform Act of 1984, 192
Involuntary hospitalization, 6, 17–70
APA position statement on, 29
duty to protect and, 83, 96
emergency provisions for. *See* Emergency
commitment
history of, 18–22
for incompetent patients only, 128
jury trials for, 20
laws governing. *See* Commitment law(s)
NGRI recidivism prevention and, 186–87
presumption of incompetence and, 119–21,
128
procedures for, 20, 27–28, 29–30, 31
psychiatrists' view of, 29–30
rates of, 211, 217
standards for, 26, 54, 120–21, 213. *See
also* Dangerousness standard; Grave
disability; Thank You Theory;
Treatment
Szasz's view of, 6
Involuntary mind control, 125, 126
Involuntary patients, 120, 123, 125, 129
Involuntary treatment, 6, 49, 125, 130. *See
also* Right to refuse treatment
Irresistible impulse standard, 167, 172, 175,
176, 183

Jackson v. Indiana, 25
Jones v. U.S., 179
Judicial activism, 22
Judicial role
in commitment, 20–22, 29, 36, 43–44, 45
in competence assessment, 129
in refusal of treatment review, 129, 130,
132, 137–39, 141, 143, 144, 145, 146,
150
substituted judgment and, 124, 129, 145
Jury, 19, 20, 24, 197
commitment procedure, 20
impervious to changes in legal standards,
193, 216
mock, studies, 191–93
Justly responsible approach, 180, 196–97
Juvenile delinquents, 24, 25, 28, 82
Juveniles' rights, 10, 24

Katz, Jay, 11
Kaufman, Irving, 172